CAMPBELL-RICE DEBATE ON THE HOLY SPIRIT

BEING

THE FIFTH PROPOSITION

IN THE GREAT DEBATE ON "BAPTISM," "HOLY SPIRIT" AND "CREEDS," HELD IN LEXINGTON, KENTICKY, BEGINNING NOVEMBER 15, 1843, AND CONTINUING EIGHTEEN DAYS,

BETWEEN

ALEXANDER CAMPBELL

AND

N. L. RICE

Published by Left of Brain Books

Copyright © 2021 Left of Brain Books

ISBN 978-1-396-31868-9

First Edition

All rights reserved. No part of this publication may be reproduced, distributed, or transmitted in any form or by any means, including photocopying, recording, or other electronic or mechanical methods, without the prior written permission of the publisher, except in the case of brief quotations embodied in critical reviews and certain other noncommercial uses permitted by copyright law. Left of Brain Books is a division of Left of Brain Onboarding Pty Ltd.

Table of Contents

RULES FOR DEBATE.	1
MR. CAMPBELL'S OPENING ADDRESS.	3
MR. RICE'S FIRST REPLY.	23
MR. CAMPBELL'S SECOND ADDRESS.	44
MR. RICE'S SECOND ADDRESS.	52
MR. CAMPBELL'S THIRD ADDRESS.	63
MR. RICE'S THIRD REPLY.	71
MR. CAMPBELL'S FOURTH ADDRESS.	80
MR. RICE'S FOURTH REPLY.	88
MR. CAMPBELL'S FIFTH ADDRESS.	96
MR. RICE'S FIFTH REPLY.	104
MR. CAMPBELL'S SIXTH ADDRESS.	112
MR. RICE'S SIXTH REPLY.	119
MR. CAMPBELL'S SEVENTH ADDRESS.	128
MR. RICE'S SEVENTH REPLY.	138
MR. CAMPBELL'S EIGHTH ADDRESS.	147
MR. RICE'S EIGHTH REPLY.	156
MR. CAMPBELL'S NINTH ADDRESS.	165
MR. RICE'S NINTH REPLY.	174
MR. CAMPBELL'S TENTH ADDRESS.	184
MR. RICE'S TENTH REPLY.	193
MR. CAMPBELL'S CLOSING ADDRESS.	204
MR. RICE'S CLOSING REPLY.	214

RULES FOR DEBATE.

The following rules governed the entire discussion:

1. The debate shall commence on Wednesday, November 15, 1843.

2. To be held in the Reform Church.

3. Judge Robertson, selected by Mr. Rice, as Moderator. Col. Speed Smith, selected by Mr. Campbell. And agreed that these two shall select a President Moderator. In case of either of the above-named gentlemen declining to act, Judge Breck was selected by Mr. Rice as alternate to Judge Robertson, and Colonel Caperton as alternate to Col. Speed Smith.

4. In the opening of each new subject the affirmant shall occupy one hour, and the respondent the same time; and each thereafter half hour alternately to the termination of each subject. The debate shall commence at 10 o'clock A.M., and continue until 2 o'clock P.M., unless hereafter changed.

5. On the final negative no new matter shall be introduced.

6. The propositions for discussion are the following:

I. The immersion in water of a proper subject, into the name of the Father, Son, and of the Holy Spirit, is the one, only apostolic or Christian baptism. Mr. Campbell affirms. Mr. Rice denies.

II. The infant of a believing parent is a Scriptural subject of baptism. Mr. Rice affirms. Mr. Campbell denies.

III. Christian baptism is for the remission of past sins. Mr. Campbell affirms. Mr. Rice denies.

IV. Baptism is to be administered only by a bishop or ordained Presbyter. Mr. Rice affirms. Mr. Campbell denies.

V. In conversion and sanctification, the Spirit of God operates on persons only through the word of truth. Mr. Campbell affirms. Mr. Rice denies.

VI. Human creeds, as bonds of union and communion, are necessarily heretical and schismatical. Mr. Campbell affirms. Mr. Rice denies.

6. No question shall be discussed more than three days, unless by agreement of parties.

7. Each debatant shall furnish a stenographer.

8. It shall be the privilege of the debaters to make any verbal or grammatical changes in the stenographer's report, that shall not alter the state of the argument, or change any fact.

9. The net available amount, resulting from the publication, shall be equally divided between the two American Bible Societies.

10. The discussion shall be conducted in the presence of Dr. Fishback, President Shannon, John Smith, and A. Raines, on the part of the Reformation; and President Young, James K. Burch, J. F. Price, and John H. Brown, on the part of the Presbyterianism.

11. The debatants agree to adopt as "rules of decorum" those found in Hedges' Logic, p. 159, to-wit:

Rule 1. The terms in which the question in debate is expressed, and the point at issue, should be clearly defined, that there could be no misunderstanding respecting them.

Rule 2. The parties should mutually consider each other as standing on a footing of equality, in respect to the subject in debate. Each should regard the other as possessing equal talents, knowledge, and a desire for truth with himself; and that it is possible, therefore, that he may be in the wrong, and his adversary in the right.

Rule 3. All expressions which are unmeaning, or without effect in regard to the subject in debate, should be strictly avoided.

Rule 4. Personal reflections on an adversary should, in no instance, be indulged.

Rule 5. The consequences of any doctrine are not to be charged on him who maintains it, unless he expressly avows them.

Rule 6. As truth, and not victory, is the professed object of controversy, whatever proofs may be advanced, on either side, should be examined with fairness and candor; and any attempt to answer an adversary by arts of sophistry, or to lessen the force of his reasoning by wit, cavilling or ridicule, is a violation of the rules of honorable controversy.

(Signed.)

A. CAMPBELL,
N. L. RICE.

MR. CAMPBELL'S OPENING ADDRESS.

Monday, Nov. 27, 10 A.M.

Mr. President.—The proposition to be discussed to-day is admitted on all hands to be of transcendent importance to the Christian. It is expressed in the following words: "In conversion and sanctification, the spirit of God operates on persons only through the Word."

Most controversies are mere logomachies—wars of words about words, and not about things. Perspicuity and precision in the definition of the terms of a proposition at the commencement, would have prevented more than half of all the debates in the world, and would have reduced the other half to less than half their size. Indeed, we yet need for daily use a much more simple and Scriptural vocabulary, on the great subject of religion, as well as in some other departments of literature and science. The cumbrous, unwieldy, and badly assorted nomenclature of certain sciences has, for centuries, retarded their progress. This is most unfortunately true in the intellectual and moral departments. Scholastic theology is greatly behind the age. The stale divinity of other times refuses to reconsider its sense or its symbols. Hence the superabundance of the barbarous gibberish and miserable jargon yet extant in our creeds and systems of theoretic divinity. Some samples of these quaint vocables may be given in the discussion of the creed question.

Meantime, we have yet to learn how much perversion, not of language only, but of the mind also, has grown out of sectarian animosities and bickerings. The periodical hobbies of religious parties generate, like our political feuds, hosts of new terms; and often change and modify the old ones, that even a well-practiced politician, with Johnson, and Webster, and Richardson by his side, can not nowadays define, either Whig or Tory, Democrat or Republican.

It is truly an interesting study to learn the new phraseology of religion—not only of religion in general, but of the different leading parties of the present church militant. An adept in this study could almost swear to a

Romanist or a High Churchman, a Presbyterian of a Methodist, in the dark, if he only heard him speak for a single hour; and that, too, without stating one of his peculiar dogmata. Certain words, like the shibboleth of the Ephraimites, invariably identify the religious tribe to which the speaker belongs.

In the midst of this babelism there is one fact which it behooves me to state. I scarcely know how, indeed, to introduce it in this place; and yet it is essential to a proper understanding of the whole subject before us. This fact is, that, in the strife of partyism, some Bible terms have been so appropriated to represent peculiar tenets and views which never occurred to their inspired authors; that, were Paul now living amongst us, he could not understand much of his own language. To this class belong the words "regeneration," "sanctification," and "conversion."

With special reference to the discussion, and to the words of my proposition, I must, therefore, notice one capital blunder, which, if not now detected, might involve the subject before us in great obscurity. I can not, however, much as I regret it, distinctly unfold my meaning in a single sentence. Allow me, then, to open it gradually to the apprehension of all.

The various conditions of man, as he was, as he now is, and as he shall hereafter be, as connected with Adam the first, and Adam the second, are set forth in Sacred Scripture, under various images and metaphors, each of which belongs exclusively to its own class, and is independent of every other one; requiring no addition or subtraction of other images, from other classes, to complete or to unfold it. For example, the present condition of sinners, in Adam the first, is set forth under such metaphors as the following: dead, destroyed, lost, alienated, enemy, going astray, condemned in law, debtor, unclean, sold to sin, darkened, blind, etc. Each one of these has a class of opposite metaphors, of the same particular idea or figure. These metaphors, just now quoted, give rise to a corresponding class, indicative of his new condition in Adam the second, such as quickened, made alive, born again, new created, saved, reconciled, friend, converted, illuminated, pardoned, redeemed, etc. The changing of these states is also set forth in suitable imagery, such as regeneration, conversion, reconciliation, new creation, illumination, remission, adoption, redemption, salvation, etc. Now, the error to which I allude, primarily, consists in not uniformly regarding each one of these as a complete view of man, in some one condition, or in his whole condition in

Adam the first, or in Adam the second; but in sometimes contemplating them as parts of one view, as fractions of one great whole, and, consequently, to be all added up to make out a full Scriptural view of man, in Adam and in Christ, and of the transition from the one state to the other. From this wild confusion of metaphors—the indiscriminate use of certain leading terms, mere images it may be—our very best and most admired treatises on theology are not always exempt. Hence regeneration, conversion, justification, sanctification, etc., etc., are frequently represented as component parts of one process; whereas, any one of these, independent of the others, gives a full representation of the subject. Is a man regenerated? he is converted, justified, and sanctified. Is he sanctified? he is converted, justified, and regenerated. With some system-builders, however, regeneration is an instantaneous act, between which and conversion there is a positive, substantive interval; next comes justification; and then, in some still future time, sanctification.

A foreigner, in becoming a citizen, is sometimes said to be naturalized, sometimes enfranchised, sometimes adopted, sometimes made a citizen. Now, what intelligent citizen regards these as parts of one process? Rather, who does not consider them as different metaphors, setting forth the same great change under various allusions to past and present circumstances? From such a statement none but a simpleton would imagine that a foreigner was first naturalized, then enfranchised, then adopted, and finally made an American citizen; yet such a simpleton is that learned rabbi, who represents a man first regenerated, then converted, then justified, then sanctified, then saved.

Under any one of these images, various distinct acts of the mind, or of the whole person of an individual, may be necessary to the completion of the predicate concerning him. Thus, in regeneration or conversion there may be included hearing, believing, repenting, and being baptized. These are connected as cause and effect, under a fixed administration or economy of salvation. So Paul asks, "How shall they call upon him in whom they have not believed? How shall they believe in him of whom they have not heard?—and how shall they hear without a preacher?—and how shall they preach unless they be sent?"

The terms of my proposition will now be easily defined and apprehended. Conversion is a term denoting that whole moral or spiritual change, which is sometimes called sanctification, sometimes regeneration. These are not three changes, but one change indicated by these three terms, regeneration, conversion, sanctification. Whether we shall call it by one or the other of these depends upon the metaphor we happen to have before us, in contemplating man as connected with the two Adams—the old or the new, the first or the second, the earthly or the heavenly. Is he dead in the first?—then he is born again and alive in the second. Has he, like the prodigal son, strayed away in the first?—he returns, or is converted in the second. Is he unclean or polluted in the earthly Adam?—he is sanctified in the heavenly. Is he lost in the first?—he is saved in the second. Is he destroyed and ruined in the first?—he is created anew in the second Adam, the Lord from heaven.

If I am asked, why I admitted the terms conversion, sanctification, or regeneration into the proposition, I answer again, I could not help it. It would have been to debate the question while settling the preliminaries. We must take the religious world as we have to take the natural or the political; that is, just as we find them, or as they find us. I seek to accomplish in this preamble, what ought to have been, but which could not be, accomplished in settling the propositions. I therefore now most distinctly and emphatically state, that with me, and in reference to this discussion, these terms, severally and collectively, indicate a moral, a spiritual, and not a physical nor legal-change.

A physical change has respect to the essence of form of the subject. A legal change is a change as respects a legal sentence, or enactment. Hence pardon, remission, justification, have respect to law. But a moral or spiritual change is a change of the moral state of the feelings, and of the soul. In contrast with a merely intellectual change, a change of views, it is called a change of the affections, a change of the heart. It is in this acceptation of the subject of my proposition that I predicate of it, "The Spirit operates only through the Word."

The term *only* is indeed redundant, because a moral change is effected only by motives, and motives are arguments; and all the arguments ever used by the Holy Spirit are found written in the book called the Word of Truth. Hence, the term is only equivalent to a denial of what I conceive to be the assumption of my respondent, viz., that the Spirit in regeneration operates *sometimes* without the Word. *Only* is, therefore, by the force of circumstances, made to mean *always*. But, indeed, this is more a matter of form than of any grave importance, inasmuch as the common admission of Protestants, and, I presume, of my opponent also, is, that the change of which we speak is a moral or spiritual change.

If, then, I prove that conversion, or sanctification, is effected by the Word of Truth at all, I prove that it is a moral change, and, consequently, accomplished by the Holy Spirit, through the Word alone.

On the subject of spiritual influence there are two extremes of doctrine. There is the *Word alone* system, and there is the *Spirit alone* system. I believe in neither. The former is the parent of a cold, lifeless rationalism and formality. The latter is, in some temperaments, the cause of a wild, irrepressible enthusiasm; and, in other cases, of a dark, melancholy despondency. With some there is a sort of compound system, claiming both the Spirit and the Word—representing the naked Spirit of God operating upon the naked soul of man, without any argument, or motive, interposed in some mysterious and inexplicable way—incubating the soul, quickening, or making it spiritually alive, by a direct and immediate contact, without the intervention of one moral idea, or impression. But, after this creating act, there is the bringing to bear upon it the gospel revelation, called conversion. Hence, in this school, regeneration is the cause; and conversion, at some future time, the result of that abstract operation.

There yet remains another school, which never speculatively separates the Word and the Spirit; which, in every case of conversion, contemplates them as co-operating; or, which is the same thing, conceives of the Spirit of God as clothed with the gospel motives and arguments—enlightening, convincing, persuading sinners, and thus enabling them to flee from the wrath to come. In this school conversion and regeneration are terms indicative of a moral or spiritual change—of a change accomplished through the arguments, the light, the love, the grace of God expressed and revealed, as well as approved by the supernatural attestations of the. Holy Spirit. They believe, and teach, that it is the Spirit that quickens, and that the Word of God—the Living Word—is that incorruptible seed, which, when planted in the heart, vegetates, and germinates, and grows, and fructifies into eternal life. They hold it to be unscriptural, irrational, unphilosophic, to discriminate between spiritual agency or instrumentality—between what the Word, *per se*, or the Spirit, *per se*, severally does; as though they were two independent and wholly distinct powers or influences. They object not to the co-operation of secondary causes;

of various subordinate instrumentalities; the ministry of men; the ministry of angels; the doctrine of special providences; but, however, whenever the Word gets into the heart—the spiritual seed into the moral nature of man—it as naturally, as spontaneously, grows there as the sound, good corn, when deposited in the genial earth. It has life in it, and is, therefore, sublimely and divinely called "The Living and Effectual Word."

I prefer the comparisons of the Great Teacher. They are the most appropriate. We frequently err when handling these, because, in our quest of forbidden knowledge we are disposed to carry them farther than he himself did. In the opening parable of the Gospel Age—a parable placed first in the synopsis of parables presented by Matthew, Mark, and Luke—he thus compares the Word of God to seed; and, with reference to that figure, he compares the human heart to soil, distributed into six varieties: the trodden pathway, the rocky field, the thorny cliff, the rich alluvian, the better, and the best of that. But we are not content with that beautiful and instructive representation of the philosophy of conversion. We must transcend these limits. We must explain the theory of vegetation. We must explain the theory of soils. We must even become spiritual geologists, and explore all the strata of mother earth; and even then there yet remains an infinite series of whys and wherefores concerning all the reasons of things connected with these varieties. These speculations, and the conflicting theories to which they have given birth, we will and bequeath to the more curious and speculative, and will farther premise some things necessary to a proper opening of the argument.

Man, by his fall or apostasy from God, lost three things—union with God, original righteousness, and original holiness. In consequence of these tremendous losses he forfeited life, lost the right of inheriting the earth, and became subject to all the physical evils of this world. He is, therefore, with the earth on which he lives, doomed to destruction; meanwhile, a remedial system is introduced, originating in the free, sovereign, and unmerited favor of God; not, indeed, to restore man to an Eden lost—to an inheritance forfeited—to a life enjoyed before his alienation from his divine Father and Benefactor. This supremely glorious and transcendent scheme of Almighty love contemplates a nearer, more intimate, and more sublime union with God than that enjoyed in ancient paradise—a union, too, enduring as eternity, as indestructible as the divine essence. It bestows on man an everlasting righteousness, a perfect holiness, and an enduring blessedness in the presence of God for ever and ever.

To accomplish this a new manifestation of the Divinity became necessary. Hence the development of a plurality of existence in the Divine Nature. The God of the first chapter of Genesis is the Lord God of the second. Light advances as the pages of human history multiply, until we have God, the Word of God, and the Spirit of God clearly intimated in the law, the prophets, and the Psalms. But it was not until the Sun of Righteousness arose—till the Word became incarnate and dwelt among us—till we beheld his glory as that of an only begotten of the Father, full of grace and truth; it was not till Jesus of Nazareth had finished the work of atonement on the hill of Calvary—till he had brought life and immortality to light, by his revival and resurrection from the sealed sepulcher of the Arimathean senator; it was not till he gave a commission to convert the whole world that the development of the Father, and of the Son, and of the Holy Spirit was fully stated and completed. Since the descent of the Holy Spirit, on the birthday of Christ's Church—since the glorious immersion of the three thousand triumphs of the memorable Pentecost, the Church has enjoyed the mysteries and sublime light of the Father, and of the Son, and of the Holy Spirit, as one Divinity, manifesting itself in these incomprehensible relations, in order to effect the complete recovery and perfect redemption of man from the guilt, the pollution, the power, and the punishment of sin.

No one, Mr. President, believes more firmly than I, and no one, I presume, endeavors to teach more distinctly and comprehensively than I, this mysterious, sublime, and incomprehensible plurality and unity in the Godhead. It is a relation that may be apprehended by all, though comprehended by none. It has its insuperable necessity in the present condition of the universe. Without it, no one can believe in, or be reconciled to, the remedial policy, as developed in the apostolic writings. And, sir, I have no more faith in any man's profession of religion, than I have in the sincerity of Mahomet, who does not believe in the Father, and in the Son, and in the Holy Spirit as co-operating in the illumination, pardon, and sanctification of fallen, sinful, and degraded man. While, then, I repudiate, with all my heart, the scholastic jargon of the Arian, Unitarian and Trinitarian hypotheses, I stand up before heaven and earth in defense of the sacred style—in the fair, full and perfect comprehension of all its words and sentences, according to the canons of a sound, exegetical interpretation.

I would not, sir, value at the price of a single mill the religion of any man, as respects the grand affair of eternal life, whose religion is not begun, carried on, and completed by the personal agency of the Holy Spirit. Nay, sir, I esteem it the peculiar excellence and glory of our religion, that it is spiritual; that the soul of man is quickened, enlightened, sanctified and consoled by the indwelling presence of the Spirit of the eternal God. But, while avowing these, my convictions, I have no more fellowship with those false and pernicious theories that confound the peculiar work of the Father with that of the Son, or with that of the Holy Spirit, or the work of any of these awful names with that of another; or which represents our illumination, conversion and sanctification as the work of the Spirit without the knowledge, belief and obedience of the Gospel, as written by the holy apostles and evangelists, than I have with the author and finishers of the Book of Mormon.

The revelation of Father, Son, and Holy Spirit is not more clear and distinct than are the different offices assumed and performed by these glorious and ineffable Three in the present affairs of the universe. It is true, so far as unity of design and concurrence of action are contemplated, they co-operate in every work of creation, providence and redemption. Such is the concurrence expressed by the Messiah in these words, "My Father worketh hitherto, and I work," "I and my Father are one," "Whatsoever the Father doeth, the Son doeth likewise"; but not such a concurrence as annuls personally, impairs or interferes with the distinct offices of each in the salvation of man. For example, the Father sends his Son, and not the Son his Father. The Father provides a body and a soul for his Son, and not the Son for his Father. The Son offers up that body and soul for sin, and thus expiates it, which the Father does not, but accepts it. The Father and Son send forth the Spirit, and not the Spirit either. The Spirit now advocates Christ's cause, and not Christ his own cause. The Holy Spirit now animates the Church with his presence, and not Christ himself. He is the Head of the Church, while the Spirit is the heart of it. The Father originates all, the Son executes all, the Spirit consummates all. Eternal volition, design and mission belong to the Father; reconciliation to the Son; sanctification to the Spirit. In each of these terms there are numerous terms and ideas of subordinate extent, to which we can not now advert. At present, we consider the subject in its general character, and not in its particular details.

In the distribution of official agency, as it presents itself to our apprehension, with reference to the subject before us, we regard the benevolent design and plan of man's redemption, as originating in the bosom of our Divine Father; the atonement, or sacrificial ransom, as the peculiar work of the Messiah; and the advocacy of his cause, in accomplishing the conversion and sanctification of the world, the peculiar mission and office of the Holy Spirit. Thus, the Spirit is the author of the written Word, as much as Jesus Christ is the author of the blood of atonement. The atoning blood of the everlasting covenant is not more peculiarly the blood of Jesus Christ than is the Bible the immediate work of the Holy Spirit, inspired and dictated by him: "For holy men of old spake as they were moved by the Holy Spirit." Now, as Jesus, the Messiah, in the work of mediation, operates through his blood, so the Holy Spirit, in his official agency, operates through his Word and its ordinances. And thus we have arrived at the proper consideration of our proposition, to-wit: In conversion and sanctification the Holy Spirit operates only through the Word of Truth.

In how many other ways the Spirit of God may operate in nature, or in society, in the way of dreams, visions and miracles, comes not within the premises contained in our proposition. To what extent he may operate in suggestions, special providences, or in any other way, is neither affirmed nor denied in the proposition before us. It has respect to conversion and sanctification only. Whatever ground is fairly covered by these terms belongs to this discussion. What lies not within these precincts comes not legitimately into this debate.

I. Our first argument in proof of our proposition shall be drawn from the constitution of the human mind.

That the human mind has a specific and well-defined constitution is as evident as that the body has a peculiar organization; or that the universe itself has one grand code of laws which govern it. Our intellectual and moral constitution, as well as our physical, has its peculiar powers and capacities, not one of which is violated on the part of our Creator in his remedial administration, any more than are our sensitive and animal faculties destroyed or violated by the physician who rationally and benevolently aims at our restoration to health from some physical malady. No new faculties are imparted—no old faculty destroyed. They are neither more nor less in number; they are neither better nor worse in kind. Paul, the apostle, and Saul of Tarsus are the same person, so far as all the animal, intellectual and moral powers are concerned. His mental and physical temperament were just the same after as before he became a Christian. The Spirit of God, in effecting this great change, does not violate, metamorphose, or annihilate any power or faculty of the man in making the saint. He merely receives new ideas, and new impressions, and undergoes a great moral or spiritual change, so that he becomes alive wherein he was dead, and dead wherein he was formerly alive.

As the body or outward man has its peculiar organization, so has the mind. Both are organized in perfect adaptation to a world without us: the one to a world of sensible and material objects, the other to that of the world, and to a spiritual system also, with which it is to have perpetual intimacy and communion. But the mind is to commune with its Creator, and its Creator with it, through material as well as through spiritual nature; and for this purpose he has endowed it with faculties, and the body with senses favorable to these benevolent designs.

Now, as the body has to subsist upon material nature, and the mind upon the spiritual system, both are so organized and furnished as to secure and assimilate so much of both as are necessary for this end. Thus, for example, the body lives, moves, and has its being in the midst of matter from which it is to draw perpetual sustenance and comfort. For doing this it is admirably fitted with an animal machinery, created for this purpose, without which animal life would immediately become extinct. The lungs are fitted for respiration, and the stomach is furnished with all the powers necessary to the reception, digestion, and assimilation of so much of material nature as is necessary to the healthful, vigorous and comfortable subsistence of the body. But nothing from without can afford it subsistence or comfort but in harmony with this organization.

Man, then, has to live by breathing, eating, and drinking; and without these operations nothing around him can afford him life and comfort. Nothing of the bounties of nature can administer to his animal enjoyments in any other way. God, then, feeds and sustains man in perfect harmony with this organization. He neither dispenses with any of these powers nor violates them in supporting physical life and comfort.

Precisely so is it in the spiritual system. The mind has its powers of receiving, assimilating and enjoying whatever is suitable to itself, as the body with which it is furnished. While embodied, it has only its own proper faculties, but it has also organs and senses in the body, by and through which it communes with matter and with spirit, with God, and nature, and man; and through which they commune with it. It receives all the ideas of material nature by outward, bodily sense, without which it could not have one idea or impression of the external universe. A blind man has no idea of colors, nor a deaf man of sounds. Neither can any one give him an idea of them without those senses. Since the world began, every man sees by his eyes and hears by his ears. Whatever knowledge, therefore, is peculiar to any sense can never be acquired by another. If God give sight to the blind, or hearing to the deaf, he does it by restoring these senses; for, since the world began, no man has ever seen by his ears nor heard by his eyes.

So true it is, that all our ideas of the sensible universe are the result of sensation and reflection. All the knowledge we have of material nature has been acquired by the exercise of our senses and of our reason upon those discoveries. With regard to the supernatural knowledge, or the knowledge of God, that comes wholly "by faith," and "faith" itself "comes by hearing." This aphorism is Divine. Faith is, therefore, a consequence of hearing, and hearing is the effect of speaking; for, hearing comes by the Word of God spoken, as much as faith itself comes by hearing. The intellectual and moral arrangement is, therefore: (1) the word spoken; (2) hearing; (3) believing; (4) feeling; (5) doing. Such is the constitution of the human mind—a constitution divine and excellent, adapted to man's position in the universe. It is never violated in the moral government of God. Religious action is uniformly the effect of religious feeling; that is the effect of faith; that of hearing; and that of something spoken by God.

Now, as faith in God is the first principle—the soul-renewing principle of religion; as it is the regenerating, justifying, sanctifying principle; without it, it is impossible to be acceptable to God. With it, a man is a son of Abraham, a son of God; an heir apparent to eternal life—an everlasting kingdom.

And what is Christian faith? It is a belief of testimony. It is a persuasion that God is true; that the gospel is divine; that God is love; that Christ's death is the sinner's life. It is trust in God. It is a reliance upon his truth, his faithfulness, his power. It is not merely a cold assent to truth, to testimony; but a cordial, joyful consent to it, and reception of it.

Still, it is dependent on testimony. No testimony, no faith. The Spirit of God gave the testimony first. It bore witness to Jesus. It expected no faith without something to believe. Something to believe is always presented to faith; and that something must be heard before it can be believed; for, until it is heard, it is as though it were not—a nonentity. But it is not enough that it be heard by the outward ear. God has given to man an inward, as well as an outward ear. The outward recognizes sounds only; the inward recognizes sense. Faith is, therefore, impossible without language, and consequently without the knowledge of language, and that language understood. It is neither necessary nor possible without language—intelligible language. An infant can not have faith; but it needs neither faith, nor regeneration, nor baptism. It was a figment of St. Augustine, adopted by Calvin, propagated in his Institutes and adopted by his children.

These infant regenerations are lame in both limbs—in the right limb of faith and in the left limb of philosophy. They move on crutches, and broken crutches, too. They have no philosophy of mind, or else they abandon it in all their theological embarrassments. They will have infants regenerated, and souls morally dead quickened by a direct impulse. The Spirit of God is supposed to incubate their souls—to descend upon them and work a grace in them—a faith without reason, without argument, without evidence, without intelligence, without perception, without fear, hope, love, confidence or approbation.

The whole system of Calvinism, of Arminianism, is crazy just at this point. They build a world upon the back of a tortoise, they pile mountains upon an egg. They build palaces upon ice, and repose on couches of ether. They have not one clear idea on the subject of regeneration. It is to them a mystic mystery, a cabalistic word, a mere shibboleth. The philosophy of mind is converted into a heap of ruins. They have the Spirit of God operating without testimony, without apprehension or comprehension, without sense, susceptibility or feeling; and all this for the sake of an incomprehensible, unintelligible, and worse than useless theory. I therefore, ex animo, repudiate their whole theory of mystic influence and metaphysical regeneration as a vision of visions, a dream of dreams, at war with philosophy, with the philosophy of mind, with the Bible, with reason, with common sense, and with all Christian experience.

II.—Our second argument is deduced from the fact that no living man has ever been heard of, and none can now be found, possessed of a single conception of Christianity, of one spiritual thought, feeling or emotion, where the Bible, or some tradition from it, has not been before him. Where the Bible has not been sent, or its traditions developed, there is not one single spiritual idea, word or action. It is all midnight—a gloom profound—utter darkness. What stronger evidence can be adduced than this most evident and indisputable fact? It weighs more than a thousand volumes of metaphysical speculations.

One would most rationally conclude that if the Spirit of God did anywhere illuminate the human mind, or work into the heart the principle of faith previous to, and independent of, any knowledge of the Holy Scriptures, he would most probably do it in those portions of the earth and amid those vast masses of human kind entirely destitute of the Word of Life—wholly ignorant of the "only name given under the whole heaven" by which any sinful man can be saved. If, then, he has never operated in this way, where the Bible has never gone, who can prove that he so operates here, where the Bible is enjoyed.

When, then, we reflect upon the melancholy fact so often pressed upon the attention of Christendom, by her missionaries to heathen lands, that not more than one-third of human kind enjoy the name of Jesus; that six-tenths or seven-tenths of mankind are wholly given up to the most stupid idolatries or delusions; that pagan darkness and Mahometan impostures cover the fairest and largest portions of our earth, and engulf the great majority of our race in the most debasing superstitions, in the grossest ignorance, sensuality, and vice; and that from these is withholden all spiritual and divine influence of a regenerating and salutary character, so far as all documentary evidence avoucheth,—if, then, indeed, the Spirit of the Bible, the Holy Spirit of our God, did at all travel out of the record and work faith, or communicate intelligence, without verbal testimony, methinks this is the proper field. And there being no evidence of his having so done, is it not a fact as clear as revelation from heaven, clear as demonstration itself, that the illuminating, regenerating, converting, sanctifying influences of the Spirit of Wisdom and Revelation are not antecedent to, nor independent of, the written oracles of that Spirit?

III.—Our third argument is deduced from the fact that no one professing to have been the subject of the illuminating, converting and sanctifying operations of the Spirit of God can ever express a single right conception or idea on the whole subject of spiritual things, not already found in the written Word. We have been favored with numerous revelations of the experiences of the most spiritually minded and excellent Christians of this, our age. And on listening to them with the strictest attention, marking, with all our powers of discrimination, every idea, sentiment and expression as uttered, I have never heard one suggestion containing the feeblest ray of light which was not eighteen hundred years old, and already found in the Holy Scriptures—read of all men who choose to learn what the Spirit of God has said to saints and sinners. Evident, then, it is, from this fact, which, I presume, I may also call an incontrovertable fact, that no light is communicated by the Holy Spirit in regenerating and converting men; which is equivalent to saying that in conversion and sanctification the Spirit of God operates only through the Word of Truth.

IV.—My fourth argument is derived from another fact which calls for special consideration just at this point, to-wit, *whatever is essential to regeneration in any case is essential to it in all cases.* The change, called regeneration, is a specific change. It consists of certain elements, and is effected by a special agency. If it be a new heart given, a new life communicated, it is accomplished in all cases, as generation is, by the same agency and instrumentality. If, then, the Spirit of God, without faith, without the knowledge of the Gospel, in any case regenerates an individual, he does so in all cases. But if faith in God, or a knowledge of Christ, is essential in one case, it is essential in every other case.

Now this being admitted, as I presume it will be, without farther argument or illustration, follows it not then that neither the Word of God, nor the Gospel of Christ, neither preaching nor teaching, neither hearing nor believing is necessary to regeneration, according to the doctrine of the Presbyterian Church?—inasmuch as that church believes and teaches that infants and pagans are regenerated, in some cases, without any instrumentality at all, but by the direct, naked and abstract influence of the Spirit of God operating immediately upon their souls. As this is a most essential affair in this discussion, it is all-important that we deliver ourselves in the very words of the

Church, and especially in the creed of that branch of the Church to which my respondent belongs.

"This effectual call is of God's free and especial grace alone; not from anything at all foreseen in man, nor from any power or agency in the creature co-working with his special grace, *the creature being wholly passive therein*, being dead in sins and trespasses, until being quickened and renewed by the Holy Spirit, he is thereby enabled to answer this call and to embrace the grace offered and contained in it; and that by no less power than that which raised up Christ from the dead. Elect infants, dying in infancy, are regenerated and saved by Christ through the Spirit, who worketh when, and where, and how he pleases; so also are all other elect persons, who are incapable of being outwardly called by the ministry of the Word."

So speaks the Confession, Chapter x, sections 2, 3.

Now, I ask, of what use is the ministry of the Word in any case, so far as regeneration is concerned? This is a point on which I am peculiarly solicitous of illumination. Surely faith, and preaching, and the Gospel ministry are all vain and useless in making a man a new creature, if dying infants and untaught pagans may be regenerated by the Spirit alone, without faith, knowledge or any illumination whatever. Nay, indeed, if my position be true, and true it most assuredly is, that whatever is essential to regeneration in any case is essential in all cases, then, although we have three classes of subjects, to-wit: Elect infants, elect pagans and elect Gospel hearers, we have for them all one and the same species of regeneration. This is one of my reasons why I have charged my Presbyterian friends, on some occasions, of "making the Word of God of non-effect by their traditions"; and, therefore, I solicit such an exposition of this dogma as will set me right if I err in this particular. As the Confession reads, we have thus, in effecting the regeneration of an infant, the Spirit alone operating by a physical power, tantamount to that which raised up to life again the dead body of the crucified Messiah.

Miracles truly never cease on this hypothesis: inasmuch as the regeneration of every infant is a demonstration of a power as supernatural as the resurrection of the Messiah. Unfortunately, however, this power is not only never displayed to our conviction at the time, nor ever so displayed after the event as to become an object of perception, much less of sensible demonstration. If, indeed, as it sometimes happens in some branches of this school, regeneration is not regarded as another name for conversion and sanctification, but a previous work, then it will be important that we be enlightened on the question, How long the interval between regeneration and conversion, between regeneration and faith, and between regeneration and the dying infant's or pagan's exit? For if the interval should be such as to preclude the possibility of conversion and sanctification, we should have the startling fact promulgated that infants, and pagans, too, dying regenerate, enter heaven without being converted! Another curious question will certainly arise here. Of what use is infant baptism according to such a theory of regeneration? For, if elect infants are regenerated without knowledge, faith, repentance, or baptism, and if non-elect infants, though baptized, are not regenerated, why have such a war of words about the matter virtually worth nothing to the living or to the dead?

V.—My fifth argument shall be deduced from the Holy Spirit's own method of addressing unconverted men; by signs addressed to the sense, and words to the understanding and affections. The Messiah himself, the seventy evangelists, and the twelve apostles were accomplished and fitted for their ministry to the world by such inspirations and accompanying powers as human nature and society, Jewish and pagan, then required, and I presume always will require. They were first sent to the lost sheep of the house of Israel; and afterwards the apostles were sent to the Gentiles. Now, in seeking to regenerate and save the human family, they, divinely guided, uttered certain words, and accompanied them with certain miracles. These were the means supernaturally chosen and used. They were certainly apposite means, appropriate and fitted to the end proposed by the donor of this intelligence and power. He seems to have sought admission into the hearts of the people by these glorious displays of divine power presented to the eye, and these words of grace addressed to the ear. They saw the sick healed, the leper cleansed, demons dispossessed and the dead raised; and, while seeing these solemn and significant arguments they heard words of tenderness—words of pardon and of life, spoken with a divine earnestness, with a heavenly sympathy and affection. Thus the Spirit sought to convert them. He used means, rational means; therefore, we argue, such means were necessary, and are still, in certain modifications of that same supernatural grandeur, necessary to conversion and sanctification. Signs, as Paul explains them, were necessary, not for believers, but for unbelievers. They were necessary to faith. The miracle opened the heart, the testimony of the Lord entered, and the Spirit of God with it, and the work of conversion was finished.

Now, may we not conclude that miracles and words are not a mere redundancy—a perfect superfluity? May we not regard them as essential means, employed by the Holy Spirit in accomplishing his work? It is, perhaps, important also to say, that the proof of a proposition is always subordinate in rank to the proposition which it proves. The life is not in the miracle, but in that which the miracle proves. The grand proposition is that Jesus is the Messiah, the Son of God, the Savior of the world. He that believes this proposition is "begotten of God." It is the "incorruptible seed." It is the "living Word." It abideth forever. The Church of the Messiah is built upon it. The premises, then, certainly justify the conclusion that, in converting and sanctifying the world, the inspired apostles and evangelists used means of divine authority; and neither did depend upon, nor teach others to depend upon any agency from above, dispensing with such an instrumentality.

VI.—Our sixth argument is derived from the name chosen by the Messiah as the official designation of the Holy Spirit. He calls him the Paracletos, and that, too, with a special reference to his new mission. This term, occurring some five times in the apostolic writings, is, in the common version, translated both *comforter* and *advocate*; and, by Dr. Campbell, *monitor*. As an official name I prefer *advocate* to either of the others. It is generic, and comprehends them both. An advocate may be a monitor or a comforter; but a monitor, or a comforter, is not necessarily an advocate. Now, as the Spirit is to advocate Christ's cause, he must use means. Hence, when Jesus gives him the work of conviction, he furnishes him with suitable and competent arguments to effect the end of his mission. He was to convince the world of sin, righteousness and judgment. In accomplishing this he was to argue from three t0pics: (1) The unbelief of the world; (2) Christ's reception in heaven; (3) The dethronement of his great adversary, the Prince of this world. Then the person, mission and character of the Messiah alone came into his pleadings. Jesus promised him the documents. And, indeed, the four evangelists are arranged upon the instruction given by the Messiah to his advocate. In converting men, the Spirit, the Holy Advocate, was to speak of Jesus. Hence, speaking of Jesus by the Spirit is all that was necessary to the conversion of men. The official service and work thus assigned the Holy Spirit is a standing evidence that, in conversion and sanctification, he operates only through the Word. And, as it has been already shown, conversion is, in all cases, the same work, he operates in this department only by and through the Word, spoken or written; and neither physically nor metaphysically.

VII.—Our seventh argument shall be deduced from the opening of the commission; from the gift of tongues, by which the Advocate commenced his operations. That the Messiah had a commission for convincing and converting the world has been already shown. That he was to use arguments has been fully proved; that he was to speak and work also; that by signs and miracles he accompanied the Word, and made it effectual. Now, that language is essential to the completion of the commission is further proved from the great fact that the first gift of the Holy Spirit, under the Messiah's commission, was the gift of tongues.

Language, not merely the various dialects of human speech, but language itself—not Hebrew, Greek and Roman, but that of which Hebrew, Greek and Roman are mere dialects, forms or modes—is essential. He gave the first and he gave the second. He made a glorious display of the use of language, of the need of tongues, in commencing his new work. He gave utterance, for utterance is his gift. So Paul to the Corinthians said, "You are enriched by him in all knowledge and in all utterance." The day of Pentecost is the best comment on this whole subject of spiritual influence ever written. We have much use for it in this discussion. It is just as useful on the work of the Spirit as on the genius and design of baptism.

It seldom occurs to us that all Christendom—the living world is now indebted for the very book that records the name and embalms the memory of the Messiah, and for all that is known of the Holy Spirit, for the very language of the new covenant, for the gospel of the kingdom, and for every spiritual idea and conception of God, of heaven, of immortality, of our origin, nature, relations, obligations and destiny, to the immediate agency of this Spirit of all Wisdom and Revelation—to the gift of tongues or of language. Yet true to the letter it is, that "no one could say that Jesus is Lord but by the Holy Spirit."

Some among us, through the ignorance that is in them on this grand theme, ascribe to the human mind the powers of the Holy Spirit. They represent the human mind as possessing some sort of innate power of originating spiritual ideas; to arrive at the knowledge of God by the mere contemplation of nature. They annihilate the doctrine of the fall, of human imbecility and depravity, and adorn human reason with a very splendid plagiarism, called natural religion. While at variance on almost everything else, the mental philosopher and the Deist, the Romanist and the Protestant, the Calvinist and the Arminian, admirably coalesce and harmonize in this self-congratulatory assumption. They say that man can, by the feeble, glimmering rush-light of his own studies of nature, either descend from his *a-priori*, or ascend from his *a-posteriori* reasoning of God—to the apprehension of his very being and perfections, human responsibility, the soul's immortality, and a future state of rewards and punishments—without the Bible and without the teaching of the Holy Spirit.

We have neither so studied nature nor learned the Bible. We subscribe to Paul's dogma, "The world by wisdom knew not God," and agree with him, that "it is by faith," and not by reason, "we know that the worlds were framed by the Word of God, so that things now seen existing did not formerly exist." We, indeed, ascribe all our ideas of spirit and of a spiritual system, our conceptions of God as Creator, of creation itself, of providence and of redemption, to one and the same Spirit, and to that Logos who, in one form or other, has been the prophet or the advocate of the Messiah and his cause for some six thousand years.

We go yet further. We assign to the Spirit of all Wisdom and Revelation the origination of the spiritual language—perhaps, indeed, of all language. The most enlightened men, whether Pagans, Jews or Christians, regard language as a divine revelation, even that large proportion of it derived from sensible objects. The philosophers, from Plato down to Dr. Whitby, have claimed for the Supreme God this honor. They have refused it to either civilized or uncivilized man, to all conventional agreement. They have handled, with great effect, that plainest of propositions, that councils could not be convened—that if they had spontaneously arisen, no motions could have been made, no debates commenced nor conducted, without the use of speech. Philosophers assume that men think in words as well as communicate by them; or, at least, have some image of the thing, natural or artificial, or they can not even think about it. The natural process, which can easily be made intelligible to all, is that the *thing* is pre-existent, the *idea* of it next, and the *word* last. The line ascending is the word, the idea, the thing. The line descending is the thing, the idea, the word. Now, as the line descending is necessarily first, we must, especially in things spiritual, admit that the spiritual things could be communicated to man only by one that comprehends them, who had seen them, and who selected from the elements of that language first given to man, when he conversed face to face with God in Eden, the proper materials for words to communicate things spiritual. In strict accordance with this assumption, Moses teaches us that God conferred with Adam, and continued his lessons until Adam was able to give every creature around him a suitable name. That language commenced in this way all admit from one fact, to wit: Every one speaks the language which he first hears. This is his vernacular. A miracle is before us; the first man spoke without being spoken to; else God spoke to him. Either is a miracle; and of the two, the latter is of the easiest credence; and, indeed, it is to the faithful evidently true from the words of Moses. With Plato then, I say, that God taught the primitive words, and from that, man manufactured the derivatives. With Newton I say, God gave man reason and religion by giving him speech. With tradition I say, that the god Thath, of the Egyptians, is the Theos of the Bible, and the Logos of the New Testament. The Logos incarnate is the Messiah of Christianity. Therefore, the Spirit of God, now the Spirit of the Word, is the origin of all spiritual words and conceptions. With Paul, therefore, I say, "We speak spiritual things in spiritual words, or words which the Spirit teacheth, expressing spiritual things in spiritual words."

I will conclude in the language of the Hebrew poet: "It is God that teacheth man knowledge, and the inspiration of the Almighty giveth him understanding." "The entrance of thy Word giveth light; it giveth understanding to the simple." The very language, then, as well as the ideas that convert the soul, is spiritual. So that truly we may affirm that in conversion the Spirit of God operates upon a person only by and through the Word, and the ideas originated by himself. Of all which the first demonstration of the Spirit in fiery tongues, words, language, and signs, is a full and ample proof.—[Time expired.]

MR. RICE'S FIRST REPLY.

Monday, Nov. 27, 11 A.M.

Mr. President—There are two principal obstacles in the way of man's salvation. The one is, that he has broken the law of God, and is, therefore, condemned; the other is, that he possesses a depraved nature, and is, therefore, disqualified for the service of God and the happiness of heaven. There are, likewise, two great doctrines which especially characterize the Gospel. The one is the atonement of Christ, by which we may be relieved from the curse of the law; the other is the work of the Spirit, by whose agency we may be sanctified and prepared for heaven. These doctrines constitute the two chief pillars in the temple of gospel truth; and he who attempts to overturn the one or the other does what he can to destroy the sacred edifice, and to expose the human race, helpless and hopeless, to the wrath of a just God.

The subject of discussion this morning is, therefore, as important as the immortal interests of the soul. Without the atonement of Christ, all must die in a state of condemnation, and without the special agency of the Holy Spirit all must die in depravity and be eternally lost.

In the discussion of a subject such as the one now before us, it is of the utmost importance that we understand distinctly the point of controversy. In this, as in his other introductory addresses, my friend, Mr. C., seems to have directed his efforts more to beauty of style and composition than to the clear statement and defense of his faith. I venture the opinion that no one individual in this large and intelligent audience has been able to gather from the address he has just read to us wherein we differ, or what is the point to be debated. If any one has been so happy as to have been enlightened concerning this important matter, I must award to him more ingenuity and discrimination than I possess. If time were allowed me, and I were capable of writing so handsome a discourse, I might afford the audience another hour's entertainment, and yet they would not know how far we agree in our views of this important subject, nor wherein we differ.

The gentleman has said a number of things which are true, and a number of things which, I suppose, are not true. Indeed, I could but admire the number of topics he contrived to introduce in the course of an hour—sectarian phraseology, the Trinity, the parts of the work of salvation assigned to each of the Persons, the nature of matter and mind, infant baptism, the origin of language, etc. I can not subscribe to much that he said with regard to theological systems and sectarian phraseology. With him it seems all churches are "sects" but his own, and yet it would be difficult to find a denomination that is more accurately described by a correct definition of the word "sect." He tells us he can at any time know a Calvinist or an Arminian by his phraseology before he has heard him an hour. And I will say that I can identify a modern reformer of his school in half the time; not by his close adherence to Scripture phraseology, but by the cant of the sect. The exclusive claims of some of our modern sects to be the church the only true church, savors more of the pride of Rome than of the Spirit of the gospel. If, however, the gentleman can establish the high claim of his Church, he will have accomplished an important work.

The proposition before us is in the following words: "In conversion and sanctification the Holy Spirit operates on persons only through the Word of Truth."

The word "conversion," as used in the Scriptures, in its most enlarged sense, expresses two important ideas, viz.: First, a change of heart; and, second, a change of conduct; or a turning in heart and in life from sin to holiness, from the service of Satan to the service of God. The word signifies literally turning from one thing to another. When an individual who has been pursuing a certain course turns to an opposite one we naturally conclude that his mind is changed. Hence, the word "conversion" came to signify both cause and effect—the change of heart and the consequent change of conduct. In this sense it is used in Matt. xviii. 3: "Except ye be converted, and become as little children, ye shall not enter into the kingdom of heaven."

The word "sanctification" is employed in the Scriptures, and by all accurate theological writers, not to signify something in its nature distinct from regeneration or conversion, but the progress of the gracious work of which regeneration is the commencement.

The difference between us, so far as this subject is concerned, is, in general terms, this: Mr. Campbell believes that in the work of conversion and sanctification the Spirit operates *only* through the Truth. I believe that the Holy Spirit operates through the truth where, in the nature of the case, the truth can be employed; but I deny that the Spirit operates only through the truth. I would not have consented to discuss the proposition, if the word "only" had been omitted. For we believe and teach that the Holy Spirit operates ordinarily through the truth, but not *only* through the truth.

That we may ascertain precisely the point in debate it is important to inquire how far we agree. I remark, then, that we agree on the following points:

First—That the Holy Spirit dictated the Scriptures—that "holy men spake of old as they were moved by the Holy Ghost."

Secondly—That the Holy Spirit confirmed the truth of the Scriptures by miracles and prophecies.

Thirdly—That in the conversion and sanctification of those who are capable of receiving and understanding the Scriptures the Spirit operates ordinarily through the truth.

Thus far we are agreed. We differ on the following important points:

First—Mr. Campbell contends that in conversion and sanctification the Spirit never operates without the truth, as the means of influencing the mind. I maintain that in the case of those dying in infancy and idiocy the Spirit operates without the truth.

Second—Mr. Campbell affirms, that in the conversion and sanctification of those capable of understanding the Word, the Spirit operates *only* through the truth—that is, the Spirit dictated and confirmed the Word, and the Word, by its arguments and motives, converts and sanctifies the soul. I desire that this point may be very distinctly apprehended, for it is of vital importance. Mr. Campbell teaches, that in conversion and sanctification, the Holy Spirit operates on the minds of men just as his spirit operates on the minds of this audience, or as the spirits of Demosthenes and Cicero operated on the minds of their auditors or their readers, viz., by his words and arguments alone. As Mr. Campbell presents words and arguments to the minds of his hearers or readers, and those words and arguments exert an influence on them, so the Holy Spirit presents in the Scriptures arguments and motives, and by these alone does he operate on the human mind.

Such precisely is his doctrine on this vital subject. I regret that he did not, in his address, more distinctly present it. To prove to you, my friends, that I am not misrepresenting him I will read several passages from his "Christianity Restored."

"Because arguments are addressed to the understanding, will and affections of men, they are called moral, inasmuch as their tendency is to form or change the habits, manners or actions of men. Every spirit puts forth its moral power in words; that is, all the power it has over the views, habits, manners or actions of men, is in the meaning and arrangements of its ideas expressed in words or in significant signs addressed to the eye or ear. All the moral power of Cicero and Demosthenes was in their orations when spoken, and in the circumstances which gave them meaning, and whatever power these men have exercised over Greece and Rome since their death is in their writings.

"The tongue of the orator and the pen of the writer, though small instruments and of little physical power, are the two most powerful instruments in the world, because they are to the mind as the arms to the body—they are but the instruments of moral power. The strength is in what is spoken or written. The argument is the power of the spirit of man, and the only power which one spirit can exert over another is its arguments. How often do we see a whole congregation roused into certain actions, expressions of joy or sorrow, by the spirit of one man. Yet no person supposes that his spirit has literally deserted his body, and entered into every man and woman in the house, although it is often said he has filled them with his spirit. But how does that spirit, located in the head of yonder little man, fill all the thousands around him with joy or sadness, with fear and trembling, with zeal or indignation, as the case may be? How has it displayed such power over so many minds? By words uttered by the tongue; by ideas communicated to the minds of the hearers. In this way only can moral power be displayed.

"From such premises we may say that all the moral power which can be exerted on human beings is, and must of necessity be, in the arguments addressed to them. No other power than moral power can operate on minds; and this power must always be clothed in words, addressed to the eye or ear. Thus we reason when revelation is altogether out of view. And when we think of the power of the Spirit of God exerted upon minds or human spirits, it is impossible for us to imagine that that power can consist in anything else but words or arguments. Thus, in the nature of things, we are prepared to expect verbal communications from the Spirit of God, if that Spirit operates at all upon our spirits. As the moral power of every man is in his arguments, so is the moral power of the Spirit of God in his arguments. Thus man still retains an image of his Creator; and from such analogy Paul reasons when he says: "For the things of a man knows no man, save the spirit of a man which is in him; even so the things of God knows no man, save the Spirit of God." And the analogy stops not here; for as he is said to resist another, whose arguments he understands and opposes, so are they said to resist the Holy Spirit who always resist or refuse to yield to his arguments."—Pp. 348, 349.

"But to return. As the spirit of man puts forth all its moral power in the words which it fills with its ideas, so the Spirit of God puts forth all its converting and sanctifying power in the words which it fills with its ideas. Miracles can not convert. They can only obtain a favorable hearing of the converting arguments. If they fail to obtain a favorable hearing, the arguments which they prove are impotent as an unknown tongue. If the Spirit of God has spoken all its arguments, or if the New and Old Testament contain all the arguments which can be offered to reconcile man to God, and to purify them who are reconciled, then all the power of the Holy Spirit which can operate upon the human mind is spent and he that is not sanctified and saved by these can not be saved by angels or spirits, human or divine.

"We plead that all the converting power of the Holy Spirit is exhibited in the divine record."—Pp. 350, 351.

These passages present, with great clearness, the views of Mr. C. on this important subject. He asserts that in conversion and sanctification the Holy Spirit operates on the minds and hearts of men only as the spirit of some one man operates on the spirit of another. Nay, he even goes further, and denies, not only that the Spirit *does* operate except simply by words and arguments, but that he *can* exert any other influence over the human mind! In the Millennial Harbinger he has given us an exhibition of his doctrine too clear to admit of any mistake as to his real sentiments. It is as follows:

"As all the influence which my spirit has exerted on other spirits, at home or abroad, has been by the stipulated signs of ideas, of spiritual operations, by my written or spoken word; so believe I that all the influence of God's good Spirit now felt in the way of conviction or consolation in the four quarters of the globe, is by the Word, written, read and heard, which is called the living oracles."—Vol. VI., p. 356.

Thus you see, according to the gentleman's doctrine, the Spirit of God has no more power over the minds of men than his spirit; except that He may present stronger arguments. That is, the only difference consists in the fact that the Holy Spirit is a more powerful preacher than Mr. Campbell, though his operations are precisely of the same kind! Against this doctrine I enter my solemn protest.

We believe and teach that in conversion and sanctification there is an influence of the Spirit in addition to that of the Word, and distinct from it—an influence without which the arguments and motives of the gospel would never convert and sanctify one of Adam's ruined race. We further believe that, although the Word of God is employed as the instrument of conversion and sanctification where it can be used, God has never confined himself to means and instrumentalities where they can not be employed. In all ordinary cases He has always clothed and fed men by the use of means; but when his people were journeying through the wilderness to the promised land, and could not obtain either food or raiment in the ordinary way, they were fed with manna from heaven; their thirst was quenched by water miraculously brought out of the rock, and their raiment was not permitted to wax old. When Elisha the prophet could no longer obtain food in the ordinary way, God sent a raven to bear it to him; and when the widow's cruse of oil was almost exhausted, it was miraculously replenished. So does He feed the soul with the bread of life, through means and instrumentalities when they are accessible, and without them when they are not.

But let it he remarked that, whilst we believe in an influence of the Spirit, in addition to the Word, and distinct from it, we do not believe that in conversion new faculties are created. The mind, both before and after conversion, possesses understanding, will and affections. There is no creation of new faculties, but a change of the moral nature—a spiritual change—a change from sinfulness to holiness, and from the love and practice of sin to the love and service of God.

Nor do we maintain that in conversion and sanctification the Holy Spirit reveals to the mind new truths not contained in the Scriptures. "For all Scripture is given by inspiration of God, and is profitable for doctrine, for reproof, for correction and instruction in righteousness: that the man of God may be perfect, thoroughly furnished unto all good works." The design of regeneration is not to reveal new truths, but to enable the sinner, who is blinded by his depravity, to see the truths of revelation in their beauty and excellency, and to incline him to embrace them, and to live accordingly. The difficulty is not, that God's revelation is not perfect, presenting every truth which is necessary to life and godliness; nor that its truths are obscurely taught; but that the hearts of men are "fully set in them to do evil"—that they "love darkness more than light"—that they are proud and rebellious, averse to the service of God, and to the plan of salvation which he has devised. The psalmist, David, sensible of his blindness to spiritual things, the glorious truths of revelation, offered this prayer: "Open thou mine eyes, that I may behold wondrous things out of thy law" (Psa. cxix. 18). The law of God, the Holy Scriptures, he knew contained wonderful things; but, in consequence of his sinful blindness, he did not behold them clearly and distinctly. He therefore prayed, not for an additional revelation, but for spiritual illumination, for sanctification, that the cause of his blindness being removed he might see those things in their true nature; that "with open face he might behold, as in a glass, the glory of the Lord."

This statement of the doctrine of divine influence is a complete answer to the argument of Mr. Campbell, that those who profess to have been regenerated by the special influence of the Holy Spirit, have received no new ideas which are not contained in the Scriptures. Regeneration consists not in giving a new revelation, but a new heart.

In further elucidation of this subject, I remark, that the "modus operandi," the manner in which the Spirit operates on the human heart, we do not pretend to comprehend. Nor is the mysteriousness of the influence, as to the mode of it, an objection against the doctrine. That God created mind and matter, is perfectly clear, and easily apprehended; but *how* he created either the one or the other, none can understand. The fact, that the mind acts through the body, is clear; but how it acts, no philosopher can explain. Nicodemus, the Jewish ruler, objected to this doctrine as mysterious, and the Savior replied, "The wind bloweth where it listeth, and thou hearest the sound thereof, but canst not tell whence it cometh and whither it goeth; so is every one that is born of the Spirit" (John iii.) We feel the blowing of the wind, and perceive its effects; but how it blows, "whence it cometh, and whither it goeth," is a mystery. The Spirit renews the heart. We can realize the effects in ourselves, and see them in others; but how he operates, we can not comprehend. No man denies that the wind blows because he can not explain how it blows; for he sees and feels the effects. The effects of the Spirit's agency are equally manifest. We see the wicked man turning from his wickedness, and delighting himself in the service of the Holy One of Heaven. We ascribe the marvelous effect to an adequate cause. That cause, the Scriptures teach us, is the Holy Spirit; but the manner of his operation they do not explain, nor does it become us to inquire concerning it.

Again, I remark, the necessity of the special agency of the Spirit on the heart, in addition to the Word of Truth, does not arise from any lack of evidence that the Bible is a revelation from God. For, to every candid mind, who will weigh the evidence, it is not only conclusive, but overwhelming. Nor does it arise from any obscurity with which its instructions are conveyed; for the inspired penmen wrote with inimitable simplicity. The great doctrines and duties of Christianity are so clearly presented, and so variously illustrated, that all who are willing to know and obey the truth, must understand them. "The King's highway" is made so plain that "the wayfaring man, though a fool, need not err therein." Nor does it arise from any defect in the *motives* presented in the Gospel, to induce men to serve God: for they are high as heaven, deep as hell, vast as eternity, and melting as the dying agonies of the Son of God. Nor is a special divine influence necessary, because man is not a free moral agent; for he is as free as an angel to consider the motives placed before him, and to choose his own course. All that we mean, or can mean, by free moral agency, is, that men, looking at the motives which present themselves to their minds, voluntarily choose their own course. They do as they please—they are under no compulsion.

Why, then, it will be asked, is it necessary that there should be an influence of the Spirit, in addition to that of the Word, and distinct from it? The necessity arises simply from the depravity of the human heart—its pride, its love of sin, and its deep-rooted aversion to the character of God, to his pure law, and his soul-humbling gospel. To secure the perfect and perpetual obedience of the angels, it is enough that the will of God be made known to them; for they are holy—they love God with all their powers, and their fellow-beings as themselves. Their highest joy is derived from his service. They fly, swift as lightning, in obedience to his commands.

But such is not the character of man. He was created in the image of his Maker; but he is fallen—greatly fallen. The divine image has been defaced. The character of God, so glorious in the eyes of angels, has no attractions for him. Pride reigns in his heart. Angels prostrate themselves with adoring wonder and love, before the throne of God; but man is too proud to kneel before Jehovah. Angels find the perfect gratification of their pure affections, and the highest possible happiness, in the contemplation of the works and perfections of God, in communion with him, and in his holy service. But man is fearfully degraded. He worships and serves the creature, and forgets the Creator. He loves earth, and its low and degrading pleasures. His affections are entwined around them. Appeals to his gratitude and to his interest fail to withdraw them from earth, and fix them on heaven.

How shall we account for the widely different and opposite courses of conduct pursued by angels and men? Both are rational and accountable creatures, under the government of the same God, having the same motives to obedience. Why do they not see, feel, and act alike? The answer is plain. The angels are holy, and men are sinful—deeply depraved. Hence the necessity of a special divine influence, in addition to, and distinct from, the Word. Motives are sufficient to secure the obedience of angels; for they are holy; they are disposed to do their whole duty. Motives will not secure the obedience of men; for they are sinful; they are disposed to rebel. Consequently if any of the human family love and serve God, it is because he "worketh in them to will and to do, of his good pleasure." If those who have entered upon his service persevere to the end, it is because "he who began the good work in them, will perform it unto the day of Jesus Christ."

What are the effects of man's depravity, with regard to his reception of the gospel of Christ? The following are some of them:

1. Their minds, their affections, and their thoughts, are occupied with earthly objects; so that, like Gallio, they "care for none of these things." They can not be induced to hear and to consider. The cares of the world, and the deceitfulness of riches, choke the word. "Israel doth not know; my people do not consider." They are unwilling to be taught the truths of revelation.

2. Others hear and think; but they are deeply averse to the soul-humbling doctrines of the cross, and its pure principles and precepts. "Man, through the pride of his countenance, will not seek after God." Desiring to take the world as their portion, they catch at every cavil against the truth of the Bible, and become infidels; or, perverting its plain instructions, and seeking a broader way to heaven, they become heretics.

3. Others still, admitting the inspiration of the Scriptures, and the truth of the doctrines of the cross, are mere speculative believers; and loving the world and the things thereof, they reject the council of God against their own souls. They barter their immortal interests for the pursuits and pleasures of earth.

Such, briefly are some of the effects of human depravity. It fills the mind with trifles, makes it averse to the truths of revelation, and to the service of God, and thus closes it against the appeals of the gospel of Christ.

In conversion and sanctification, this corruption of nature is to be subdued and eradicated. No individual, it is certain, will ever become a true Christian, until he sees sin to be odious, and hates it; till he sees the character of God to be glorious, and loves it; till he perceives his lost condition, and the precise adaptation of the Gospel to secure his salvation, and cordially embraces it; in a word, till the service of God is his joy and his rejoicing. A radical moral change must be experienced, before the sinner will, or can, become a disciple of Christ.

That I have given a correct account of the character of man, I will now prove, by a number of plain declarations of Scripture. Indeed, it is scarcely necessary for me to enlarge on this branch of the subject; for we have just heard read, by Mr. Campbell, several passages of Scripture, which present a very dark picture of human nature. To those I will add several others. In John iii. 6, the Savior, giving the reason why the new birth is necessary, says: "For that which is born of the flesh is flesh; and that which is born of the Spirit is spirit." The meaning of this passage will be clear, if we can ascertain the meaning of the word "flesh." This word has, in the Scriptures, several meanings but when used with reference to moral character, it always signifies depravity, sinfulness. Thus it is used in Galatians v. 19-21: "Now the works of the flesh are manifest, which are these, adultery, fornication, uncleanness, lasciviousness, idolatry, witchcraft, hatred, variance, emulations, wrath, strife, seditions, heresies, envyings, murders, drunkenness, revilings, and such like." These are the works of the flesh, the legitimate products of man's corrupt nature, left to itself. Here we can be at no loss to understand the meaning of the word. It is the cause in man from which flow the dreadful evils here enumerated; it is his corrupt nature or disposition. And let it be remarked, no good is said to proceed from this nature; its fruits are "evil, and only evil, continually." In the same sense the word "flesh" is used in the epistle to the Romans (viii. 1, 6, 8, 9,) "There is, therefore, now no condemnation to them that are in Christ who walk not after the flesh, but after the Spirit." "To walk after the flesh is to be wicked, to walk after the Spirit is to be holy." Again: "So, then, they that are in the flesh can not please God. But ye are not in the flesh, but in the Spirit, if so be that the Spirit of God dwell in you." They who are in the flesh can not please God. It is evident, therefore, that there is nothing morally good in them; for God is pleased with goodness wherever he sees it. But who are in the flesh? All are in the flesh, unless the Spirit of God dwell in them. It is, then, perfectly clear, that the passage, "That which is born of the flesh is flesh," means, that by the natural birth all are depraved, entirely depraved; for the flesh, as we have seen, produces nothing but evil.

The same doctrine is taught in Gen. viii. 21: "And the Lord smelled a sweet savor; and the Lord said in his heart, I will not again curse the ground any more for man's sake; for [or though] the imagination of his heart is evil from his youth." I do not read the description of man's character, as given in Genesis vi., because some have pretended that it applied only to the corrupt generation then living; and I desire to prove, that after the flood, when only Noah and his family remained on earth, the same doctrine was taught in the most unqualified terms—"The imagination of his heart, [the human heart] is evil from his youth." It is evil from the earliest period of his being.

The same doctrine is taught, in the strongest language, in Psa. li. 5: "Behold, I was shapen in iniquity; and in sin did my mother conceive me." Again, Psa. lviii. 3-5: "The wicked are estranged from the womb; they go astray as soon as they be born, speaking lies. Their poison is like the poison of a serpent; they are like the deaf adder that stoppeth her ear; which will not hearken to the voice of charmers, charming never so wisely." These passages teach the doctrine of the original and entire depravity of man from his birth, in language so clear and so strong, that comment is unnecessary.

The same exhibition of the character of man is made by the prophet Jeremiah, chap. xvii. 9, 10: "The heart is deceitful above all things, and desperately wicked; who can know it? I, the Lord, search the heart; I try the reins, even to give every man according to his ways, and according to the fruit of his doings." Observe, he does not say the hearts of *some* men, or of some *classes* of men, are thus deceitful and desperately wicked; but the *heart,* using the most general expression in human language, without qualification. How dark is the picture—"deceitful above all things, and desperately wicked; who can know it?"

In the third chapter to the Romans, Paul gives an infallible description of man, as he is in heart and in life. "There is none righteous; no, not one; there is none that understandeth, there is none that seeketh after God. They are all gone out of the way; they are together become unprofitable; there is none that doeth good; no, not one. Their throat is an open sepulchre; with their tongues they have used deceit; the poison of asps is under their lips; whose mouth is full of cursing and bitterness. Their feet are swift to shed blood. Destruction and misery are in their ways; and the way of peace have they not known. There is no fear of God before their eyes." Thus Paul presents the deep and total corruption of man's nature. The description belongs not to one class, or to one nation, or to one age. He pronounces it a correct exhibition of the character of both Jews and Gentiles. All men do not actually commit all kinds of sin; nor do all proceed to the same length in any one course. But there are in man the seeds of all evil—a nature which, freed from restraint, and exposed to temptation, will run headlong into crimes of all kinds. Such is, in fact, the character of the human race, that John, the apostle, says, without qualification, "The whole world lieth in wickedness (1 John v. 19).

In further confirmation of the doctrine of man's total depravity, if indeed the evidence can be increased, I will state an important fact, viz., that all that is morally good in any man is by the Scriptures ascribed to a radical change of heart, of which God is the author. Does any one do good works? Paul ascribes it to a new creation. "For we are his workmanship, created in Christ Jesus into good works, which God hath ordained that we should walk in them" (Eph. ii. 10). Does any one love God and his fellow-creatures? John says: "He that loveth is born of God" (1 John iv. 7). Does any one believe that Jesus is the Christ? The same apostle says he "is born of God" (chap. v. 1). Since, then, all that is good in man is ascribed to a great change wrought in his heart by the Holy Spirit, and all that is evil is ascribed to his nature, it follows inevitably that he is entirely corrupt.

Such being the character of men, it is impossible, till their hearts are renewed, that they shall love God, his law, or his Gospel, or find pleasure in his service. The reason is this: No human being ever admired and loved a moral character just the opposite of his own. Both the judgment and the conscience of a wicked man may constrain him to acknowledge that his virtuous neighbor is better than he; but he will not choose him as a companion, because of his purity of heart and life, nor find pleasure in his society. "The light shineth in darkness; and the darkness comprehendeth it not." Our Savior appeared amongst the Jews in all the perfection and loveliness of human nature, and in the glory of divinity—"the glory as of the Only-begotten of the Father"; and yet they hated him, because his character was to theirs as light to darkness. "For what fellowship hath righteousness with unrighteousness? and what communion hath light with darkness?" (2 Cor. vi. 14.)

It is, then, perfectly clear, that every individual must experience a radical change in his moral character, before he ever will love God or embrace the Gospel of Christ. But are the truths of revelation sufficient to effect this change? They are not. If a man has conceived a strong prejudice against his neighbor, through a mistaken view of his character and conduct, you may remove the prejudice by giving him correct information. Or if one man entertains unkind feelings towards another, only because of some peculiar circumstances in which they happen to be placed in relation to each other; a change of circumstances may, produce a change of feelings—reconciliation may take place. Thus Joseph's brethren hated him, because they looked upon him as a successful rival in the affections of their father. But when the circumstances were changed, and, instead of regarding him as a rival, they looked up to him as a benefactor, their feelings were changed, and they were reconciled. But if a man hate the true character of his neighbor, if he dislike him, not viewed through erroneous information, but as he really is, the one or the other must greatly change, or they will never come together as friends. You can not induce the man who hates the real character of his fellow-man to love him by presenting the hated qualities more distinctly to his view. The more distinctly he sees that which he dislikes, the stronger, of course, is his aversion to it. Suppose, for example, an individual has a most inveterate dislike to some particular color, red, if you please. Will you be able to make him admire it by placing it before his eyes in the clearest possible light? The color is the very thing he dislikes, and you present it to him in its scarlet hue with the hope of inducing him to admire it! Evidently until his taste, if I may so call it, is changed, no clearness of light through which it is seen will cause him to admire it.

Let me apply the illustration. God is infinitely pure; his law is "holy, just and good," and his gospel is like its glorious author. The character of man is just the opposite. Consequently his aversion to God does not arise either from mistake, or from any unfavorable circumstances, which might be changed. He is sinful; God is infinitely pure; therefore there is in his heart a deep-rooted aversion to God. "The carnal mind is enmity against God." The Word of God is compared to light. It is the medium through which we see the objects of revelation. Light is the medium through which you see objects around you. It presents to your view many things that please, and many that offend. Select, if you please, one of the objects to which you have the greatest aversion. Concentrate upon it as much light as possible, so that you distinctly see its every feature. Now let me ask, will this concentration of light upon an object to which you have the strongest aversion cause you to admire and love it? You say, it will not. Light can not change your feelings toward an object which you dislike. Either the object must change, or you must change before you will love it. Let your mind be changed, and the same light which before revealed its apparent deformity will now reveal its beauty and loveliness.

So through the light of revelation we have presented to our minds the character of God, his law, his gospel, heaven and hell. This revelation presents these objects in their true character; but men, because of their depravity, feel a strong aversion to them. They are not averse to the character of God and the Gospel of Christ through mistake, but they dislike these glorious objects in their real character. Now when a man whose heart is enmity to God in his true character has that character presented to his mind by the light of Divine Truth, will the light cause him to admire and to love it? Or will he whose proud heart rises in rebellion against the pure and soul-humbling gospel be induced to love and embrace it by having it very clearly presented to his view? Surely not. It is clear, then, that man must experience a radical moral renovation—must be greatly changed—or he never will love God and obey the Gospel of Christ.

This I take to be the correct philosophy, as well as correct theology. There is no mysticism and no abstruse speculation in it. It requires not the mind of a Newton, a Locke, or a Bacon to perceive its truth. It strikes the common sense of every reflecting mind; and it presents to view the reason why conversion and sanctification never can be secured, in the case of any one of our race, without an agency of the Holy Spirit in addition to the truth, and distinct from it.

Having thus briefly explained the doctrine for which I contend, and proved the necessity of a direct divine influence in conversion and sanctification. I wish now to offer some further arguments against the doctrine believed and taught by Mr. Campbell.

I. My first argument is this: It prescribes to the power of God over the human mind, an unreasonable and unscriptural limitation. I can never subscribe to the doctrine that God can exert over the human mind no more power than I, except that he may employ stronger arguments; that the Creator can influence men morally, only as they may be pleased to listen to his arguments. I can never consent to place the Holy Spirit on a perfect equality with man, except that he is a better preacher.

First.—The doctrine which thus limits the power of the Spirit is most unreasonable, as well as most unscriptural. God created man holy in the beginning, and he did it without words and arguments. Gen. i. 26, 27: "And God said, Let us make man in our image, after our likeness. So God created man in his own image, in the image of God created he him." "Lo, this only have I found, that God hath made man upright, but they have sought out many inventions. Now, if God could originally create man holy, without words and arguments, who shall presume to assert that he can not create him anew, and restore his lost image, without them; or that he has now no power over the human mind, beyond that of argument and motive? The gentleman may philosophize and speenlate as much as he pleases, to prove that God has no more power over the heart of man than a fellow creature; but the simple fact now stated, that originally he made him upright, without words or arguments, is abundantly sufficient to refute his theory.

As he created man holy, so can he new-create him. As he created Adam in his own image, without words, so can he renew the infant mind, and prepare it for heaven, though it can not receive the truth.

Mr. Campbell will not deny that God created man upright, since in his "Christian System" he has so taught (pp. 26, 28):

"Man, then, in his natural state, was not merely an animal, but an intellectual, moral, pure, and holy being."

Again:

"God made man upright, but they sought out many inventions. Adam rebelled. The natural man became preternatural," etc.

If, then, God made man upright without words and arguments, exerting a moral influence over his mind without motives, who can prove that now his power is limited to mere words and arguments?

It is admitted that the light of revelation is necessary to call into exercise proper feelings and affections, and to prompt to a right course of conduct; for we can not love an object of which we know nothing, nor obey a law concerning the requirements of which we are not informed. But whether the light will call into exercise such feelings depends upon the moral character or state of the mind. The Jews beheld the miracles wrought by the Messiah in proof of his divinity and of his mission to save men; but such was the state of their minds that they were either unconvinced or unwilling to become his followers. Thus Paul accounted for their blindness in reading the Old Testament, and yet rejecting the very truths which it most clearly revealed. "But their minds were blinded, for until this day remaineth the same veil untaken away in the reading of the Old Testament" (2 Cor. iii. 14).

The gentleman would make the impression on your minds that according to our doctrine there is no need of the gospel at all. But this is not true. The light is necessary as the medium through which we may see the objects around us; but the light will not open the eyes of the blind. The sun may shine with noonday brightness, but the blind man will be blind still; or if a man hate the light and shut his eyes against it, he will not see. This is not owing to any defect in the light, but to the defect in his eyes in the one case, and to hatred of light in the other. So the light of revealed truth is necessary to present to the mind the objects calculated to call into exercise holy affections; but whether the effect will be produced, depends upon the state of the heart. The fact that men love darkness more than light, and turn from beholding it, argues no imperfection in the light.

The light is still necessary, though of itself it can not cause the blind to see. The gospel is equally necessary, though of itself insufficient to renew and sanctify the depraved hearts of men. If a man were suddenly made as holy as an angel, he could not love God, unless he knew him; nor embrace the gospel unless it were presented to him; nor do his work unless it were made known to him; nor aspire to heaven unless it were revealed to him. But when, by the Holy Spirit, the heart of the sinner has been renewed, he is filled with adoring gratitude, and with deep penitence, as the cross of Christ is presented to his view. He beholds an adaptation in the plan of salvation to his situation which he never saw before, and a glory in the character of the blessed Redeemer he never before beheld. In the beginning God made man upright; yet a revelation of himself and of his will was absolutely necessary that he might love and obey him. For similar reasons the gospel is necessary, though alone it can not purify man.

Second.—That Mr. Campbell's doctrine prescribes an unreasonable and unscriptural limitation to the power of God over the human mind, is proved conclusively by the fact that God does, in the course of his providence, exert over the moral conduct of man a controlling influence, which is not simply nor chiefly by words and arguments. And if he can control them at all without words and arguments, he can control them to any extent. This fact I will prove by several declarations of Scripture. (Exod. xxxiv. 24.) All the adult males of the Jews were required to go to Jerusalem thrice every year, to attend their three principal festivals. But how could they safely leave their families and their possessions exposed, as they must be, to the incursions of malignant enemies on their borders? To free their minds from apprehension God gave them the following promise: "For I will cast out the nations before thee, and enlarge thy borders; neither shall any man desire thy land when thou shalt go up to appear before the Lord." Does not this promise proclaim the truth that God could and would exercise a controlling influence over the desires of the surrounding nations? He not only said that they should not invade the territory of his people, but that they should not desire their land. Had he no power to control their desires? or did he restrain them by words and arguments?

Again, Prov. xxi. 1: "The king's heart is in the hand of the Lord, as the rivers of water; he turneth it whithersoever he will." Does Solomon mean that God turns the hearts of kings by words and arguments? Observe, the language is very emphatic—expressing the entire control which God can and does exercise over the hearts of kings. "He turneth it whithersoever he will, even as he turns the rivers of water." And if he can and does thus completely turn the hearts of kings, can he not, and does he not, also turn the hearts of others, not by words and arguments only? We can not avoid seeing that in this passage God claims to govern men by an influence far more powerful than mere motive.

The same truth is taught with equal clearness in Ezra vi. 22. The Jews, who had returned from captivity in Babylon, "kept the feast of unleavened bread seven days with joy: for the Lord had made them joyful, and turned the heart of the king of Assyria unto them, to strengthen their hands in the work of the house of God, the God of Israel." Here we have a very remarkable instance of the exertion of a divine influence over the moral conduct of a pagan king—a man who believed not in God's revelation, but was an idolater. He turned the proud heart of this king to his people, so that he aided them in the building of the temple at Jerusalem. Did he influence this king by words and arguments? Was this remarkable conduct of the king the effect of mere motives?

Again, chap. viii. 27, 28: "This Ezra went up from Babylon; and he was a ready scribe in the law of Moses, which the Lord God of Israel had given; and the king granted him all his request, according to the hand of the Lord his God upon him." Ezra having obtained a decree of the king, in favor of the work of building the temple, uttered the following language: "Blessed be the Lord God of our fathers, which hath put such a thing as this in the king's heart, to beautify the house of the Lord, which is in Jerusalem; and hath extended mercy unto me before the king and his counsellors, and before all the king's mighty princes." Ezra recognized the hand of the Lord in his success; a divine influence on the hearts of proud and ungodly idolaters; and he, therefore, offers thanks to God for this remarkable interposition. Was this an influence exerted by words and arguments? Did not God control the moral conduct of those men by another and more powerful influence?

The same doctrine is illustrated and confirmed by Neh. i. II. Nehemiah had heard of the deplorable condition of Jerusalem and its inhabitants; and he desired to go and rebuild the temple and the city. It was necessary to gain the consent of the king of Babylon; and, therefore, he prays: "O Lord, I beseech thee, let now thine ear be attentive to the prayer of thy servant, and to the prayer of thy servants, who desire to fear thy name; and prosper, I pray thee, thy servant this day, and grant him mercy in the sight of this man." Nehemiah prayed for what? That the Lord would so influence the mind of the king that he would grant him his request. And his prayer was answered: "And the king granted me, according to the good hand of my God upon me" (chap. li. 8).

These passages, and many others, prove, beyond controversy that God can and does exert upon the minds of men a controlling influence, distinct from words and arguments. Consequently the doctrine of Mr. Campbell, which denies that he does or can exert any other moral influence than that of mere motives, is not true.

I will now offer a second argument against the gentleman's doctrine. By the way, I should have been disposed to follow him in his argument, if he had made any distinct statement of his doctrine, and attempted to prove it. But it can not be expected that I should follow him in such a dissertation as that we have heard this morning, in which there is no clear and definite statement of the points at issue, and, of course, no clear and pointed argument. It has, therefore, become necessary for me to state his doctrine from his published works, and to advance arguments against it.

II. The argument I was about to offer is this: Mr. Campbell's doctrine necessarily involves the damnation of all infants and idiots. I do not say that he holds the doctrine of infant damnation, but I do say that, to be consistent, he must hold it, for it follows, as a necessary consequence, if his doctrine concerning divine influence is true.

The gentleman, I must so far digress as to remark, is yet in trouble on the subject of infant baptism. He has brought it up again. I did suppose, that, after calling it up in almost every speech since the subject was disposed of, he had at last fully delivered himself upon it; but I was mistaken. If I understand his remarks correctly, he said that all infants, baptized or not, are saved. Is he not aware that no Presbyterian, Methodist, or evangelical Pedobaptist baptizes infants for the purpose of saving them from hell, should they die in infancy? Many things in the plan of salvation we regard as useful, that are not absolutely essential to the salvation of the soul. We esteem it a precious privilege and a solemn duty to enter into covenant with God to train up our children in his nurture and admonition, and humbly to claim his promise to be a God to us and to our seed. God has commanded us to bring our children with us into the covenant and into the church; and we think it wise and useful to obey him. I hope the gentleman will now be satisfied, but if he still feels uneasy, he must still scatter his remarks about infant baptism through all his speeches to the close of the debate.

But to return. The gentleman's doctrine, I have said, necessarily involves the damnation of infants and idiots. This is an important argument, for more than one-third of the human race die in infancy. And although I do not suppose that his views will affect the safety of infants, still it is a subject which very deeply interests the feelings of every affectionate parent. It would indeed be difficult to induce them to believe that infants, incapable of knowing right or wrong, are sent to hell.

It is a truth, clearly taught in Scripture, and admitted by Mr. C., that infants and idiots are by nature depraved. Our Savior said: "That which is born of the flesh is flesh." By the natural birth all are depraved. This, I say, Mr. Campbell admits. I will read an extract or two from his "Christian System" where he has presented his views on this subject:

"This alarming and most strangely pregnant of all the facts in human history proves that Adam was not only the common father, but the actual representative of all his children. * * * There is therefore a sin of our nature, as well as personal transgression. Some inappositely call the sin of our nature our 'original sin,' as if the sin of Adam was the personal offense of all his children. True indeed it is, our nature was corrupted by the fall of Adam before it was transmitted to us; and hence that hereditary imbecility to do good, and that proneness to do evil, so universally apparent in all human beings. Let no man open his mouth against the transmission of a moral distemper until he satisfactorily explain the fact that the special characteristic vices of parents appear in their children as much as the color of their skin, their hair, or the contour of their faces. A disease in the moral constitution of man is as clearly transmissible as any physical taint, if there be any truth in history, biography, or human observation.

"Still man, with all his hereditary imbecility, is not under an invincible necessity to sin. Greatly prone to evil, easily seduced into transgression, he may or may not yield to passion and seduction. Hence the differences we so often discover in the corruption and depravity of man. All inherit a fallen, consequently a sinful, nature; though all are not equally depraved. * * * Condemned to natural death, and greatly fallen and depraved in our whole moral constitution though we certainly are, in consequence of the sin of Adam, still, because of the interposition of the second Adam, none are punished with everlasting destruction from the presence of the Lord but those who actually and voluntarily sin against a dispensation of mercy under which they are placed."

This system is indeed quite orthodox, and since this is the gentleman's second confession of faith, we may hope that his third will bring him very nearly right. There is, then, he acknowledges, "a sin of our nature, as well as personal transgression"; there is "a disease in the moral constitution of man"; and he is "greatly fallen and depraved in his whole moral constitution." Now the question is, how are infants, thus fallen and depraved, to be saved? The gentleman, with singular inconsistency, admits their depravity, denies any divine influence by which they can be sanctified, and still expresses the opinion that they may be saved!

Infants, it is admitted, are depraved. Then, concerning all that die in infancy, one of three things is necessarily true, viz.: either they go to hell, or they go to heaven, in their depravity, or they are sanctified by the Spirit without the truth. But we know that they can not go to heaven in their depravity; we know that they can not be sanctified through the truth, which they can not comprehend; and Mr. Campbell denies that they can be sanctified without the truth. We are, therefore, forced to the horrible conclusion, if his doctrine be true, that they die in depravity, and are forever lost. With his *opinions* on this subject I have nothing to do. They directly contradict his *doctrine*, and, therefore, the one or the other is false. But here I will, for the present, close my argument. (Time expired.)

MR. CAMPBELL'S SECOND ADDRESS.

Monday, Nov. 27, 12 o'clock P.M.

Mr. President.—I have had reasons numerous and various, before to-day, to conclude that my zealous opponent has fallen upon a rather singular mode of conducting the defense of the dogmata of his party, and of assailing us. When the Presbyterians first proposed the discussion to me, it was distinctly stated and agreed upon that we should severally maintain and defend the doctrines which we teach, in such words and propositions as we respectively preferred. The points selected were supposed to comprehend the points at issue. It was also always contemplated and understood on my part that we should have an equal number of affirmatives and negatives, as our correspondence will exhibit, when examined from first to last. We have now had the experience of ten days, and upon an impartial retrospect of the past, and of the speech of this morning, I must say that I have never before been placed exactly in the same circumstances. I have had some little experience in conducting popular discussions, and have had a considerable variety of opponents, some that sought always to lead, and some who preferred to follow; but I have never before found just such an opponent as my friend, Mr. Rice—one that will neither lead nor follow. [A laugh.] This is precisely the state of the case. He has conducted the discussion of two affirmatives. I did not wish to form an estimate of the man, his talents, or his policies, from his management of the first. But I have now all the data before me which the present occasion will afford. He has done with his affirmative propositions. He is now, for the third time, on the negative.

On the first affirmative I was curious to comprehend his resources, and to form a proper estimate of his powers of defense. After speaking nearly half an hour, he took out his watch, and during twenty minutes looked at it no less than five times. Finally, before his time expired, he asked the moderators if his time was not nearly expended. On learning that he had still a few minutes, he sat down. Thus toiled he under the "onus probandi" of an infant subject of baptism. On Saturday last, as most of you will remember, when his other affirmative was on hand, after various efforts in his opening speech, to advance into the merits of the question, after the fourth appeal to his tardy watch, he sat down at the end of forty minutes!

He looks to me, sir, for matter of argumentation. He is made for contradiction. I have then to furnish materials for both sides. Instead of responding to the proper issue, already formed, he seeks in my addresses new points from which to digress into new regions of negations; that is to say, I must give him data out of which to excogitate new, adventitious, and foreign subjects, on which to wrangle in the way of digression. He endeavors to make me always affirm, even while on the negative side, that he may occupy a negative position as often as convenient.

Of all this I ought not, probably, to complain. It is the best, the very best mode of defense which his cause affords. I must, however, because of his boastful manner, expose the awkwardness of his position, and the barrenness of the soil which he occupies. He can do no better.

The gentleman knew that he had not one argument, not one precept or precedent in the Bible in support of either of his affirmations. His hope, then, rested upon remote questions, far-off inferences, involved reasonings, irrelevant or false issues and contingencies. And while I affirm and file off my arguments numerically, challenging investigation, why does he not, why can he not, respond to them as in duty bound, according to all the laws of disputation? Has he, then, sirs, at all responded to my opening speech on this grand proposition? With all reasonable emphasis, I pronounced argument first, second, third, etc., in order to challenge his special attention. But I could not succeed. The gentleman is not to be moved in that way. I have, then, sir, really and in truth, no opponent on this occasion. In a speech of one hour he did not come up to one of my arguments, as though he felt it neither necessary nor important formally to encounter them.

These arguments I introduced by a considerable preface, containing very important items of thought, and even of argument, as I supposed, demanding some notice. Even that, too, the gentleman found it most convenient to pass in a respectful silence. But he was pleased to say that I do not state the issue, nor make out the difference between us. Did I not read the proposition? Did I not distinctly affirm "that the Spirit of God operates in conversion and sanctification only through the truth"? This I solemnly affirm as my belief. This he denies. He maintains another proposition, viz., that the Spirit of God operates in conversion and sanctification, not only through the truth, *but sometimes without it.* The issue, then, was fairly stated and definitely made out. There is no necessity for expatiating much more on this subject. I submitted seven arguments in proof of the issue agreed upon. He has formally responded to none of them. In so doing I can not but conclude that the argument, the real issue, is given up, and the gentleman *can not* at all respond to my proof. This is my conscientious conviction. I may, then, either sit down or proceed for the gratification of the audience to state some other arguments and proofs. I opine the gentleman will never answer those now on hand; indeed, I feel confident he can not.

He has given us a few of the dry remains of some old harangues or lectures upon total depravity, which he may have preached around the country I know not how many times. This matter is wholly foreign to the subject. The question is not about total depravity. I believe man is depraved. He is proving a proposition, wide as the breadth of the heavens of the subject before us. I believe that God presides over all the works of his hands. But that is not the point of debate, nor is the question about what God can or can not do, whether or not he turns the hearts of kings and mortals, as the channels of the rivers or the seas are turned. Whether he disposes the hearts of men, without words, is nor the question; for were it proved that he can move kings and princes, and men of all ranks and degrees, as I believe, without the Bible, and without words, that reaches not this issue at all. The question before us is about *sanctification*, about *conversion*. These are but sallies, feints, mock assaults, wholly alien to the issue. The question is whether God *converts* men to Christ or *sanctifies* Christians *without the truth of the Bible.* If I could now marvel at any course the gentleman might adopt I would at his present singular attitude. Neither as affirmant or respondent will he keep to the Bible. I truly regret this truckling and catering to vulgar prejudices—this ad captandum rhetoric. When he will rise he may tell you with a smile, "Well, I can not please my friend, Mr. Campbell, nor do I expect to please him." Mighty logic, indeed! Unanswerable argument, truly! Alas! as my friend would say, alas! for the cause that depends upon such logical legerdemain!

While on this subject, I beg leave to expatiate for a moment on the scenes transpiring around us. I came here, at considerable sacrifice, to debate certain great principles with the elect representative of a respectable religious denomination, claiming the advantages of an elevated clerical character, and some antiquity in some its tenets and forms. During ten days I have carefully observed the management, the tactics and developments of my respondent and his party. I do not recollect on any occasion, certainly at no discussion of any great religious question, to have noticed so much homage and condescension to catch, if not to manufacture, public opinion, and to set on foot the opinion that Mr. R. had gained a glorious victory, in the cause of immersion at least. Touching the love of partisan triumph, I am aware that this is common to such occasions; but the means by which it is sought on the present occasion really surpass everything I have ever known or witnessed.

I was, indeed, expecting something of the kind; but my anticipations have been greatly transcended. On arriving in this city I asked a gentleman whom I now see standing in this audience how many newspapers were published in this city and by whom, and to what parties the editors belonged? Being informed on these points, the gentleman wished to know my reasons for making these inquiries. I responded that I simply desired to know what facilities my Presbyterian friends might have for manufacturing public opinion. My experience led me to expect that efforts of this kind would be made, for, in my debate with Mr. McCalla, past twenty years ago, that indefatigable party had spared no pains to propagate and circulate a glorious Pedobaptist victory, and so continued for several days, until Pedobaptism became so perfectly bald and naked that none seemed disposed to do it homage. For at least two or three days rumors were sent abroad all over the land that Mr. McCalla had gloriously maintained the cause. A reverend gentleman, now in this assembly, one of the moderators of that discussion, on his return to Flemingsburg, as I learn from good authority, very ingeniously explained the result of that discussion, very much to the credit of the party. The excited community, on hearing of his arrival, were anxious to hear his opinion as to the final result. Some of the elders of his church, approaching him, said, "Well, sir, what of the debate? How did it close?" "Why, sir," said he, "Campbell would prove that a crow was white if you would listen to him."

This sage remark saved the cause, at the expense of my reputation. It was the man that was defeated, and not the cause of infant baptism.

On the present occasion I learn a more extended system has been got up. Runners spread the tidings abroad—letters are written to distant places. Even the Presbyterian press has proclaimed all over the land a glorious victory. To the old system more thoroughly carried out, has, in this age of the march of mind, been added a new invention. True, indeed, something like it in days of yore seems to have occurred at Drury Lane and other London theaters, when some new actor was about to make his debut. In order to stimulate his energies, and to manufacture fame, a few friends were stationed in the galleries above, with a previous understanding when to clap, express their plaudits and to encore his performances. As an improvement, I learn a laughing committee has been organized, with a clerical fugleman, at whose signal certain persons are to smile a little broad, and thus encourage my worthy friend! I have, indeed, in these particulars been somewhat disappointed. My Pedobaptist friends have rather gone ahead of all my past experiences and expectations.

During the Roman Catholic discussion at Cincinnati, in 1836, I had a second lesson in this school of experience. A certain Protestant editor, who would at this day take rank among Puseyites of the first class, soon as the discussion began set on foot a manufacturing of public opinion. He observed, very frankly one day, that it was due to Protestantism that I should not triumph over the Bishop, on some of the questions at least, for, said he, we ought all to know that our bishops stand or fall with those of the Roman hierarchy. "If Mr. Campbell destroys the succession, on what shall we hang our plea? Our episcopacy goes by the board!" Still I was not prepared for all that I have seen, and read, and heard on this occasion. I had hoped the dignity of the discussion and solemnity of the occasion would have prevented anything of this sort.

For myself, I contend for truth, and not for victory without truth. My prayer is that truth, immutable, eternal truth, may prevail. The occasion demands a calm, dignified, religious investigation of these grand principles. It is all important that it should be so. We are getting up a book for the public, and we desire to give it to them without prejudice and without bribe. Our motto is, "Read, think, judge and decide every man for himself."

I did not come here to gain a triumph of that sort. I did not consider there were any laurels to be won, nor any honors to be gained in this field, nor from my present opponent. I presume no one of reflection thinks otherwise. I never felt more the dignity, grandeur and power of truth than on the present occasion. She, standing erect, with lofty mien and heaven-directed eye, deigns not to use any other arguments or to employ any other means than conscience, religion, and the God of truth will sanction and approve. Her reliance is not on human passion, temporal interest, nor fleshly policies; but on solid facts, substantial reasons and dignified argumentation. Entering upon a new week and upon a new subject, I regard it due to myself, my brethren, the public and the triumphing cause of Divine Truth to offer this critique upon the past—that, if possible, we may redeem time and proceed in a manner more worthy of ourselves and the cause we advocate. To proceed, then, to the subject offered by Mr. Rice in his last speech.

Human depravity and special providence are not the topics on hand. The gentleman must reply to me, or admit that he can not. It is my duty now to lead, and his to follow, if he can. Meantime, I have nothing to defend and nothing to do in further maintaining my position. It seems to be established. I will, therefore, make some remarks on the gentleman's use of my writings. I do not shrink from the discussion of anything I have ever written on this subject. Yet it would be more than human, more than any mortal man has yet achieved, if, in twenty years' writing, and in issuing one magazine of forty-eight octavo pages every month, written both at home and abroad, in steamboats, hotels and in the houses of my private friends and brethren, I should have so carefully, definitely and congruously expressed myself on every occasion on these much-controverted subjects as to furnish no occasion to our adversaries to extract a sentence or a passage which, when put into their crucible and mixed with other ingredients, might not be made to appear somewhat different from itself, and myself, and my other writings. To seal the lips of cavilling sectarians and captious priests is a natural impossibility. The Great Teacher himself could not, at least he did not do it.

I state it as a fact somewhat curious that for several years I have not looked over my first volumes, nor do I, when about to write upon a subject, feel it necessary to examine all that I have previously said about it. I am at no such pains to prevent contradictions—real or apparent. The secret is, I have, like the four cardinal points, certain grand principles clearly defined and solidly fixed in my own mind. These I can not forget, nor contradict. I can affirm, off-hand, what I have *not* written, if I can not always say what I *have* written. I can not contradict these fundamentals. They are sternly fixed in my mind. As the first principles of mathematics can never be forgotten, nor lost sight of, while the mind is master of itself, so the grand fundamental principles of Christianity can never be forgotten by him who has once clearly apprehended and sincerely embraced them. We may not, however, always express ourselves with equal clearness and precision.

As respects the passages read from "Christianity Restored," I will say that the gentleman has very greatly misrepresented me. I was explaining what is usually called *moral* power in contradistinction from *physical* power, or what some call *spiritual* power, as defined by some of our schoolmen. Physical force and the power of motives are very different things. Reasons, containing *motives*, constitute the elements and materials of all moral, converting or sanctifying power, so far as known to man. God's power is omnipotent, but it is consistent with himself and itself. The Gospel, Paul says, is "the power of God unto salvation." Hence, the moral omnipotence of God is in the document called the Gospel. God's moral power is infinitely superior to ours. Yet all that power is in the Gospel, and this is all we mean by all the converting power being in the Word of God. God may employ other means, other power, if you please, in converting men; but nothing finally converts them but the light and love of God in the Gospel.

Every word of God has life in it. If I might explain myself by one of the divine metaphors: The seed, said Jesus, is the Word of God. Now every grain of wheat, sound and good, has life in it; but it must be placed in a soil and under circumstances favorable to its development. It will not germinate nor grow but under those circumstances. Hence, when the Word of God is sown in the heart it will grow and develop itself in all the fruits of righteousness and holiness. The question is not, *how* it is sown, how it gets into the heart; but the question is, as to the power developed and exhibited when there. Whenever the seed of the Word is planted in the moral constitution of man I believe it will vegetate, grow, blossom and fructify unto eternal life.

With Mr. Rice conversion and sanctification seem to be by the Spirit alone. If this be so in one case, it is so in all cases. This is one of my main arguments, for, as before affirmed, whatever will produce one ear of corn will produce an indefinite number; seeing that all that is essential in any one case, is essential, neither more nor less, in every other case. So observation and experience testify in all vegetable and animal products. Is it not so, also, in the spiritual? If the Bible is to be our only guide, that it is so, can be made most evident. It is thus that we use and apply those offensive words that all the converting power of the Holy Spirit is in the Word. All the motives, arguments and persuasions of the Holy Spirit are found in the record. He uses no other in the work of conversion, or in the work of sanctification. "Sanctify them through thy truth." "The law of the Lord is perfect, converting the soul." So far as moral influence is concerned there is none besides, none beyond this.

If there be any other moral or spiritual influence in the new creation of man, we call for the testimony and the definition of it. If the Lord converts, sanctifies and saves an infant without the Word, the Gospel of Christ—sanctification or conversion, then, is independent of the Word, and seeing it is so, the Word ceases to be *the means* of grace and of conversion. The fact that whatever is essential to one product, whether animal, vegetable, intellectual, moral or spiritual, is essential to every other result of the same kind, will one day explode this mystic, unintelligible, unscriptural jargon, which makes void and of non-effect the Word of the living God.

The doctrine which I oppose, so far as it is really believed and acted upon, neutralizes preaching, annuls the Bible, and perfectly annihilates human responsibility. I know of no doctrine more fatal. For if God, by some mysterious power, without light, knowledge, a new idea, view or reflection, touch the soul of A, B or C, and make it holy by "infusing a holy principle," if he does this without any thought, motive or argument, instantaneously and immediately, what comes of the doctrine of human responsibility! Of what use is preaching, or the name of the Lord Jesus, or any instrumentality whatever! While, then, I believe and teach, and rejoice in the presence, and power, and positive influence of God's Spirit in the work of conversion and sanctification, I do repudiate a doctrine full of desolation—which makes man a mere machine, annihilates all rational liberty, destroys human responsibility and makes the Word of God a mere superfluity, of no essential importance, of no salutary instrumentality in the great work of regeneration.—[Time expired.]

MR. RICE'S SECOND ADDRESS.

Monday, Nov. 27, 12:30 p.m.

Mr. President—I have had some little experience in public debate, and I have uniformly observed, that when men find themselves pressed with arguments which they are conscious of being unable to answer, their effort is to induce the audience to believe that their opponents are saying absolutely nothing to the point. Such, as you are aware, has been the course pursued by my opponent from the commencement of this discussion. Fearful that the audience, in their simplicity, would believe that his arguments had been answered, and his doctrine overthrown, he has again and again most solemnly asseverated, as if divinely commissioned, that I had advanced not an argument, had said not one word bearing on the subject before us. Such are the means by which he vainly seeks, in his trouble, to save a sinking cause. Such are the means to which it is common for men to resort when defending a bad cause.

But the gentleman has, at length, put forth his high decree, that Mr. Rice *must* follow him, or confess that he can not. And it is now time for me to say to Mr. Campbell distinctly that we have moderators, whose business it is to determine when I am out of order, to whose decisions I shall cheerfully submit; but that Mr. Campbell can not moderate me. To his dictation I most assuredly will not submit.

His statements concerning my previous course in this discussion are not true. I will not say that he knows them to be untrue. I will not violate the rules of this discussion, and of common courtesy, as he has repeatedly done, by throwing out against him personal imputations; but I will say he is mistaken.

Mr. Campbell—I submit to the moderators whether I have violated the rules of this discussion?

Mr. Rice—I will, then mention some of his expressions: "Licentiousness of the tongue," "base aspersion," etc.

Mr. Campbell—If I say an author has written a base aspersion, does this involve the moral character of my opponent?

Colonel Speed Smith—I understand the expression "base aspersion" to be used concerning the author read.

Mr. Rice—I read only two authors, Perrin and Jones. Perrin wrote a hundred years before Jones, and, therefore, could not have written against him a base aspersion. The charge was against myself.

Mr. Campbell—It was Faber to whom I referred, and not Perrin.

Mr. Rice—I have never seen anything from Faber on this subject. I read the paragraph from Perrin, and compared Jones's quotation with the original, proving that whilst he professed to quote from Perrin, he omitted what related to infant baptism. The gentleman can not escape.

When a man so accustomed to debate as Mr. Campbell, and so remarkable for his coolness and self-possession, displays so much temper as the audience witnessed in his last speech there is sad evidence that something is wrong. Men do not ordinarily lose their temper when successful in argument. I will not now detain to reply to his singular assertions concerning my course in this discussion. I verily believe that the sole cause of his trouble is, that I adhere too closely to the point. Every argument I have advanced bears directly on the subject in debate unless when I am diverted from it, in pursuit of my opponent.

He, of course expects you to believe that he never wanders from the subject. Yet a part of his first speech was against infant baptism! The argument, I presume, would be this: Infants ought not to be baptized; therefore the Spirit, in conversion and sanctification, operates only through the truth! He is always in order—precisely to the point! All this is very easily understood.

His statements concerning the debate with McCalla—the runners who proclaimed victory, etc., require proof. Moreover, the assertion that McCalla was defeated needs to be proved. I also desire some evidence that Mr. Burch, one of the moderators, made the remark charged upon him. I have the very best reason for asserting that it is not true. No doubt Mr. Campbell has been so informed; but when he makes statements that are to be stereotyped, and go forth to be read by thousands, he is solemnly bound to have his proof at hand. Who does not know that thousands of rumors get afloat on such occasions which have absolutely no foundation in truth? The gentleman really seems to have greedily swallowed all that his friends and his flatterers told him, and, hence, he found no difficulty in believing that everybody ascribed to him a glorious victory.

But what has all this to do with the subject under discussion? Quite as much, no doubt, as his ad captandum closing speech on Saturday had to do with the administrator of baptism. To prove, of course, how closely he always adheres to the subject in debate he gave us a long harangue about going for faith to Geneva, to Westminster, to Rome, etc.! So now he has given us a variety of statements, none of which are true, about my mode of conducting the discussion; the debate with McCalla; manufacturing public sentiment, etc.—all, of course, to prove that in conversion and sanctification the Spirit operates only through the truth!

In reading the gentleman's writings for the purpose of having his views distinctly before the audience, I was acting precisely in accordance with our written agreement, as the correspondence will show. I was not pleased with the wording of the proposition now under discussion, and I agreed to debate it with the distinct understanding and agreement on his part that I would appeal to his writings in determining its true meaning. But I discover that he is never so much out of temper as when I read to the audience from his own works!

But the gentleman, in his excitement, told you that I was delivering to you the dry remains of old harangues which had been delivered he knew not how often. This he asserts as a fact. Now, pray, how does he know? What are we to think of a man who will stand up and boldly assert facts, of the truth of which he can not have evidence?

But he tells the audience, as usual, that his arguments have not been answered. Let us see whether they have or not. True, I did not choose to number them one, two, three, etc.; but they have been effectually answered.

His first argument to prove, that there can be no divine influence on the human mind except words and arguments, was based on his notion concerning its nature and constitution. This I was under no obligation to answer. If he will produce a "Thus saith the Lord," to sustain his doctrine, I will at once yield the point; but I am not concerned to answer a long metaphysical argument, based on what he conceives to be the constitution of the mind. He has professedly repudiated human philosophy, and taken the Bible alone as his guide; and yet, in the discussion of a Scriptural doctrine he hurries us immediately into the dark regions of metaphysical speculation! Does the Bible say that such is the constitution of the human mind that the Spirit of God can exert over it no moral influence except by words and arguments? Mr. Campbell's philosophy says so; but where is the passage in God's Word that does so teach?

Now although I was under no obligation to answer such an argument, I did expose it by presenting the simple and indisputable fact that originally God did create man holy, and that he did it without words and arguments. I also proved, by the Scriptures, that God in his providence, can, and does, exert a controlling influence over the moral conduct of men by his Spirit, and not simply or mainly by argument and motive. These simple and incontrovertible *Bible facts* demolish effectually his fine-spun metaphysical argument, written out with so much labor.

His second argument was, that there are among pagans, who have not the Bible, no spiritual ideas. This was answered by showing that, according to our views, regeneration by the Holy Spirit is not designed to communicate new ideas, but to enlighten the mind by removing sin, the cause of its blindness, that it may see, in their true light, the truths contained in the Scriptures. The gentleman could not hear my reply.

His third argument was, that whatever is essential to regeneration in one case, is essential in all cases; and, therefore, if the Word of Truth is necessary in any case, it is necessary in all. This was fully answered by proving that God has never limited himself in the bestowment of his blessings to any particular means and instrumentalities. Ordinarily, he has given his people food in the use of means; but when they have been placed in circumstances where means could not be employed, as in their journey through the wilderness, he has fed them without means. When the multitudes were with the Savior in a desert place, he gave them bread miraculously. So when infants are called from earth before they can be sanctified through the truth, they are sanctified without it. Surely if God would feed the bodies of his people without the ordinary means, he would not refuse to the soul of an infant the bread of life. The soul is worth infinitely more than the body, and eternal life than the temporal. Such was my reply to his third argument, and I regard it as perfectly conclusive.

His fourth argument was, that the Holy Spirit has addressed words and arguments to men. This is true; but does this fact prove that in conversion and sanctification he operates *only* through the truth? He can easily prove that ordinarily the Spirit operates through the truth; but he can not prove that he operates *only* through the truth. Yet this is precisely what he has undertaken to prove. His proof, therefore, falls very far short of his proposition.

His fifth argument was, that the Holy Spirit is called an Advocate. This is but a repetition of the other. But as an Advocate, does he influence the mind only by words and arguments? The gentleman has not produced a passage of Scripture, which so teaches. He boasts, that for every article of his faith he has a "Thus saith the Lord." Has he, I ask you, my friends, produced one passage of Scripture that sustains his proposition? He has not, and he can not. Yet he has heaped on me no slight reproach and abuse, because, as he pretends, I did not answer all his metaphysics.

Before proceeding farther in the regular course of argument I must make a few remarks which I forgot at the proper time. The gentleman, in the recklessness of despair, has charged the Presbyterians of this community with attempting by unfair means to manufacture public sentiment against him. The charge is not true—not a word of truth in it. If he believes what he has said, it only proves that a man in trouble can persuade himself to believe the greatest absurdities. The truth is, my friends have been more than satisfied with the expression of public sentiment relative to this debate. So clear, so strong, so unanimous has been the verdict against him, by the crowds of intelligent persons of all classes, of different denominations, and of no denomination, that they have had no temptation to seek to change it. I rejoice that such is the power of truth, that it, and not Presbyterians, has made public sentiment what it is. I would not have it changed. I am more than satisfied.

But Mr. C. goes not for *victory*. I wish he would. I am anxious to see his gigantic powers brought fully to bear on the subject. It may be true, as he fretfully intimates, that he can not gain very great fame by triumphing over one so feeble as your humble servant; but it is also true that he may gain the more disgrace by failing, as he evidently has, to sustain himself. What opinion will the public form of the strength of his cause, when he, who would affect to look down with contempt upon men of ordinary powers, fails to sustain it! What must be thought of this boasted reformation, and of its invincible champion, when both sink under the feeble strokes of a mere pigmy! It is truly cause for alarm, if, surrounded and sustained by almost an hundred of his preachers, and crowds of his people, who came to this place in the most confident expectation of a complete triumph, he can not keep public sentiment from going strongly against him! Alas, for this vaunted reformation!

It would appear, if we are to believe the gentleman, that I misrepresented him by reading his own book. He says, he maintains, that *moral* power is exerted only by words and arguments; but he makes a distinction between *moral* power and purely *spiritual* power. I will again read from "Christianity Restored" (pp. 347, 349), and leave the audience to judge whether I misrepresented him:

"We have two sorts of power, physical and moral. By the former we operate upon matter; by the latter upon mind. To put matter in motion we use physical power, whether we call it animal or scientific power; to put mind in motion we use arguments, or motives addressed to the reason and nature of man. * * * Every spirit puts its moral power in words; that is, all the power it has over the views, habits, manners or actions of men is in the meaning and arrangement of its ideas expressed in words, or significant signs addressed to the eye or ear."

Again:

"No other power than moral power can operate on minds; and this power must always be clothed in words addressed to the eye or ear. Thus we reason when revelation is altogether out of view. And when we think of the power of the Spirit of God exerted upon minds or human spirits, it is impossible for us to imagine that that power can consist in anything else but words and arguments. Thus, in the nature of things, we are prepared to expect verbal communications from the Spirit of God, if that Spirit operates at all on our spirits. As the moral power of every man is in his arguments, so is the moral power of the Spirit of God in his arguments."

Now, observe, the gentleman tells us we have only two kinds of power, viz., physical and moral; and he asserts that no other power than moral power can operate on minds. He further affirms that every spirit puts forth its moral power in words; that as the moral power of every man is in his arguments, so is the moral power of the Spirit of God in his arguments, which must be addressed to the eye or ear. I gave you the doctrine precisely as he himself stated it. If he will say that he was in error when he wrote this book we will certainly admit that he has the right to change; and since he is accustomed to change, it can not injure him much. I once heard of a Dutchman and an Irishman who had been condemned to be hanged, and were in the same prison. The Irishman was greatly bewailing his fate. The Dutchman reproached him for his cowardice. "Ah!" said the Irishman, "ye're used to it." Mr. C. is used to changing.

I must occasionally illustrate a point by an anecdote, since the gentleman has charged me with having a "Laughing Committee" here; or they will have nothing to do. He has dealt out to this imaginary committee, which must be large, quite a lecture for their unworthy employment!

Let it be understood that he has asserted that only moral power can be exerted on mind, and that all the moral power of the Spirit must be put forth in words and arguments. He even goes so far as to say that "if the Spirit of God has spoken all its arguments; or, if the New and Old Testaments contain all the arguments which can be offered to reconcile man to God, and to purify them who are reconciled, then all the power of the Holy Spirit which can operate upon the human mind is spent; and he that is not sanctified and saved by these can not be saved by angels or spirits, human or divine."—(Ib., p. 350.) If all the converting power of the Spirit is spent, there is, of course, no further influence that he can exert to save man. The gentleman, either to illustrate or to prove his doctrine, told us that a grain of wheat or of corn, has life in it, and that when it is placed in the earth it will grow; and so the Word of God, the seed, when it gets into man's moral nature, will bring forth fruit. But the wheat and the corn will not grow without the heat of the sun and rain; and man can not create either the one or the other. I am pleased with the illustration, for the Scriptures teach, that though "Paul planteth and Apollos watereth, God giveth the increase." In conversion and sanctification there is a work for man and a work for God; and he who rejects God's part of the work must be forever undone.

The gentleman objects to the doctrine for which we contend that it makes the Word of God wholly unnecessary. Light can not heal the eyes of the blind man, nor open the eyes of him who hates it. But is light therefore worthless? Light is the medium through which objects are seen; but if my eyes are diseased the light, however brightly it may shine, can not cause me to see. But let my eyes be healed, and then I can see by means of the light. As the light is absolutely necessary to vision, though it can not cause the blind to see, so is the Gospel necessary, though alone it can not purify the depraved heart.

Again, Mr. Campbell objects that the doctrine of a special divine influence in conversion and sanctification destroys the accountability of man. That this objection is wholly unfounded is perfectly plain. Man is a free moral agent. In view of motives he freely chooses and refuses. But his heart, as Solomon says, "is set in him to do evil." In the exercise of his freedom he deliberately chooses to sin. Is he then a mere machine? But God works in him to will and to do—inclines him to turn from sin to holiness. Is his free agency thus destroyed? Can not God incline the sinner to the path of righteousness without interfering with his freedom and accountability? The gentleman would have us believe that he never makes assertions without adducing the proof. I venture to say that he can not find a passage in the Bible, nor an acknowledged principle of mental philosophy, by which to sustain his objection.

When I closed my last speech I was proving that Mr. Campbell's doctrine necessarily involves the damnation of infants and idiots. He admits their native depravity. He denies that they can be sanctified without the truth. We know that they can not receive the truth; consequently they must die in their depravity; and wherever they may go, certain it is that they can not go to heaven. He may express the opinion that they may be saved, but his opinion contradicts his doctrine. There is no way of escaping the difficulty but by abandoning the doctrine. He can not answer the argument—it admit of no answer.

But the Scriptures clearly teach the necessity of regeneration in the case of infants, as well as of adults. Our Savior said to Nicodemus, "That which is born of the flesh is flesh; and that which is born of the Spirit is spirit" (John iii. 6). Infants, it will be admitted, are born of the flesh; consequently they must be born of the Spirit, or they can not enter into the kingdom of God. By the natural birth they are sinful; by the spiritual birth they become holy. But if, as Mr. C. teaches, infants can not be born of the Spirit, they can not be saved.

He complains that I do not follow him in his train of remark, as the respondent should follow the affirmant. Whether I will follow him or not depends very much on the course he takes. Every passage of Scripture which he may adduce in support of his doctrine I will notice; but in his metaphysical dissertations I shall not feel bound to follow him.

III.—My third argument against his doctrine is—that it contradicts the doctrine of human depravity, as taught in the Scriptures; for, if his doctrine is true, men sin only through ignorance or mistake. All that is necessary in order to convert and sanctify those, at least, who ever will be saved, is, according to Mr. C., simply to teach them the truth—to present before their minds words and arguments. Only teach them the truth, and they will turn and serve God, and go to heaven. Why, then, did they not sooner turn? Because they were laboring under mistaken notions. They had adopted erroneous views of the character of God, of his law, and his Gospel! All that is necessary, therefore, according to this doctrine, is to correct their mistakes.

This doctrine, I say, is contrary to the Scriptures. Let us examine a few passages, which prove clearly that men do not sin simply through mistake, but willfully. Eccl. viii. II: "Because sentence against an evil work is not executed speedily, therefore the heart of the sons of men is fully set in them to do evil" Ch. ix. 3: "Yea, also, the heart of the sons of men is full of evil, and madness is in their heart while they live, and after that they go to the dead." Psa. x. 4: "The wicked, through the pride of his countenance, will not seek after God; God is not in all his thoughts." The reception with which the Gospel meets men is set forth in a parable by our Savior, in which he says, "And they all with one consent began to make excuse" (Luke xiv. 18). Paul accounts for all the abominations of the heathens by saying, "And even as they did not like to retain God in their knowledge, God gave them over to a reprobate mind" (Rom. i. 28).

These Scriptures and many others teach most distinctly that men sin, not because they are ignorant or are under mistaken impressions, but knowingly, willfully, deliberately—that their actual transgressions flow from a corrupt and rebellious disposition. It is true that men do fall into error; but it is not so much the error that causes them to sin as it is sin that causes them to err. Paul, in his Epistle to the Romans, proves the depravity of the heathen, first, by their errors in belief, and secondly, by their immoralities in practice. The former affords as decided evidence of a sinful disposition as the latter. If a man stumble over everything in his way in daylight, we know that he is blind. So if any man with the Bible in his hand, err fundamentally, we know that a sinful heart has blinded him.

The doctrine of Mr. C. makes men, at least those who will ever be saved, sin only through mistake. The Scriptures teach that they sin knowingly, willfully, and deliberately. His theory, therefore, contradicts the teaching of the Scriptures concerning human depravity. It is, therefore, false.

I fear I shall look at my watch too often for the comfort of my friend, but I do not like to commence a new argument when my time is near out. So I will, for the present, close.

Here Mr. Campbell arose and said: "I beg the decision of the moderators upon the point, whether the respondent is not bound, according to the established usage of debate, to answer and respond to such matters as may be advanced by the affirmant."

One of the moderators then arose and remarked as follows: It is the most appropriate mode of procedure for the affirmant to open his ground of debate with such arguments as he may be able to adduce, and for the respondent to notice those grounds; but in his own way. The object of each is to prove his own position; but he must do it in his own mode. Men's minds are differently constituted. Their reasoning faculties run in different channels; and while one is making an argument, the other may suppose that he is evasive, and his remarks not appropriate; while the party replying may deem them perfectly so. All that we can decide is, whether or not the parties indulge in extraneous or irrelevant matter.

Mr. Campbell: Is it not usual for the respondent to reply in some way or other to the matter presented by the affirmant?

Moderator: It is certainly expected that he will notice the matter presented by the affirmant.

Another moderator remarked that it had devolved upon him to offer a few words with reference to the course of procedure thus far. He had on several occasions observed the boundaries of good order to have been very nearly trodden upon; but it was always unpleasant, on such an occasion, to check the speaker; and, though he had been more than once upon the point of striking, when, by an explanation from the speaker, the debate had been permitted to proceed. If he might be indulged in the suggestion, he would here intimate the propriety of avoiding, in future, everything of a personal character, and he trusted they would be able to get along without again touching so nearly upon the line.

The former moderator said he would add another suggestion. He thought that, generally, the debatants had conducted themselves with great propriety and decorum, which, to the moderators, had been highly gratifying. It could not be denied, however, that on some occasions there had been digressions from the true line of logical argumentation, and he would add, that these things would never do good, and that such matter would not look well in print. The propositions should alone be considered, and nothing but authorities and argument ought to be introduced into the discussion.

Mr. Fishback said, as a friend, he would recommend the reading of the rules.

Mr. Campbell: Under these rules I have thought that my friend was out of order, in upbraiding me with the consequences of a doctrine which I do not teach. If I understood, he ascribes to my teaching the consequences of sending infants to hell; which I have ascribed to those cruel decrees.

Mr. Rice: I have stated that I did not charge upon my friend with actually holding the doctrine of infant damnation.

Moderator: We can not decide whether the argument is persuasive or conclusive. Mr. Rice has assailed and endeavored to disprove the doctrine advanced on the other side; and he has a right to try that argument and except to its absurdities. But whether he can maintain his ground, we are not prepared to decide.

MR. CAMPBELL'S THIRD ADDRESS.

Monday, Nov. 27, 12:30 o'clock P.M.

Mr. President.—Sir: There are several small matters that require attention. Among these is the remark of Mr. Burch on the result of the McCalla debate, as to the conversion of a black crow into a white one.

Mr. Rice: Mr. Burch says he did not say so.

Mr. Campbell: Of course, the gentleman means he did not remember his having said so. He could not testify in such a case. No man could testify in a case of this sort, after an interval of twenty years, what he did not say on such an occasion. One single good witness declaring that he heard him say so, would, in a court of evidence, set aside his want of recollection in the case, and would stand in law. A person's having no present recollection of what he said twenty years ago is no proof that he did not say so. This is, indeed, a matter of very small moment; it is only the occasion that gives it any consequence.

Mr. Rice desires to know how I could say that he had been delivering the fragments of old harangues on total depravity. He seems to intimate that Christian morality might be implicated in such a saying. I have satisfactory evidence of the fact from two sources. First, I have heard of his discourses on this subject round the country, in different places; and again, I have positive written evidence of the fact of his promulgation of these views in his controversy, in one of our periodicals, with President Shannon.

The remarks on the subject of my excitement I will reserve to another occasion. I shall, then, proceed to the argument which closed my last speech.

If there be the slightest apparent relevancy in the arguments of my opponent to anything I have advanced, or to the true and proper issue before us, I hold myself in duty bound to respond to it. But when there are many things of the same class, it is not necessary to respond to them individually and severally. I will, in such case, select the strongest particular or incident introduced; and in disposing of that, as a matter of course, the others of that class are disposed of.

To illustrate and apply this observation, I must remind you that in my introductory address it is my aim to express, in a written form, the more cardinal principles and classes of evidence and arguments relied on, as fixed points, to which, at any time after, in the course of discussion, we may recur with certainty. In my opening address, therefore, I very formally propounded one invaluable principle or argument in support of this thesis—that God has given to the human mind a certain constitution as he has to the body of man, or to the universe; and that, whatever be the process of regeneration, conversion, or sanctification, it must, from the universal laws of the universe, be in perfect harmony with that constitution; hence no power or faculty of the human mind is changed or destroyed, in this great moral revolution of which we speak. A fact this, which, when duly appreciated, forever annihilates the system which I oppose. Mr. Rice gives evidence of its clearness and power. He felt it, and how does he seek to dispose of it? He tells us that God made man holy at first, and that he can do it again! He created Adam holy, and he may create others. This is, in reality, an admission of the unanswerable force of this argument. He therefore seeks to go beyond its dominions—beyond the present constitution of man, and affirms, that if God can not violate his present constitution, he can do as he did before, make an original constitution or create him holy as he created Adam! That is, he can create a new Adam out of the old Adam, as he created Adam out of the dust of the ground, etc.! Truly, this is a triumph of no ordinary character. He commences a response by conceding my position, and asking for God the power to literally create a new man. But this is not the question before us. I admit that God could have created another Adam, and that he can now literally create a holy man; but it is not an original physical primordial creation, but a moral change, a moral renovation and creation of which we speak. It is not the origination of a new constitution, but a change of heart, a transformation moral that we are inquiring into.

Will the gentleman say that creation, providence, and redemption are the same process of divine power? Was not creation a miracle? Was there a previously existing constitution of the universe and of man? Did God make man after man's own previously existing constitution? Because God did at first give to man a constitution after his own image, follows it, therefore, that God will create for him a new constitution, now that he is fallen, and make him new by miracle? And would not man be as perfect now as he was at first, according to this hypothesis? For when God made Adam holy, he was perfectly holy. Does God thus make Christians perfectly holy? When these objections to his presumptive assumption are responded to, he shall have others.

Infants and adults are then created holy by the same direct and positive fiat, the same specific miracle that made Adam holy. Avaunt, then, all secondary causes, all ministerial means, all Bible preaching and moral argumentations! God makes infants, adults and pagans holy by the same means that he made Adam holy; that is, by a miracle. With Mr. Rice every conversion is just as great a miracle as the creation of Adam; for, recollect, his only escape from my argument is, that as God could and did give to Adam a holy constitution, so does he now give a holy constitution to infants, pagans, Jews, and all other persons whom he pleases thus to create anew. Was there ever a more perfect fatalism than this? Every infant and adult now made holy is a miracle—a new and original demonstration of Omnipotence. Yet still the wonder is, that this new creation is not perfectly holy, inasmuch as all other works of God are perfect.

Now, according to my introductory speech and fourth argument, I insist, that if one infant be regenerated *without moral instrumentality*, all can; and if one perfect and complete regeneration, without the Word of God, can, in any case whatever, be consummated, then in all other cases the Word is wholly unnecessary. For if I can produce one apple without a tree, or one ear of wheat without earth, then I can do it ad infinitum. No living man, as I conceive, can in these points refute my introductory address. I will insist that Mr. Rice explains to us why preach the Word; why print Bibles; why send missionaries to foreign lands; why set on foot any human instrumentalities whatever, on the assumption that God makes men and infants holy, as he did Adam. I never objected to a spiritual religion. Nay, I love it, I preach it, I contend for it. I never would have jeopardized my reputation in questioning the popular notions of spiritual influence, but to aim a blow at the root of all fanaticism, and of a wild, irrepressible enthusiasm. I believe not only in the Holy Spirit, but in a religion of which this divine agent is both the substance, origin, cause, and reason. But, sir, in my humble opinion this metaphysical abstraction, this theological speculation, this electric, immedial operation, that makes an infant or a pagan holy in a moment, has been the most soul-ruining dogma ever invented, preached, or propagated. It has slain its tens of thousands. It has made skeptics, fanatics, despondents, and visionaries without number, and without limit.

These elect infants, elect pagans, elect idiots, on whom God acts when, where, and how he pleases, but makes them holy in a moment, without light, knowledge, faith, or love (for though these may be called by them effects of the regeneration, the thing, the work, the operation itself, is anterior to them, above and independent of them, without any human agency whatever,) are figments of distempered brains, the creatures of religious romance, the offspring of a metaphysical delusion, for which there is no cure, but in the rational reading and study of the Book of God.

Mr. Rice seems, if I understand him, to have drunk deep into these muddy waters, and to have adopted the fable of infant regeneration as a choice of evils. His dilemma is, Infants are saved or lost. Not lost truly! Well, then, they are saved. With, or without, regeneration! Without regeneration is to him inadmissible, because then they would be saved in a state of wickedness. His theory is, therefore, adopted to get rid of a metaphysical difficulty. It owes its origin to a mystic knot which he can not untie, and which he dares not cut. The regeneration of these infants is, then, not moral, but physical. Well, perhaps we may yet agree in their physical regeneration. I believe those dying infants, and with me they are all elect, are fitted for heaven by a physical regeneration, of which we shall hereafter speak. But in the meantime the question is lost, if we lose sight of the regeneration of which we now speak, and which is an essential part of the system we oppose.

What, then, let me ask, is the philosophy of regeneration according to Mr. Rice? It is a change of heart. There we agree again. What sort of change? Not of the flesh, but of the spirit—a change of the affections, of the feelings and sympathies of the soul. Agreed!—a change so great that we love our former hates, and hate our former loves. We love God and our Savior supremely, and our brethren fervently. We hate Satan, falsehood, and sin. Hence comes the annihilation of his hypothesis—can an infant love or hate, without previous knowledge, faith or apprehension of things amiable and hateful! No, says every man; where there is no light, no understanding, no intelligence, there can be no disposition at all, no moral feeling, no change of affections, no change of heart; consequently no infant moral or spiritual regeneration. It is impossible—it is inconceivable! No man can demonstrate, illustrate, or prove it. Whenever Mr. Rice can show that a man, a child, or an infant, can love what he never heard, saw, felt or thought of, and that he can love, fear, or eschew that of which he has no conception whatever, then, but not till then, can he offer one argument, reason, or evidence, of infant moral regeneration. Whenever he shows a man loving Jesus Christ, righteousness, and holiness, who has never heard of him—and hating Satan, sin, and impurity, who has never heard of them, then I will believe that he can find a dying infant regenerated and sanctified in its spiritual and moral nature. Till then I shall regard it as a mere phantasy, an idol, or chimera of the brain, and the whole doctrine growing out of it a miserable delusion.

But now with regard to our physical regeneration of infants, my faith is in the Lamb of God, who hath taken away the sin of the world. The atonement of the Messiah has made it compatible with God, with the honor of his throne and government, to save all those infants who die in Adam. He has made an ample provision for extending salvation from all the consequences of Adam's sin to whomsoever he will. Ever blessed be his adorable name! The Lamb of God has borne away the sin of the world. Infants then need that same kind of regeneration that Paul, and Peter, and James, and John, and all saints need—the entire destruction of this body of sin and death. The most perfect Christian that I have seen needs a regeneration to fit him for the immediate presence of God. The infant that falls asleep in its mother's bosom, and after a few short days breathes out its spirit gently there, needs no more change to fit it for Abraham's bosom, than that which the Spirit of God will effect in the resurrection of the dad, or in the transformation of the living saints at the time of his coming. Philosophy, reason, and faith are alike silent on the subject of any infant regeneration before death. It is all theory—idle, empty, suicidal theory. Experience lifts her ten thousand voices against it. Whoever saw a child regenerated growing up from birth a pure and exemplary Christian? Persons have been sanctified; that is, set apart to the Lord from their birth; but that any one was, in our sense of regeneration, changed in heart from birth, reason, revelation, experience, observation, depose not; on this subject they are all as silent as death. While, then, I believe in the physical regeneration of infants after death, I repudiate their spiritual or moral regeneration in life, because unscriptural, irrational and absurd.

This delusive doctrine operates very differently on two classes of subjects—the sanguine and vain, the imaginative and elate. Those of high self-esteem are often the victims of a conceit that they have been touched by a supernatural impulse, a sort of celestial electricity, which in a moment regenerated and gave them religion. Some of them tell right marvelous tales of mighty shocks of this sort. A lady of whom I recently heard, from a highly credible source, in describing her conversion, said, "The Holy Spirit went through her from head to foot, bursting off the nails from her fingers and toes." This was, truly, an extraordinary case; yet many of the same class, not so well marked, daily occur. These persons often live and die without any right conception of God, of his Son, or of his salvation, yet are they joyful, happy, riding on the clouds communing with spirits, and filled with rapture, which neither poetry nor philosophy can reveal. They carry with them through life, the notion that they were once truly regenerate, and, therefore, can never perish.

But there are some rather of a melancholy temperament; somewhat atrabilious and desponding. They are more rational, though less imaginative—they have little hope, and less self-esteem; but they feel their need of this regeneration, without feeling that sensible touch Divine, which instantly brings them out of nature's darkness and death into supernatural light and life. They are too rational to dream of it. They are too sensible to imagine it; and sometimes they fall into a frightful melancholy, which, in instances not a few, bereaves them of reason and sends them into an asylum, where, although surrounded with all that science and humanity can bestow, leaves them without the comforts and assistance of relatives and friends, those best palliatives of mental alienation and woe.

The gentleman has given us another exemplification of his freedom in quoting Scriptures. Paul may plant and Apollos water, but God gives the increase. His meaning is: Paul may plant the seed of religion in the heart of A, B and C; Apollos may water that seed, but God alone makes it to grow. I rejoice in the truth of the fact here stated, but I pronounce the application of the passage to the point before us a gross misconception and perversion of its meaning. Paul may plant churches and Apollos may water churches, but God makes the churches grow. So says the context, and so say I with all my heart.

I do not wish to lose time in expositions of the various sophisms of false quotation and application of Scripture. I do not even choose to defend my own writings from such illogical torture. I should give no argument if I stopped to wrangle about all these misquotations and misapplications. I only request those who choose to examine more accurately these quotations, to read the whole contexts from which they are illegally arrested. The gentleman is very emphatic (for effect, no doubt) in telling you how often he calls my attention to certain matters, which, but for his manner of quoting them, deserve no real regard, because irrelevant. He said the other day, he called my attention three times to a verse, and finally affirmed that he could neither make me see or hear it, although I had two or three times replied to it in common with its whole class. And when it was for the third or fourth time replied to by me, what use did the gentleman make of my reply? All those passages I have shown, like the oft-repeated case of the thief on the cross, are misapplied, because they were spoken of things and persons as they were before the gospel age commenced—before the Christian ordinances were instituted or the church began. The thief indeed was saved without baptism; not merely because there was no Christian baptism then; for if there had, he being converted as he was, and having no opportunity, would have been saved without it, as all are who are providentially prevented from receiving it. Scriptures are generally quoted wrong when applied to prove a proposition not of the same species with that in the writer's mind.

The gentleman fights for victory, and he will have it in any and every contingency whatever. He has at proper intervals the mournful alas. Alas! alas! for the reformation! The unfeeling crowd, so perfectly destitute of sympathy, however, smile at his wailings! He can hardly proceed under the dreadful weight of arguments on his side, and yet he can not utter them. For who has heard them! I do not think it either edifying or important to notice these matters, for any other reason than to express my pleasure in reflecting upon the dignity of my cause and its self-respect; that it needs not such ephemeral and political appliances to sustain or commend it.

Mr. Rice may express all his conceptions of himself and his cause without any offense to me whatever. I presume that owing to his education he honestly thinks so, whether or not I am obliged to so regard him, and I will so continue till the end. What is said here is to be read by all parties; and my only desire on that subject is that the book may be read impartially, and that the argument may be duly weighed on both sides. Let every man take up the book and read it as though it had fallen from heaven into his hands. Let him read it candidly, decide according to evidence and fact, and then let him act in perfect harmony with his convictions and may the Lord bless him in so doing! (Time expired.)

MR. RICE'S THIRD REPLY.

MONDAY, NOV. 27, 1:30 P.M.

Mr. President:—I have but a remark to make in reply to the singular logic of Mr. Campbell, concerning the alleged statement of Mr. Burch. No man, he would have us believe, can testify, that twenty years ago he did not make a certain statement! I presume Mr. Burch may very well know he never did believe that Mr. C. triumphed over Mr. McCalla, and, therefore, that he never did make a statement which implied such an admission. He never believed that Mr. C. triumphed, and, consequently, never so said. The gentleman's anonymous evidence is worth absolutely nothing.

The gentleman attempts to justify his assertion that I am delivering scraps of old harangues by saying that he has heard of my preaching on these subjects, and has seen, in my discussion with President Shannon, some of the same arguments I have advanced on this occasion. Why, I have read in his publications almost everything he has advanced on this subject; and a considerable part of his closing speech, on Saturday, I heard almost verbatim some three years ago. Why, then, may I not charge him with delivering scraps of old harangues?

But he can not so easily escape the difficulty into which his temper hurried him. For it is not true that I have ever before discussed this subject just as I have done to-day. I have occasionally, it is true, discussed all these subjects, though not so thoroughly and extensively as now.

Regeneration, the gentleman says, must take place in harmony with the powers of the human mind. This is true. I have not said that in regeneration men are deprived of any of their faculties, or that new faculties are created. But he tells us, that creation is one thing, and the renewing of the heart quite another; and he seems to consider the idea of creating holiness quite absurd. The doctrine of Mr. Campbell, as stated by himself, is, that no other than moral power can be exerted on the human mind; and it must always be exerted by words and arguments. In refutation of this assumption, I stated the

Scripture fact, that God created man holy, and consequently there must have been a moral influence exerted, not by words or by arguments. We do not regard holiness as a distinct substance or essence. It is, however, true, that God created man with a holy heart or nature. How he did it I know not, nor does Mr. C. Inasmuch, then, as he understands not how that influence was exerted, which made man originally holy, he can not possibly prove that the Spirit may not now exert a moral influence, distinct from motives.

It is worthy of special remark, that Paul, in speaking of the sanctification of the human heart, uses the word "create." "We are his workmanship, created in Christ Jesus unto good works" (Eph. ii. 10). There is not, in any language, a stronger word than the word "create." Yet this word is employed, without qualification, in regard to the renewal of the human heart. If, then, this word does not express a direct divine influence, distinct from the word, and in addition to it, by what word, I ask, could the idea be expressed? God did not create the heavens and the earth by words and arguments; neither did he thus create the body or the soul of man. The very word "create" expresses the putting forth of divine power. Can it, then, be true, that God creates the heart anew by words and arguments? Is it not perfectly absurd to talk of creating by arguments? It is an abuse of language. God created man in his own image; and now, by the new creation he restores that image. In the latter, as in the former, there is an exertion of divine power; and in both the modus operandi is equally mysterious.

Mr. C. objects to the doctrine of special divine influence; that it makes every instance of conversion or regeneration a miracle. So it does, if we take his definition of a miracle; but if we take the definition given by all correct writers on the subject, regeneration is not a miracle. A miracle is a suspension of the laws of nature, by the immediate interposition of divine power, of which men can take cognizance, for the purpose of confirming the truth of God's revelation. God sends rain, and in a time of dearth we pray for rain, not expecting God to work a miracle, and yet expecting him to put forth his power in answer to our prayers, so as to grant the desired blessing. Elisha prayed that it might not rain; and during the space of three years and a half it rained not. He prayed for rain, and it descended in torrents. In one sense, perhaps, these divine interpositions might be called miracles; but so far as man could see, the laws of nature were uninterrupted, both whilst the long drought continued, and when the rain descended. Properly speaking, therefore, there was, in this case, a divine interposition, but not a miracle.

So the Holy Spirit operates, though invisibly, on the hearts of all who are renewed. The change is wrought by supernatural power; but it is not a miracle because it is invisible, nor is it a suspension of the fixed laws of nature. The effects of the divine influence we do see. The man who, yesterday, delighted only in sin, to-day turns from his iniquities, and rejoices in the service of God. The effects are manifest; and common sense compels us to ascribe them to some adequate cause. The Bible teaches us, that the cause of the visible change is a new creation wrought by the Holy Spirit. "We are his workmanship, created in Christ Jesus unto good works."

Mr. Campbell objects again, that if, in one case, regeneration takes place without the Word, it must be so in all cases; and then, of what use is the Word? He has often told us that it is far easier to assert than to prove. It is admitted that regeneration is the same in all cases; but it is not admitted that the means employed are, in all cases, the same. He asserts that the same means must always be employed, but he can not prove the truth of the assertion, either Scripturally or philosophically. I know of no part of God's Word that teaches that if God should sanctify a soul in one instance without the truth, because it can not be employed, he must, of course, sanctify all others without the truth. God is a sovereign; and he works by means or without means, as his infinite wisdom directs.

But the gentleman asks of what use is the Word, if regeneration can take place without it? If the question has any meaning, it is this: Of what use is the Word to adults, if infants, that can not receive it, can be regenerated without it. This is a singular question. Or does he mean to ask, of what use is the Word to adults, if there is necessary a distinct divine influence? I presume if he had been in the camp of Israel, in the days of Joshua, he would have asked, why should the priests compass the walls of Jericho seven times, and blow rams' horns, since the walls will not fall without a direct interposition of divine power? The Lord commanded, and that is sufficient. Or, perhaps, he would have found fault with our Savior, because, in healing the eyes of the blind man, he used clay and spittle. He might ask, of what use are the clay and spittle, since they will not open his eyes without a direct exertion of divine power? Such is the logic of my friend. It is in vain to reason against facts. God has often employed means, when, without an immediate exertion of his power, they were wholly inadequate to accomplish the end. So he employs the Word ordinarily, though alone it is not adequate to effect the conversion and sanctification of men. Yet God has never confined himself to means and instrumentalities; and no man has the right to limit him where he has not limited himself.

The doctrine of special divine influence, Mr. Campbell believes, leads to a great deal of fanaticism; and he has told us an anecdote about some very fanatical woman. It is admitted that there have been, and now are, many fanatics in the world; but his is quite as conclusive against the truth of Christianity as against the doctrine I am defending. Multitudes of those who have professed to be Christians, have been, or now are, fanatics; therefore, says the infidel, Christianity leads to fanaticism, and, of course, it can not be true. The infidel adopts Mr. Campbell's principle, and argues quite as conclusively as he. It is a trite remark, that the abuse of a doctrine, or of a principle, does not prove it false. Does the doctrine of special divine influence generally make fanatics of those who embrace it? There is not a body of people in this world who are more free from fanaticism than Presbyterians; and yet there are none who more firmly believe in the special agency of the Spirit than they; nor any who more zealously contend for the constant use of means, in order to conversion and sanctification.

I could also tell an anecdote concerning a convert in Mr. C's church that would be quite a match for the one he has related, but I could not do so without treating this solemn subject with unbecoming levity.

The gentleman has at length produced one passage of Scripture in support of his doctrine. I am gratified to see him leaving his metaphysical speculations, which he has, indeed, long professed to repudiate, and entering upon this Scripture proof. The passage is in John xvii. 17: "Sanctify them through thy truth: thy word is truth." It is really one of the most conclusive proofs of the truth of the doctrine I am advocating. Does not the Savior pray to his Father to sanctify them? But if Mr. C's doctrine is true, why should he have prayed? He did not pray that new truths, new arguments, might be revealed to his people. According to his doctrine, it was necessary only to give them the truth. But the Savior prayed to his Father to do something for them, and to do it by certain means—to exert on their minds a sanctifying influence distinct from the truth, but in connection with the truth.

Mr. Campbell asks, how can an infant be born of God before it has any knowledge of God? There can be no disposition, he says, where there is no knowledge. I thought he had repudiated metaphysics; but really, he appears to rely upon his speculations more than upon the Bible. But his philosophy is most unphilosophical and unscriptural. Who does not know that there are a thousand things which we admire at first sight, and as many to which we feel a decided aversion? Does not this prove that there may, and does, exist in the mind a disposition or inclination to love some objects, and to dislike others, even before we have any knowledge of them? There are dispositions existing in the mind, as well as tastes and appetites in the body, before the knowledge of the appropriate objects calls them into existence. A child loves sweetness the first time it tastes it; and is charmed by music the first time it hears it. Why, then, may not the soul be in such a moral state, that when first it is made acquainted with the character of God, it will admire, love and adore him; or, that it will turn from him with strong aversion? There is neither sound theology nor sound philosophy in the gentleman's objection.

But he is not willing to give up the salvation of infants; and he complains of me for urging the argument against his doctrine, that it necessarily involves the damnation of infants. He does not find fault with me for maintaining that they are depraved; for, although he now denies that there can be moral disposition where there is no knowledge, he admits and teaches, that infants are by nature depraved!—that they have a proneness, a disposition to sin! This being admitted, my argument against his doctrine is most certainly legitimate and conclusive. It is what logicians call the "reductio ad absurdum"—proving that it leads necessarily to results which he admits to be false and absurd. I was indeed surprised that he thought it necessary to appeal to the moderators to protect his doctrine against the force of this argument.

He attempts, however, to escape from the difficulty by saying that nothing more than the atonement of Christ is necessary to the salvation of infants. Does the blood of Christ purify the heart? The atonement secures the remission of sins; but does the Bible teach that it takes away depravity? Why, the very idea is absurd. There is not a word in the Bible to countenance such a notion. The difficulty still remains. Infants, as the gentleman admits, are depraved. How, then, shall they be sanctified and prepared for the enjoyments of a holy heaven? They can not be sanctified through the truth; and Mr. C.

asserts that they can not be sanctified without it. Therefore they must die in sin, and be forever lost! Such are the results to which his doctrine necessarily leads, whether he is willing consistently to carry it out or not.

There is nothing in the Bible, he tells us, that favors the idea of infant regeneration. He takes care, however, not to reply to the argument founded on John iii. 6, "For that which is born of the flesh is flesh, and that which is born of the Spirit is spirit." Infants are born of the flesh; and therefore they must be born of the Spirit; and if not born of the Spirit, they can not enter into the kingdom of God—they must be lost. They can not go to heaven in their depravity.

But, says the gentleman, adult believers must, at death, undergo as great a change in order to enter heaven as infants need experience. For this assertion he can find no authority in the Bible; and it is vain for him, on a subject such as we are now discussing, to give us either his opinions or his assertions. Death will produce on the mind no moral change, such as infants must experience before they can enter heaven.

It is, no doubt, true, as the gentleman says, that some persons who have believed in the doctrine of the special agency of the Spirit have been melancholy, under the conviction that they were not serving God faithfully, or from other causes; but it can not be proved that the doctrine has any such tendency. On the contrary, thousands and tens of thousands have felt their hardened hearts melt under the blessed influences of the Spirit, have renewed their strength as they have waited on God in prayer, and have in their affections and joys mounted up as on the wings of an eagle, have run without weariness, and walked without fainting. "The Spirit itself," says Paul, "beareth witness with our spirit, that we are the children of God; and, if children, then heirs, heirs of God and joint heirs with Christ." Convince the man who has become acquainted with his true character that there is no such special influence of the Spirit; that he must prepare himself by his unaided exertions for heaven; and he will lie down in deep despair. He will never again entertain a hope that he can see God in peace, or enter into his rest. It is a holy heaven to which he desires to go; a holy God reigns there; holy angels worship around his glorious throne; and none but "the spirits of just men made perfect" can ever enter there. If, then, sinful man is left to prepare himself for such a heaven, well may he weep in despair.

In my last address I directed your attention to the language of Paul in 1 Cor. iii. 6: "I have planted, Apollos watered; but God gave the increase." But the gentleman says Paul spoke of planting churches. There is no such expression in the connection. On what evidence, then, does he found the assertion? Paul was rebuking the Corinthian Christians because there were contentions among them, one saying, I am of Paul; another, I am of Apollos; and a third, I am of Cephas; and a fourth, I am of Christ. All this, he tells them, is most unwise as well as very sinful; for, says he, "who, then, is Paul, and who is Apollos but ministers by whom ye believe, even as God gave to every man? I have planted, Apollos watered; but God gave the increase." Paul had planted the seed, had first preached the Word in Corinth; Apollos had succeeded him with his eloquent exhortations; and God had by his Holy Spirit caused the seed to spring up and bring forth fruit.

But if Paul were speaking of planting a church (though this is not a Scripture expression) his meaning must be that he had induced Christians to remove from other parts of Corinth and settle there. You may plant corn; but you must first have corn to plant. A church might be planted; but the members must be there before it could be planted. But Paul planted the seed, the Word, and God blessed it to the conversion of many; Apollos preached and exhorted, and God blessed his labors to their growth in grace.

But if Paul could really plant a church, and Apollos could water it without any special divine influence, could they not keep it alive, and cause it to extend? Or what are we to understand by the declaration that "God gave the increase"? The figure used by the apostle is both beautiful and striking, and the meaning can not easily be misunderstood. Before you plant your seed the ground must be prepared; and then the sun must shine and the refreshing rains descend upon it. Man plants his seed and sometimes waters it; but there is no artificial sun to shine upon it. God must give the increase. So the ministers of Christ are to preach the Word, to proclaim the glorious gospel to men, and look up to God for that divine influence, the outpouring of the Holy Spirit, which only can cause men to turn to God.

My friend can not forget the past days of this discussion. He constantly calls up the subjects that have been disposed of. He says that on the third proposition he did answer my argument from John iii. 18: "He that believeth on him is not condemned." I certainly did not hear his answer. It must have been extremely brief. The truth is, it admits of no answer. The obvious and only meaning is that no believer, baptized or not, is condemned; but all believers are justified.

The last note I took of the gentleman's speech relates to the charge he had made that great pains have been taken to bias the public sentiment, to make the people believe that he has failed to sustain himself. He tells you he has heard the fact from various quarters. I will not condescend to gather up floating reports and state them here as facts for the purpose of producing effect. When I state facts, and they are denied, I will prove them. These reports, which would seem to have given him so much trouble, are not only false and slanderous, but unspeakably ridiculous. Does the gentleman expect to make the impression that the intelligent people who have come together from all parts of the country to hear this debate can not judge for themselves, but will believe just what Presbyterians tell them they must believe? This most ridiculous charge I pronounce to be utterly false. There is not one word of truth in it.

I know not whether it is necessary for me to introduce any additional arguments in favor of the doctrine for which I contend, until Mr. C. shall have advanced something to sustain his proposition. I will, however, quote a few passages of Scripture which clearly teach the doctrine of a special divine agency in conversion and sanctification. Ezekiel xxxvi. 26, 27: "A new heart also will I give you, and a new spirit will I put within you; and I will take away the stony heart out of your flesh, and I will give you a heart of flesh. And I will put my Spirit within you, and cause you to walk in my statutes, and ye shall keep my judgments and do them." Does not God here proclaim himself the author of that radical change of heart which causes men to turn from sin and keep his commandments? The passage is a promise and a prediction of the converting and sanctifying influences of the Spirit which should be exerted upon the Jews in a future day. Does this language teach that the Spirit can exert on the heart no other moral power but that which is contained in words and arguments? The Bible is, on all important points, a plain book; and its obvious meaning is generally its true meaning. Now I ask, what idea would this language convey to the mind of any one who has no theory to support? When God says, I will give you a new heart, would not such a person understand that he would exert an influence quite different from mere argument? I cheerfully leave every candid hearer to determine whether there is not here the promise of an influence of the Spirit in addition to the Word, and distinct from it.

The next passage I quote is Jer. xxxii. 37: "Behold, I will gather them out of all countries whither I have driven them in mine anger, &c., and I will give them one heart and one way that they may fear me forever, for the good of them and their children after them." Does the prophet mean that God would by arguments give to his people one heart and one way? He promises to gather them from their wanderings, and to exert such an influence on their minds that with one heart they would turn from their sins to his service, and fear him forever. I ask again, what idea would be conveyed by such language to the unsophisticated mind, to a plain, honest man, who has no theory to support? What is the obvious meaning of the language? I verily believe that there is not an intelligent man living who, on hearing this passage read, would not, if he had no favorite theory to bias his judgment, understand it to teach the doctrine of a special divine influence distinct from mere words and arguments.—(Time expired.)

MR. CAMPBELL'S FOURTH ADDRESS.

Tuesday, Nov. 28, 10 o'clock A.M.

Mr. President.—Before proceeding to the business of the day, I must make a few introductory remarks. In reference, then, to the incidents of yesterday, I ought, perhaps, to advert to some of them which were not of so pleasant a character as usual. And, first, as to the incident in the after part of the day which called for an allusion to Mr. Burch. I did not, indeed, name that gentleman; Mr. Rice named him in your presence. My remarks could not in the least involve the moral character of that gentleman. I did not intend to impeach the moral character of Mr. Burch or any one else. It was, sir, I repeat, the most remote thing in my mind to violate the feelings, unnecessarily, of any one present, much less the moral reputation of Mr. Burch. The fact stated I believed then, and I believe now, to be strictly true. But having ascertained that Mr. Burch's feelings have been wounded, and a desire having been expressed that it should not go to record, I cheerfully consent that it be not published. I have no desire to put anything on record which might at all tend to mar good feelings.[1]

As respects the imputation uttered on yesterday by Mr. Rice, that in some of my remarks touching the management of affairs here I spake under excitement. If by excitement the gentleman means animal passion or anger, I can not admit it. Exciting as have been some of the circumstances in which I have been placed in conducting this discussion, I have not allowed myself to yield to any temptation of that sort. If I appeared so to him or any one else, I certainly am not conscious of it. It must be because they thought I had provocation enough. It is with me a principle, confirmed by habit, on all occasions, especially one so solemn as the present, to hold in abeyance those passions which might be wrought up into effervescence. Knowing that the

---

[1] Understanding from Mr. Rice that Mr. Burch desired this incident to go to record, I have consented to the publication. A. C.

wrath of man worketh not the righteousness of God, I feel myself always admonished to avoid even the slightest appearance of it. I have, therefore, on no occasion of this sort, in all my life, been accused of anything of this kind. Indeed, as the troubled water is generally muddy, and the calm, gently flowing stream clear, excited passions are no way auxiliary to the ascertainment of truth, but rather of a contrary tendency. Mr. Rice is fully comprehended in this maneuver.

I shall now proceed to the business of the day. The proposition before us is: "In conversion and sanctification the Spirit of God operates only through the Word of Truth," or always through the Word of Truth. Mr. Rice admits it sometimes so operates, but not always; sometimes operating without the Word of Truth. The proper difference between us is the difference between *sometimes* and *always*. That the Spirit of God does operate in both conversion and sanctification we both admit. But I affirm and he denies that it operates *only* in that way. In sustaining the affirmative, my method has been to show that as these works of conversion and sanctification are specific works—works uniformly the same, as any of the products of the animal or the vegetable kingdom—there must be uniformity in the operation. This the constitution of the human mind requires; and hence, whatever is in any one case essential to any one result, such as regeneration, is necessary in each and every other case whatever. So far we have reasoned on the inductive plan; these being the results of innumerable multitudes of facts, such as no man can suggest an idea, or view, or feeling, of a moral or spiritual character, which has not been borrowed from the Bible; and again, the person destitute of that book is destitute of all those ideas, impressions and sensations.

To these views Mr. Rice has simply affirmed that there is no such uniformity; that it is not necessary. We call, but we call in vain, for an example of conversion by the Spirit alone, or where the Word was wholly unknown. Such a case, even were it plausibly alleged, would be entitled to very high consideration. He will not attempt such a case; he presumes upon no such evidence. His, then, is a position purely metaphysical, and belongs to the science of abstract speenlative theology. It is wholly and forever insusceptible of any appreciable demonstration or proof. We have not only Bible declarations, but facts and analogies innumerable, on our side of the question. One of my axioms is, whatever is essential in one case is essential in every case.

But as the gentleman has not met, and, I presume, will not meet me in a debate on any one of these great positions, I shall proceed to a new argument, more intelligible to all minds, and more in support of these conclusions than any merely analogous or abstract reasonings could be. I open the New Testament at once and read as my

Eighth argument, 1 Peter i. 23: "Being born again, not of corruptible seed, but of incorruptible seed, by the Word of God which liveth and abideth forever." Now, as you all remember, our Lord compares his Word, or the Word of God, to seed planted or sown; and, under the parable of the sower, represents its various fortunes, and beautifully teaches the true philosophy of conversion in the fact that the good ground is the man who "receives the Word of God in an honest heart." Under both metaphors, drawn the one from the vegetable, the other from the animal kingdom, the Word of God is the seed of which we are born again or renewed in heart and life. This Word of God liveth and abideth, for God lives and abides forever.

First.—With regard to the essentiality of the seed. We all know that, in the vegetable kingdom, without that there is no harvest, no fruit. And, as certain it is, that when the Word of God is not first sown in the heart, there can be no regeneration, or renewal of the spirit, and, consequently, no fruit brought forth unto eternal life. So the metaphors taken from the animal and vegetable kingdoms teach the same lesson. But does not the mere fact that Peter says, that we are born again of incorruptible seed, declare that where this incorruptible seed is not, there can possibly be no birth! Unless, then, Mr. Rice can shew that it is just as true to say, we are born again, neither by corruptible nor incorruptible seed, without the Word of God,—this single passage settles this question forever, as I honestly conceive.

Is it necessary now to traverse the whole face of nature, to explore the whole kingdom of botany, to find a planet without a seed, in order to prove the proposition, that every ear of corn comes from one grain of seed deposited in the earth? No more is it essential to my argument, that I should first hear all the conversions in the world, before I conclude that there is one that originated without one word of God having been sown in the human heart. Will not all the word believe me, if I prove in one case that without the specific seed,—corn, wheat, etc.,—we can not have the crop, that it is true in all other cases, without a particular examination; and from every principle of analogy, if I prove the Word in one case of a new heart to be necessary, it needs not that I prove it to be so in every other heart, in every other case. The mere fact of calling the Gospel the incorruptible seed, is enough. Where that seed is not, the fruit of it can not be.

The phrase, "the incorruptible seed" of anything, indicates, in the ears of common sense, that it is essential to that thing; and if so, then who can be a Christian without being born?—and who can be born but according to one uniform and immutable law? Now, in the theory of Mr. Rice, there is no uniformity; there is a plurality of ways of being born, which, to my mind, is most palpably at fault in every particular.

But I will adduce some other testimonies under this head of argument. We shall hear James the apostle, chapter i. 18: "Of his own will begat he us by the word of truth, that we should be a kind of first fruits of his creation." Hence the truth again appears as an instrument of regeneration. God's will is the origin of it; his Spirit the efficient cause of it; but the Word is the necessary instrument of it. By the Word of Truth, then, we are begotten, and not without it, according to James. We may add testimonies without increasing either authority or evidence; but, for the sake of illustration, if not for authority, we shall offer a few other testimonies to complete this particular argument. We shall hear Paul, as a father, speak to his sons in the faith in Corinth (1 Cor. iv. 15): "As my beloved sons I warn you: for though you have ten thousand instructors in Christ, yet have you not many fathers; for in Christ Jesus have I begotten you through the gospel." Paul regards the gospel just in the same attitude in which James represents it. The gospel is here the seed, the instrument of the conversion of the Corinthians.

But the whole oracle of God is unique on this subject. God "purifies the heart by faith," that is, the truth believed—not by believing as an act of the mind, but by the truth believed, which constitutes "the faith." Paul also told the Thessalonians that God had, "from the beginning, chosen them to salvation through sanctification of the Spirit and belief of the truth." Here again the belief of the truth is the instrument of sanctification and salvation. I shall conclude this little summary of a portion of the direct and positive testimony of God, in proof of my grand position on the Holy Spirit's work of conversion and sanctification, by the testimony of the Messiah, in person: "Sanctify them through thy truth, O Father, for thy Word is the truth."

Whether, then, we call the truth the Word, the Word of God, the gospel, it is called the seed, the incorruptible seed of the new birth; by which a sinner is quickened, begotten, born, sanctified, purified, and saved. I regard this my eighth argument as a host in itself—nay, as the solemn, direct, and unequivocal declaration of God, in attestation of the entire truth and safety of the proposition concerning both conversion and sanctification. I wish Mr. Rice and the whole community to know that I regard this argument, when fully canvassed and developed, as enough on this subject. I am willing to place the whole cause upon it.

I shall now go on to review some portions of Mr. Rice's speeches not yet noticed, which may by some be considered as constituting some objections to my former reasonings on the subject. The gentleman rallied with great zeal and warmth, upon the passage, "Paul planted and Apollos watered." He expressed some astonishment at my presuming to give such an interpretation, and I am just as much astonished at his pertinacity. It fully proves how much he is the slave of bad commentators. I have all good translators, commentators, and critics with me; but, better still, I have got good Dr. Common Sense with me, and he will make it plain to all. Indeed, no really learned theologian thinks differently from me. But let us look to the context. The Word of God is not mentioned in the passage—as the gentleman said, Canaan was not found in the Epistle to the Galatians. Paul speaks of men and not of the Word. I planted you men in God's field or husbandry, and Apollos watered you, but God gave the increase, the growth. He presents the same persons under three distinct figures, in the same context, and connects with each an appropriate imagery. But we shall confine ourselves to two of them—the husbandry, and the building. As a husbandry, Paul planted them; as a building, a temple, he laid the foundation. But if I must make it still plainer, I will then suppose it to be the Word. Well, then, Paul planted the Word in the people's heart; and Apollos watered it in their hearts, and God made it grow in their hearts. Paul, in this case, planted the Word by preaching the Word, and Apollos watered the Word by exhorting them through the Word; and God made it grow by his Spirit operating through the Word. Well, now Paul is placed in a most awkward attitude. He is converted into a school-boy, confounding all laws and usages of the schools. He has Paul planting the Word by the Word! and Apollos watering the Word by the Word! Suppose we convert it into corn;

then all the world will comprehend Paul's beautiful rhetoric. Paul planted corn by scattering corn in the fields; Apollos came along and watered that corn by scattering some of the same corn upon it!

But my friend superciliously asks, How can any one plant a church? would you stick it in the ground! Profoundly erudite objection! How do men plant a colony of men?—stick them in the ground! Men have been said to plant churches and colonies from time immemorial! The field or husbandry is the place where Paul figuratively planted men; and as living stones, he also builded them together, under another figure, "for an habitation of God through the Spirit." The apostle's rhetoric is classic, rich, and beautiful. As a field, Paul brought the Corinthians into it, and planted them in the nursery. Apollos came next, and refreshed them much by his exhortations; and thus, through their joint labors, Corinthians became God's husbandry. I take pleasure in avowing my conviction that it is the blessing of God upon the labors of Paul and Apollos, that made these Corinthians grow. I do not labor this passage to oppose that idea, but to expose this most licentious way of quoting the Scriptures, and forcing them into the sectarian service. The improvements in the science of hermeneutics will, I hope, move westwardly.

A favorite passage, which has been quoted oftener many times than any other text in the Bible, during this discussion, and for no reason that I can see, but because the word "sprinkle"—that blessed word "sprinkle," is found in it, along with clean water—I must quote it once, out of courtesy: Ezek. xxxvi. 25: "Then will I sprinkle clean water upon you, and ye shall be clean from all your filthiness; and from all your idols will I cleanse you." This is not literally water free from mud, but an allusion to the water mixed with ashes, which purified the unclean—a mere symbol here of the cleansing of the Jews. He says in verse 24: "For I will take you from among the heathen, and gather you out of all countries, and will bring you into your own land." Here there is an express declaration that God would bring them back to their own land. "Then will I sprinkle clean water upon you, and ye shall be clean from all your filthiness, and from all your idols." It was to cleanse them from their idols by the water of purification. "A new heart also will I give you, and a new spirit will I put within you; and I will take away the stony heart out of your flesh, and I will give you a heart of flesh. And I will put my spirit within you, and cause you to walk in my statutes; and ye shall keep my judgments, and do them. And ye shall dwell in the land that I gave to your fathers, and ye shall be my people, and I will be your God." Now, with regard to this strong phrase—"a new heart will I give you"—suppose I should affirm that men make their own hearts new? As he proves his positions, so would I prove it. Ezek. xviii. 31: "Cast away from you all your transgressions, whereby ye have transgressed; and make you a new heart and a new spirit; for why will you die, O house of Israel?" Here, I say, Israel is commanded to make for themselves a new heart; could I not prove that they were thus "commanded by the sound of these words? My friend says that God does create a clean heart. But in what sense? There is nothing to be gained by thus quoting Scripture out of its proper connection. Paul says: "Be renewed in the spirit of your minds." I doubt not the propriety of both these forms of speech. The Lord does everything that is good. He says: "I, the Lord, create light, and I create darkness; I create good, and I create evil; I, the Lord, do all these things." How does he do them? by his own immediate power? Certainly not. But by various instruments—permits some, and appoints others, in various ways. He does not always create good and evil by the same means.

The word "create" does not only mean to make a thing out of original nonentity, but to change its relations, and sometimes only to new-modify it. In creating light, God does something. In creating darkness, he withholds something. In creating good, he imparts something. In creating evil, he withholds good. Men make to themselves a new heart; and God makes for them a new heart. He institutes the means, gives his Spirit, and they receive and obey the truth.

The gentleman, in an attempt to reply to the just objection that he makes conversion in every case a miracle equal to the resurrection of the Lord, went into the definition of a miracle, instead of removing the difficulty, and asks what need of the instrumentality of angels in the world? We always admit that an angel's visit is a miracle. But what has that to do with the subject before us? I do not admire his definition of a miracle. I sometimes define it as "a display of supernatural power in attestation of the truth of some proposition." That supernatural power may be either intellectual or physical, such as raising Lazarus, or foretelling the destruction of Jerusalem. But this is no place for such matters. God never squanders power unnecessarily. He never does by miracle what he can do without it. He works by secondary causes, unless some great emergency in the universe calls for the primary, original, creating power. God does not work without the laws of mind, nor change the laws of mind. He does not violate the constitution of the mind, nor give a man new powers, intellectual or moral, through any moral or supernatural change in this life. To work salvation, or a change of heart, without the laws of mind or contrary to the laws of mind, would be a miracle as great as the resurrection of Lazarus. And such, I presume, to be Mr. R.'s theory of regeneration—without knowledge, argument, faith, hope, or love, etc.; a direct, immediate operation of omnipotence upon the naked soul, without any instrument between.

The gentleman gave a singular definition of moral disposition. He made it a sort of animal instinct—for a child was disposed to love music! Hunger and thirst are also dispositions upon the same philosophy! And, sir, this was the answer given to a very important question, viz.: If moral disposition be a part of regeneration, and if moral disposition be to love God and hate Satan, to love righteousness and hate iniquity—query, Can an infant then be regenerated? Can it love or hate a being or a thing concerning which it knows nothing more than a rock? Mr. R. can not explain this difficulty, and it is fatal to his theory. If a child be regenerate, it must love holiness and hate iniquity; but this can not be without knowledge, because in religion, as in everything else, intellect pioneers the way, while the affections and the heart follow. We must see beauty before we can love it. We must see deformity before we can hate it. And, therefore, "the love of holiness and the hatred of sin" are impossible to an infant. (Time expired.)

MR. RICE'S FOURTH REPLY.

Tuesday, Nov. 28, 10:30 o'clock A.M.

Mr. President—Before proceeding to the discussion of the subject before us, I must briefly notice Mr. Campbell's statement concerning Mr. Burch, who was one of the moderators in the debate between him and Mr. McCalla. When he made the statement, on yesterday, about an opinion expressed by one of the moderators in that debate, there were present many who knew that Mr. Burch was alluded to. I wish now to say that I am authorized by Mr. B. to deny most positively that he ever expressed or entertained the opinion that in that debate Mr. C. was victorious; and to state that from that day to this, he has expressed precisely the opposite opinion. It is taking an unfair advantage of a man who, according to the rules of this discussion, can not be permitted to reply, to prefer such charges.

The gentleman says he has not spoken, at any time during the debate, under the influence of passion. I will not dispute the truth of his statement; but I must say that he has said many things which would have been more excusable, if uttered under excitement, than if spoken deliberately.

It is of the first importance in this discussion that we keep distinctly in view the point in debate. I stated it clearly on yesterday; but it has not been brought prominently to view in the speech of this morning. Indeed, I believe it would be utterly impossible to learn, from all the gentleman has said this morning, wherein we differ.

The main point in the debate is not whether the Spirit always operates through the truth. I was surprised to hear him read the proposition in this way, "only and always." I was not aware that the words "only" and "always" are synonymous. I presume that no dictionary can be found that defines "only" to mean "always." If you will substitute "always" for "only," it will make a proposition radically different from that we are now discussing. What, then, are the points in regard to which we differ? First, we differ concerning the sanctification of infants and idiots. This, however, is not the only difference between us, nor the most important. For, second, we differ widely concerning the influence of the Holy Spirit in the conversion and sanctification of adults. Mr. Campbell contends that the Spirit operates only through the truth. I believe that the Spirit operates ordinarily through the truth, but not only through the truth. The word *only*, in the proposition before us, is an emphatic and an important word. He maintains that the Spirit dictated the Word, and confirmed it by miracles, and that the Word, presented to the mind by any instrumentality, converts and sanctifies it. That is, the Spirit, according to his doctrine, converts and sanctifies men, just as the spirit of Demosthenes and Cicero affected their hearers or readers; and as the spirit of Mr. Campbell affects this audience! He exerts on your minds no other influence than that exerted by his words and arguments. Just so, according to his doctrine, the Spirit of God operates.

We believe and teach that the Word is ordinarily employed in conversion and sanctification. Yet there must be, and there is, an influence of the Spirit on the heart, in addition to the Word, and distinct from it; and by this influence, especially, man is converted and sanctified. This is, practically, the great point on which we differ.

As I have heretofore distinctly stated, we do not believe in a physical change of the faculties of the soul. Mr. C.'s remarks about physical regeneration are, therefore, out of place. Our Confession of Faith does not teach the doctrine, nor do we hold it.

He desires me to follow him in his train of argument. I will now do so, as far as time will permit. I have adduced against his doctrine some four distinct arguments, viz.: 1. That it prescribes to the power of God over the human mind an unreasonable and an unscriptural limitation. 2. That it necessarily involves the damnation of infants and idiots. 3. That it contradicts the Scripture doctrine of human depravity, making it arise from mere mistake; whereas the Bible teaches that men sin willfully and deliberately. 4. I have quoted several passages of Scripture directly teaching the special agency of the Holy Spirit in conversion and sanctification.

I will now pay my respects to the gentleman's new arguments. He refers us to Luke viii. II: "The seed is the word of God"; and to 1 Pet. i. 23. Do these passages prove that in conversion and sanctification the Spirit operates only through the truth? Do the seed of themselves produce the harvest? Who ever heard of obtaining an abundant harvest only by seed? Does not the farmer first prepare his soil? He does not scatter his seed amongst thorns and weeds. The human heart is like the unprepared earth; and in the parable to which the gentleman referred, the seed that produced the harvest are said to be sewn in, "good ground"—in soil previously broken up and prepared. But when the soil has been prepared, and the seed sown, the sun must shine, and the rain must descend, or there will be no harvest. God has a most important agency in these things. He only can cause the sun to shine, and the showers to refresh the earth. In these things there is human agency, and there is divine agency. So the servants of God sow the seed of life; but God prepares the hearts of men to receive it, and the Holy Spirit, like showers on the thirsty ground, causes it to spring up and bear fruit to the glory of God. The argument from the passage under consideration is decidedly in favor of our views. I prove my doctrine by the very arguments brought forward to overthrow it!

He has repeatedly asserted if the Word of God is employed in conversion and sanctification in one case, it must be necessary in all. But this is bare assertion. Let the gentleman prove it if he can. I should like to see him attempt to prove that God has bound himself always to employ in this work the same means and instrumentalities. If he has thus limited himself, let the passage be produced; if he has not, who dares limit him?

The next argument used by Mr. C. is founded on James i. 18: "Of his own will begat he us with his Word of Truth." The argument is mine. I prove the doctrine of special divine influence by this very passage. Observe, it presents two influences exerted on man in regeneration—the agency of God who begets him, and the instrumentality of the truth through which he is begotten or renewed. Does James say he begat us only by his Word? He does not. God begat us; he put forth power, and he did it in connection with his Word as the means. How, then, can it be said with truth, that the means or instrumentality did the whole work? James says, God did the work, and that he did it by the Word, not *only* by the Word. This is precisely the doctrine for which I am contending.

The next argument offered by Mr. C. is founded on the language of Paul, in 1 Cor. iv. 15: "For in Christ Jesus I have begotten you through the Gospel." There are commonly three agencies employed in the conversion and sanctification of the soul: First, the agency or influence of the Word; second, the agency of the minister who preaches it; and, third, the agency of the Holy Spirit on the heart, inducing men to receive the truth in the love of it, and to live according to its divine principles and precepts. There are some passages of Scripture which present particularly the agency of man; some which present the influence of the Word; and some which speak directly and clearly of the agency of the Holy Spirit. I believe in the importance of all these three. The special agency of the Spirit is taught as distinctly and as frequently as either of the others. It is unsafe, therefore, to reject any one of the three. We have not the right to do so.

I must now notice the remarks of the gentleman on 1 Cor. iii. 6: "I have planted, Apollos watered, but God gave the increase." He insists that Paul speaks here of planting the church. Yet not a word is said about planting the church in the chapter, nor in the epistle. But, he asks, if Paul planted the Word, how did Apollos water it? And I ask him, if Paul planted the church, how did Apollos water it? By preaching. He says I make Apollos water the Word with the Word. But if there is any inconsistency, is he not equally guilty of it? He makes Paul plant the church by preaching the Word, and Apollos water it by preaching the Word; so that the planting and the watering are thus made to be the same operation. The truth is, Paul planted in the hearts of the people the seed of divine truth; God by his Holy Spirit caused the seed to grow; and then Apollos came and continued to proclaim the truth, in connection with which the Spirit still descended like refreshing showers on the parched earth, and brought the fruit to maturity.

That a special divine influence was exerted is evident from the fifth verse: "Who, then, is Paul, and who is Apollos, but ministers by whom ye believed, even as the Lord gave to every man?" Does not the apostle here teach that God inclined each one to believe, to receive the Gospel?

But, says the gentleman, we talk of planting a colony or a city. [Mr. C.: I did not say planting a city, but founding a city.] Very well, I have nothing to do with the word "founding." We are speaking of planting. When we speak of planting a tree, we mean removing it from one place and setting it in another. When men speak of planting a colony, they mean transferring people from one place, and establishing them in another. Did Paul transfer Christians from Antioch and from other churches to Corinth? The Scriptures never speak of planting a church.

The gentleman is quite tired of hearing me quote Ezekiel xxvi. 25, 26. True, I have had occasion frequently to quote it, for it presents the emblem of purification in connection with the work of the Spirit. I have referred to it as illustrating both the mode and the design of baptism; and I now have use for it in proof of the doctrine, that in conversion and sanctification there is an agency of the Spirit distinct from the truth. "A new heart also will I give you, and a new spirit will I put within you; and I will take away the stony heart out of your flesh, and I will give you an heart of flesh. And I will put my Spirit within you." Here God promises to give a new heart and a new spirit. How could language more fully teach the doctrine we hold? I have no occasion to say anything more about the sprinkling of clean water. That part of the passage belongs to subjects that have been disposed of.

Mr. C. attempts to evade the force of this and other plain and unequivocal declarations of Scripture by telling you that God commanded men to make themselves new hearts, and that Paul exhorted Christians to be renewed in their minds.

And he says he could thus prove that men do renew their own hearts. So he perhaps could if he could only prove that men always do their duty. It is the duty of all men to love and serve God—to be holy; but the question is, Do they do it? God commands them to repent, believe, and be perfectly holy; but do they do so? But in the passage under consideration God does not command men to do their duty; but he tells his people what he will do. "A new heart will I give you; and a new spirit will I put within you; and I will take away the stony heart out of your flesh. And I will put my Spirit within you, and cause you to walk in my statutes." Here we have most clearly exhibited the radical change of heart, and the consequent change of life, of which God is the glorious author. The cause must be bad that leads a man to attempt to evade the force of language so perfectly unequivocal.

I rejoice to know that in the Bible, as in the book of nature, the truths which are essential to the safety and happiness of men are revealed in language so clear and so simple that the uneducated, as well as the wise, may understand them. Not more certainly are we taught that God sends rain upon the thirsty earth than that he pours out his Spirit upon the hearts of men; and he who can pray for the former, that his seed may produce an abundant harvest, may also pray with stronger faith for the latter, that he may bear the peaceable fruits of righteousness. The gentleman repeats the assertion that regeneration, according to our views, is a miracle. He admits that it is not a miracle in the common acceptation of the word, but he chooses to use it in a new sense. If he chooses to say that every event brought about by divine interposition is a miracle, he must be permitted to do so; but such is not the meaning of the word as used in the Bible. Daily, in the course of his providence, God puts forth his almighty power. If he does not, why should we pray for his protection? If all things are now governed by fixed laws, our prayers are worse than vain.

It is true, God does not directly interpose supernatural power without means, when means can be employed. But when an infant dies, that could not receive the Word, nor be sanctified through it, there is occasion for God to work without means. Mr. C. admits that infants are depraved; and therefore he must admit that if they are not sanctified and prepared to enter heaven, they must be lost. And is not the soul of an infant of sufficient value to call for a divine influence without means to sanctify it? It is immortal; it will live through endless ages. It is worth more than the whole world. When such a spirit is called to leave the world, and is unfit for heaven, shall we be told that God can not sanctify it by his Spirit? that he can not prepare it for the joys and glories of heaven?

The gentleman reasserts his unphilosophical principle that there can be no moral disposition where there is no knowledge. A child, he says, can not love God before it knows him. But it is absolutely certain that the mind may be in such a state, that it will love some objects and feel an aversion to others on first sight. This is a fact known to everybody. Thousands have experienced its truth, for they have loved or disliked persons and things the first moment they ever saw them. This love or aversion depends upon a previously existing character or state of mind.

Everything has its nature. The lion, however young, has a lion's nature. All lions, in all climates and countries, manifest the same disposition, as soon as capable, proving that they possess a common nature. Plant two trees in the same soil, and let them be watered by the same stream, and one will produce sweet fruit and the other bitter. They possess different natures. This very illustration is by the Savior applied to the subject now under discussion. He said: "Make the tree good, and the fruit will be good." Make the heart pure, and the life will be pure. Again, he says: "A good man out of the good treasure of the heart bringeth forth good things; and an evil man out of the evil treasure bringeth forth evil things" (Matt. xii. 35.) Such may be the moral disposition of a man's heart, that an object of compassion will in a moment call forth his sympathy and his benevolence. So may an infant possess a holy nature; so that when first it shall look upon God in heaven, it will love, adore, and worship him. This, I think, is perfectly clear to every one but my friend, Mr. C.

I think I have answered every argument he has offered, for I was careful to note them all. I will now adduce some further arguments in favor of a special agency of the Holy Spirit in conversion and sanctification.

The first passage I will read is Ezekiel xi. 18, 19, which contains a prediction concerning the spiritual blessings which God would bestow upon the Jews: "And they shall come thither, and they shall take away all the detestable things thereof, and all the abominations thereof from thence. And I will give them one heart, and I will put a new spirit within you; and I will take the stony heart out of their flesh, and will give them an heart of flesh." Are we to understand by such language as this that God intended at a future day simply to present the truth before their minds—the very truth which they now rejected? Or are we not plainly taught, that he purposed to exert upon their hearts such a spiritual influence as would cause them to return to his service? The meaning of the passage is so perfectly plain that no criticism can obscure it.

Again, I will read Isaiah liv. 3: "For I will pour water upon him that is thirsty, and floods upon the dry ground: I will pour my Spirit upon thy seed, and my blessings upon thine offspring; and they shall spring up as among the grass, as willows by the water courses." This is one of the precious promises made to the church in her affliction. The day was coming when the Lord would pour water upon the thirsty—would cause the influences of his Spirit to be abundantly enjoyed by his people and by their descendants. Here we have the emblem and the thing signified. This outpouring of the Spirit was to result in the conversion and sanctification of their seed.

Now compare this language with that employed by the prophet Joel, which was fulfilled on the day of Pentecost. "And it shall come to pass in the last days, (saith God,) I will pour out of my Spirit upon all flesh; and your sons and your daughters shall prophesy," etc. This language of Joel is admitted by all to denote a divine agency distinct from words and arguments. Then, when

Isaiah employs the very same expression—"I will pour my Spirit upon thy seed"—is it not clear that he also speaks of an influence of the Spirit distinct from arguments? Mark, too, the happy results of this spiritual influence. The blessing of God was to descend upon their offspring; and they were to grow up spiritually as willows by the water courses. They were to bring forth the peaceable fruits of righteousness. (Time expired.)

MR. CAMPBELL'S FIFTH ADDRESS.

Tuesday, November 28, 11 o'clock A.M.

Mr. President.—On yesterday morning, sir, I gave reasons why I sometimes read the word "always" for "only"—not as its grammatical import, but its contextual import in the proposition, as it relates to our respective views. Mr. Rice might, therefore, have saved his time for a more important purpose. The terms "only" and always," as before explained, have here an equivalent value; and, therefore, I lay no stress whatever upon any preference, except for sake of perspicuity.

The legitimate point of discussion in this proposition, is not whether the Word operates, but whether the instrumentality of the Word be necessary, according to the words, only through the Word. The gentleman is shifting the ground. I never said, nor wrote, that the Word was the original cause of man's salvation, nor even the efficient cause. I have never ranked it above the instrumental cause. All that has been offered by Mr. R. upon the subject, in any other view of the matter, is gratuitous and irrelevant. It is to change the proposition, and hide the point in his system, which I repudiate. The proposition is, in its own language, a refutation of all these insinuations. It affirms that the Spirit of God operates. The question is not upon operation, but upon instrumentality—"only through the Word." This is the question to be debated here. If there be any controversy at all, this is just the point. If Mr. Rice will make the Word the uniform and universal instrument, he agrees with me. There is, then, no controversy about it. This is the true and real issue. Any other issue is false, feigned and deceptive. I have, during a protracted controversy for many years, given my views on physical, moral and spiritual influences; upon physical and metaphysical regeneration—but these are other questions than that now before us. What the Spirit of God does is not the question; but by what means the Spirit of God operates in conversion and sanctification. The gentleman is seeking to get off from the question; still, he perceives the real point, for he has offered arguments which have no relevancy, if that be not the point.

He argues against my views, because they "limit the power of God." That is, of course, in confining the operation to the instrumentality of the Word. It limits, but does not deny the operation. He is right here. This is the issue, and the objection was made in a just view of it. Well, now, I meet the objection as a legitimate one. We shall try its merits. The Universalian says, the Unitarian, the Calvinist, and especially the Presbyterian, limits the power of God, because he makes salvation depend upon faith and a holy life. When Mr. Rice defends himself from that charge, his defense shall be mine from his charge of limitations. The Unitarian, too, talks against limiting the great God, in extending salvation beyond the precincts of Bible influence. But all this is idle talk. I do limit the power of God only because he himself has limited it. God can only do by his power, what his wisdom and benevolence approve. He has no power beyond that, though almighty to do what these two perfections approbate. Therefore, "He can not lie"; "He can not deny himself." Therefore, he can not make a wicked man happy; and, therefore, he can convert men only through the Gospel. There are physical as well as moral impossibilities. God can not make two mountains without a valley. He can not make light and darkness cohabit the same place at the same time. He can not lie. This is another ad-captandum argument. God can do many things he will not do. I say again, he can only do what is in harmony with all his perfections. There are, also, moral impossibilities. A virtuous and kind father could kill all his children, and yet he could not. He has physical, but not moral, power. His arm could, but his heart could not; and, therefore, the moral sometimes triumphs over the physical. God can only save through the means his wisdom, justice and benevolence dictate.

But a second objection, pertinent to the true issue, is couched in the following terms: My doctrine "leads to infant damnation." That is, if the Spirit operates only through the Word, then infants can not be saved, because they can not understand or believe the Word. Now, if his views of faith and spiritual influence were correct, then the objection would lie against my affirmation, "only through the Word." But his views being erroneous on these points, the objection is idle and impotent. These words, "infant damnation," are ugly words—and they come not so consistently from one who believes and teaches the Confession. His creed divides infants into two classes—the elect and the "non-elect." Of course, then, infant damnation is inevitable, if the Confession be true. Now, if we were to proportion the number of "elect infants" by the number of elect men, according to appearances, there would be a hundred non-elect, for one. And yet this gentleman upbraids my doctrine as objectionable, because it might, perchance, involve the possibility of infant damnation, when his own Confession consigns an awful overwhelming majority of all infants to eternal perdition! Think not that I exaggerate the relative proportions. Look at the whole world! Pagans of all castes; Greek and Roman parties; Jews, Turks, Atheists, and all the reprobate Protestants! What disproportion between the good and the bad! It is as one to the hundred!

There is nothing more repulsive to the human mind than the doctrine of infant damnation. It was the first item of Calvinistic faith at which my infant soul revolted. I still remember my boyish reasonings on that tenet of elect and non-elect infants. I dared not to say that it was absolutely false, seeing my creed and my ancestors recognized it. But, thought I, can it be true? How can it be true? An infant is born, yet could not help it; it opened its eyes but once, and shut them forever—and went to everlasting anguish!!! That millions should be forced into existence, and forced out of it in a day, a month, a year, or some six or seven, and go down to everlasting agonies! My soul sickened at the thought!—and yet, I had lived full fourteen years before I presumed to utter to any mortal what my heart felt. I thank God, this doctrine of reprobate infants is not found anywhere but in the creed; and there they are found only in minced form, by implication, in the words "elect infants."

There are various assertions and negations, and sometimes oft repeated, the only object of which, as it seems to me, is to call me off from the main issue. I should like to refer to all these matters, some of them several times repeated, if I had time, or if it were incumbent on me. We should lose nothing by a full examination of them all. Meantime, I am just reminded of the speculation on the word "holy."

The gentleman's speculations on the word "holy," and God's making man holy, and a holy house, etc., have not been full of light to my reason. Holiness is not a positive creation, an entity, a substantive existence, nor an attribute like wisdom, power, or goodness. It is a relative attribute. Were there no impurity there could be no holiness. In contrast with impurity, God, and angels, and saints, are holy beings. The gentleman's positions would apply as much to Eden and paradise as to man. He might say, God created Eden and paradise holy, as well as man. In that acceptation the universe was made holy. I must be permitted, though perhaps not in a way adapted to universal intelligence and acceptance, to offer a remark or two on man, tending to illustrate my position at least.

Man, with me, when contemplated in his whole person, is a plural unit. He is one man, having a body, a soul, and a spirit. So both my philosophy and my Bible teach. Paul prayed for the Thessalonians that God would sanctify them wholly (*holoteleis*), their body, soul and spirit. Their *pnuema, psuche, soma*. Not only have the Greeks these three names, but the Latins also. They had their *animus*, their *anima*, and their *corpus*. So had the Hebrews. So have the moderns, as we have—body, soul, spirit. The body is a mere organized material machine—the soul is the seat of all the passions and instincts of our nature, and is intimately connected with the blood. It is the animal life. The spirit is a purely intellectual principle, as intimately connected with the soul as the soul with the blood, and the vital principle. Now the spirit, or intellectual principle, in man is not the seat of corruption, or of depravity abstractly, any more than the mere materials of human flesh. The understanding or intellect is indeed weakened, and sometimes perverted by the passions, the animal instincts and impulses. But the soul is the great seat of all those corrupting and debasing propensities and affections that involve the whole man in sin and misery. Man was not condemned for reasoning illogically; nor was he condemned because he was either hungry or thirsty, or had these appetites, but because captivated by his passions, he was led into actual rebellion. This is still the depravity of man. His spirit is enslaved to his passions and appetites. Its approvings and disapprovings are all more or less contaminated, biased, and tinged by these rebellious elements, this "law of sin which is in his members," warring against the law of his mind, reason and conscience. Now these not being developed in infancy, any more than reason or conscience, places them under quite a different dispensation and destiny. Dying in that undeveloped state, they are not the subjects of condemnation eternal, never having disobeyed God, nor refused the Gospel. They need not those operations of the Spirit of which the theory of Mr. Rice so often speaks, and with which it is so replete, all of which originated, too, in the brain of one Saint Augustine.

Hours might be consumed in the development of these principles; and without a full development, perhaps they ought not to be introduced. I have, indeed, spoken thus far merely to show that we have reason to repudiate the notion of the abstract, undefinable metaphysical regeneration of an infant, as essential to its salvation. It only needs, as before observed, a physical regeneration; a destruction of that body in which those seeds of passion and sinful appetites are so thickly sown, in consequence of the animal and sensitive having triumphed over the intellectual and moral man, and so entailing upon our race this natural proneness to evil. Hence the necessity of physical regeneration. The adult saint needs it as much as the infant. "That law (or power) of sin" in the members, of which Paul complained—that "body of sin and death," under which he groaned, and which made him, in his own esteem, a "wretched man," must be destroyed. While "the inward man delighted in the law of God, he saw another law in his members, warring against that law of his mind and bringing him into captivity to the law of sin, which was in his members." This will be destroyed in the saint before admission into heaven— and that is what I mean by physical regeneration; and this is destroyed before development in the dying infant, and, therefore, through the Lord Messiah; the Resurrection and the Life; the sin-atoning Lamb of God; the Second Adam—it slumbers in the bosom of its Father and its God, till the great regeneration of heaven and earth.

Mr. R. says he believes not in physical regeneration. Why, then, believe in infant regeneration, without the moral means of the Word? Without a regeneration of the heart, he says, they can not be saved; and that being without knowledge, faith, love or hope, must be either physical or metaphysical, or both. I plead the physical regeneration of the body and animal soul, he the physical and immediate regeneration of the spirit while in the body. This, however, is all aside from the great question. It comes in by the way, to illustrate or support the fact, that with him regeneration is not according to my eighth argument, through the incorruptible seed of the Word, but without it. I will dismiss this episode by a quotation from Paul (Rom. v.): "By one man's disobedience many were constituted sinners, so by one man's obedience shall many be constituted righteous"; and as death reigned, before the law, over them that had not sinned, as Adam did, by violating a positive precept, so grace will reign by another man, over them that never obeyed a precept; who, by reason of their infancy, never on earth could discern between good and evil. So I opine, and in so thinking, I have much countenance, if not positive testimony, from my Father's Book.

Our Savior's death has laid such a broad, strong, and enduring foundation, that the Divine Father of humanity can, with the most perfect propriety, so far as mortal vision can pierce, throw the arms of his sublime philanthropy around the dying millions of our race, whose only Son was in their flesh, and not only snatch them from the desolation of the grave, but also train them in the skies, as he does their parents on the earth, for the high beatitudes of an eternal fruition of him that made and redeemed them from the earth.

Mr. Rice has not yet explained to us his views of faith. He has a regeneration without it; indeed, in all cases, I presume, a regeneration anterior to faith. Faith, as I perceive, is the effect of regeneration, not the cause, according to his theory. A holy principle is immediately infused, and then faith is a holy act of a holy soul, regenerated by immediate contact with the Divine Spirit. Hence his adult and infant regeneration are, if I understand him, alike physical, or without the Word of God. Faith or regeneration must be prior—a simultaneous existence is not supposable. With me faith is first, and repentance, or a change of heart, next in the order of things—in the order of nature and causation. If regeneration be the cause of faith, anterior to faith, without faith, then again, of what use are all human instrumentalities preaching, Bibles, etc.? I wonder, except to save appearances, why any one should be taught to read the Bible, or go to meeting, until he is born again. If regeneration is not within the control of any mortal instrumentality—if no means are to be used with reference to it, I ask, then, how do men make faith void, and the Gospel of none effect? If the Bible be not a moral instrument in this matter, what kind of instrument is it?

With me every Christian is a new man. His heart is changed. His soul is renewed in the image of God, "in knowledge, righteousness, and true holiness." God's Holy Spirit is the agent—his Gospel is the instrument. Instrumental causes are not original nor procuring causes. Without the instrumental, however, it can not be accomplished. No man can see without the instrument called an eye, or the instrument called light. Truth, and faith are the grand means, or the conjoint means, of conversion and sanctification.

Mr. R. must again have up Paul and Apollos. It is a small matter, but he may have it again. I have not opened a commentator as an authority for my views in any case in the discussion, but I will read a few words from Henry confirmatory of them. (Here Mr. C. read a passage from Henry, the copy of which is lost.)

I repose no confidence in Henry as a critic, but I do in McKnight, who paraphrases these words thus: "I have planted you in God's vineyard; others have watered you by giving you instruction; but God hath made you to grow." Henry, in his common-sense view, very well agrees with McKnight. I know not how many critics agree with me, but I have the context.

Paul preached the Word, and Apollos watered the Word! A little better acquaintance with Paul and Apollos would relieve him from this strait. Paul was a powerful reasoner, and Apollos was an eloquent exhorter. Now, the reasoner is the strong man, and therefore grubs and plants. The exhorter follows him, and refreshes with his zeal, his ardor, his eloquence. They do well to go together. Two by two, let them go. One reasons and one pleads. Sinners are converted, and saints are built up, and churches made to grow, by such joint laborers in God's field. While the idea of a church is in our mind, the figure is apposite and beautiful. But substitute the Word, and it is destitute of consistency, propriety, and beauty. It is peculiarly unfortunate for the development of the great principles involved in these propositions, that I have no respondent. Eight arguments are now before us, without any response or closing upon any one, in the form of a direct issue. In my last I brought the united testimony of Peter, Paul, and James, and of the Messiah himself, on the indispensable instrumentality of the Word. I gave all emphasis to the figure of *seed*, consecrated as it is by Jesus and the apostle Peter. It appears as though Mr. R. feared the figure and the argument deduced from it. He can not but perceive that if the Word be so compared to seed, with regard to the new creation, whether traced in its animal or vegetable associations, it is made essential to the product of a new man. Where that is not the offspring, the product can not be. Our Savior carries the figure so far as to say that if even the seed be sown in the heart, and the devil should take it away by any stratagem, then there is no change, no salvation. May I not then conclude that the gentleman's neglect to reply is an indisputable evidence of his lack of ability to reply. Well, we shall expect to hear from him on the subject of physical regeneration, and especially on faith, as the cause or the effect of moral renovation. The gentleman has indeed said, the seed is not everything! And so say we.

An acquaintance with Mr. Rice's manner of assertion, attack, and negation, makes it the more incumbent on me to keep the proper issue before you, fellow-citizens; and frequently to assert my views on the subject on which we have been most calumniated. Our reformation began in the conviction of the inadequacy of the corrupted forms of religion in popular use, to effect that thorough change of heart and life which the Gospel contemplates as so essential to admission into heaven. You may have heard me say here, (and the whole country may have read it and heard it many a time,) that a seven-fold immersion in the river Jordan, or any other water, without a previous change of heart, will avail nothing, without a genuine faith and penitence. Nor would the most strict conformity to all the forms and usages of the most perfect church order; the most exact observance of all the ordinances, without personal faith, piety, and moral righteousness—without a new heart, hallowed lips, and a holy life, profit any man in reference to eternal salvation.

We are represented, because of the emphasis laid upon some ordinances, as though we made a Savior of rites and ceremonies—as believing in water regeneration, and in the saving efficacy of immersion; and as looking no farther than to these outward bodily acts; all of which is just as far from the truth and from our views as transubstantiation or purgatory. I have, indeed, no faith in conversion by the Word without the Spirit; nor by the Spirit without the Word. The Spirit is ever present with the Word, in conversion and sanctification. A change of heart is essential to a change of character, and both are essential to admission into the kingdom of God. "Without holiness no man shall enjoy God." Though as scrupulous as a Pharisee, in tithing, mint, anise, and cummin, and rigid to the letter in all observances, without those moral excellencies usually called righteousness and holiness, no man can be saved eternally; "for the unrighteous shall not enter the kingdom of God." (Time expired.)

MR. RICE'S FIFTH REPLY.

Tuesday, November 28, 11:30 o'clock A.M.

Mr. President—I do not deny that Mr. Campbell believes in the necessity of a change of heart; but the great difficulty is that he rejects the only agency which can effect it. It is of little advantage for him to urge the necessity of such a change, so long as his doctrine makes it unattainable. He teaches that without holiness no man shall see the face of God, but denies the only agency that can prepare him for the bliss of heaven.

I do not know what he means when he says the Spirit is always present with the Word, nor does he convey any definite information concerning his views when he says men are converted and sanctified by the Spirit and the Word. We desire to know what he means by these expressions. Does he mean, that in addition to the words and arguments contained in the Scriptures, there is an influence of the Spirit on the heart? If so, what are we contending about? But if I am to learn his views from his publications, he does not so believe. The manner in which he has illustrated his views on this subject, leaves no room to doubt what they are. The Holy Spirit, he has said, operates on the minds of men just as the spirits of Demosthenes and Cicero operated on the minds of their hearers or readers. But, I ask, would there be any propriety in saying that the spirits of Demosthenes and Cicero are always present with their writings? Who ever heard of such language being employed? If his illustration is not wholly deceptive, the Holy Spirit is with the Word in no other sense than the spirits of those ancient orators are present with their writings which still are extant!

It is very important that we do not lose sight of the real difference between us. I will, therefore, again read a passage from his Christianity Restored, which I read on yesterday:

"Every spirit puts forth its moral power in words; that is, all the power it has over the views, habits, manners, or actions of men, is in the meaning and arrangement of its ideas expressed in words, or in significant signs addressed to the eye or ear. * * * The argument is the power of the spirit of man, and the only power which one spirit can exert over another is its arguments."

Observe, he says only moral power can be exerted on minds, and every spirit puts forth the only power it can exert over others in words and arguments. The whole converting and sanctifying power of the Holy Spirit, he contends, is in the written Word. The Spirit dictated and confirmed the Word, and the Word accomplishes the whole work of conversion and sanctification. It is against this doctrine that I enter my solemn protest.

Mr. C. says, he holds, that the Word is only the instrument in conversion and sanctification. This, however, like his other statements, is entirely ambiguous, for the words of Demosthenes and Cicero were the instruments by which they sought to produce an effect on the minds of their hearers and readers. But he does not come out plainly and tell us whether he believes in any influence of the Spirit direct from the Word. Does the gentleman now believe in any such additional influence in conversion and sanctification, or does he still hold the doctrine taught in his publications? Does he retract his former views?

In our correspondence, so far as I had anything to do with it, I was careful to have a perfect understanding that I should have the right to explain the proposition by his published writings. To this he agreed, and I have read them. And most certainly he does deny any influence of the Holy Spirit in conversion and sanctification, except the mere force of words and arguments!

I am truly gratified that the gentleman has brought forward the charge against us of holding the doctrine of the damnation of infants, because it is believed by many who are unacquainted with our views. He says our Confession of Faith teaches this doctrine This is not correct. It is true that it speaks of elect infants. "Elect infants, dying in infancy, are regenerated and saved by Christ through the Spirit." Are all infants dying in infancy elect? All Presbyterians who express an opinion on the subject so believe. The expression, "elect infants," the gentleman seems to think, implies non-elect infants; but I call on him to produce one respectable Presbyterian author who ever interpreted the Confession of Faith as he has. I never heard a Presbyterian minister, nor read a Presbyterian author who expressed the opinion that infants dying in infancy are lost. Mr. Campbell boasts of his familiarity with the doctrine of our Church. He, then, is the very man to make good this oft-repeated charge. I call for the proof.

So far as I know the sentiments of Presbyterians on this subject, they believe that all that die in infancy are of the elect—are chosen of God to eternal life, and are sanctified by the Holy Spirit, and saved according to his eternal purpose. Infants do not die by accident. He whose providence extends to the falling of the sparrow, takes care of every human being; and we believe that his purpose is to save those whom he calls from time before they are capable of knowing the truth.

But the gentleman has made the charge that the Presbyterian Church holds the doctrine of the damnation of infants, and now I demand the proof. What proportion of the human family are chosen to eternal life, our Confession of Faith does not profess to determine. The calculations of Mr. C., therefore, is an affair of his own, for which we are not responsible. The very worst that any candid man can say of our Confession, so far as this subject is concerned, is that it does not profess to determine whether all infants are saved. It gives not the least intimation that any are lost.

But the gentleman tells us that, when quite young, his mind was shocked at this doctrine. Is it not, then, most marvelous that whilst his mind revolted at the imagined doctrine that some infants may be lost, he should have embraced a doctrine that makes it utterly impossible that any of those dying in infancy can be saved! It was certainly a most singular effect of his early dislike of what he imagined to be the doctrine of our Church!

I must say a word or two in reply to his remarks concerning the limiting of the power of God over the human mind. He says he does limit the power of God, and that the Universalists complain of him for so doing, and he has specified two things which God can not do, viz.: He can not lie, and he can not make two hills without a valley! I was not aware that these things were the objects of power. Absurdities are not the objects of power. There is no objection to his speaking of the exertion of God's power as limited where God has so spoken; but I call on him now to show us where, in the Bible, God has said that he can not, or that he will not, exert on the human mind any power except through words and arguments. Or where has he said that he can not or will not sanctify the hearts of any of the human family without the Word! There is not such passage from Genesis to Revelation. And since God has not limited himself, who dares undertake to limit him?

Mr. C., let it be remembered, not only denies that God does exert on the human mind any other power than that of words or arguments; but he even goes so far as to assert that he can not operate except by the Truth!!! Where has God said that he can not? Nowhere. How, then, can any man venture to say so?

I was quite pleased with the gentleman's last speech. For our cause it was the best he has made since the debate commenced, except that remarkable one on yesterday morning. His doctrine has driven him into absurdities so glaring that all must see them. He asserts that God did not create man holy, and says we might as well talk of making the Garden of Eden holy! Solomon said, "God made man upright, but he sought out many inventions." What is the meaning of the word "upright"? What is the difference between uprightness and holiness? If the gentleman chooses to charge Solomon with talking foolishly, let him do it. It is the language of Divine revelation.

Mr. C. says that there is no depravity in intellect—that it is all in our animal passions, which belong to the body. I was pleased to hear him advance this doctrine. Not that I desire to see any one run into dangerous error, but I am glad when false principles lead to such results as to prove to every one their erroneousness. The doctrine that depravity is in the body, not in the mind, is indeed quite ancient. The Manicheans held that matter is inherently evil, and that the soul is not depraved. Hence, they believed that to become holy it was only necessary to afflict, starve, and emaciate the body! If all sin is in the body, the sooner we get out of it the sooner we shall get clear of sin. If sin belongs to the body, let us get the body into a proper state, and all will be right!

But I understand that "sin is the transgression of the law," not that it consists in corruption of the body. The works of the flesh, as enumerated by Paul, are "Adultery, fornication, uncleanness, lasciviousness, idolatry, witchcraft, hatred, variance, emulations, wrath, strife, seditious, heresies, envyings, murders, drunkenness, revellings, and such like." By the word "flesh," as I have repeatedly remarked, he means the depraved nature of the human mind, and these are its works. Yet Mr. C. tells you that depravity is in the appetites and passions belonging to the body! This is not only a contradiction of Paul, but of his own doctrine, as stated in his Christian System, where he says:

"Man, then, in his natural state, was not merely an animal but an intellectual, moral, pure and holy being."

Admitting and teaching that God created him holy. Again:

"There is, therefore, a sin of our nature, as well as personal transgression. Some inappositely call the sin of our nature our 'Original Sin'; as if the sin of Adam was the personal offense of all his children. True, indeed, it is, our nature was corrupted by the fall of Adam before it was transmitted to us, and, hence, that hereditary imbecility to do good, and that proneness to do evil, so universally apparent in all human beings. Let no man open his mouth against the transmission of a moral distemper until he satisfactorily explains the fact that the special characteristic vices of parents appear in their children, as much as the color of their skin, their hair, or the contour of their faces. A disease in the moral constitution of man is as clearly transmissible as any physical taint, if there be any truth in history, biography, or human observation. * * * All inherit a fallen, consequently a sinful nature, though all are not equally depraved. * * * Condemned of natural death, and greatly fallen and depraved in our whole moral constitution, though we certainly are, in consequence of the sin of Adam," etc.—(Chap. IV., Sec. 4, pp. 29, 30.)

Now, observe, he here distinctly states that there is a sin of our nature, as well as personal transgression. Yet he has positively asserted, during this discussion, that there can be no disposition where there is no knowledge! In his last speech he located sin in the body; but here he says, "Let no man open his mouth against the transmission of moral distemper until he can satisfactorily explain the fact," etc. "A disease in the moral constitution of man is as clearly transmissible as any physical taint, if there be any truth in history, biography, or human observation!" And on the next page, "All inherit a fallen, therefore a sinful nature"; or would he say a sinful body? Again, he represents man as depraved in his whole moral constitution! Ah, when a man, in order to sustain his tenets, is forced into such palpable contradictions, concerning subjects so clear, he must feel that his cause is hopeless!

A word about physical regeneration. He says regeneration, without means, as in case of infants, is physical regeneration. Let him prove it. He has asserted it, but the Bible does not so teach. I deny that the regeneration of a soul, without means, is physical, and an assertion is, I think, properly met by a denial.

Mr. C. says I have not defined regeneration. I have explained conversion to mean a change of heart, followed by a change of life. The former is commonly called regeneration, and the latter conversion. Regeneration is a change of heart from sinfulness to holiness, and, consequently, from the love and practice of sin to the love and service of God. When the heart is renewed, man loves that Savior against whom heretofore it rose in enmity. He sees a divine beauty and loveliness where before he saw, as it were, a root out of a dry ground. It is of this blessed work of the Spirit Paul speaks, when he says: "It is God that worketh in you to will and to do of his good pleasure." The heart is renewed by the Holy Spirit, and the result is that the sinner wills and acts in obedience to God's commands.

The gentleman has read Henry's Commentary to prove that in 1 Cor. iii. 6 Paul spoke of planting a church. I have not examined Henry on this passage, but I observed that he read Henry's comment, not on the passage in dispute, but on the 10th verse, in which Paul says: "I as a wise master-builder have laid the foundation!" What was the foundation? It was Christ crucified—the doctrine of the cross. "Other foundation can no man lay than that is laid, which is Jesus Christ."

But I will admit, for the sake of argument that Paul, when he used the word "planted," meant planting the church. I see not how this can help the gentleman's argument. Paul planted the church, but God caused it to grow—gave the increase. Paul planted it instrumentally; God, by his spirit, gave efficiency to the work. I have no objection, so far as this argument is concerned, to this interpretation. I will cheerfully admit that Paul planted the church instrumentally; but I also contend that God caused it to grow—gave it life and increase. The gentleman, however, overlooked the fifth verse: "Who then is Paul, and who is Apollos, but the ministers by whom ye believe, even as the Lord gave to every man?" This passage speaks distinctly of a divine influence leading the Corinthian Christians to believe; but my friend did not see it!

He says there was never a tree without a seed, and hence he infers that no one was ever converted without the Word. This is running out figurative expressions, so as to make them contradict the plain teaching of the Bible. God at first created trees without seeds, and made all things without means. He fed the Israelites in the wilderness without means, because means could not be employed. The gentleman might as well deny that Elijah was fed by a raven, because persons are not commonly thus supplied with food. God clothes and feeds men only in connection with means, when by the exertion of the power he has given them the means can be used; but he has never confined himself to means. Nor has he ever said that he will, in no case, regenerate and sanctify without the written Word.

I wish the audience distinctly to see the contradictory positions of the gentleman. Yesterday he assumed one position, and to-day the opposite. In my argument, showing that his doctrine necessarily involves the damnation of infants, I stated the fact that infants are depraved. I stated, what all admit, that they can not be sanctified through the truth. The conclusion, then, is unavoidable, that if they are not sanctified by the Spirit without the truth, they must, dying in infancy, either go to heaven in their depravity, or be forever lost. He admits their depravity, and therefore he is forced to admit that if not sanctified without the truth, they go to heaven in unholiness, or to hell!

To escape the force of this argument he told us, on yesterday, that only the atonement of Christ is necessary to save infants. But I replied that the blood shed on the cross does not change the heart; and that the difficulty in the way is that they are unholy. Now, to escape the difficulty in which he is involved, he has located their depravity in the body. But this is not only absurd and unscriptural, but it is contradictory of his own writings on this very subject!

The difficulty, then, returns upon him with double force. If the doctrine taught in his Christian System is true, infants are depraved in their whole moral constitution; and, I ask, can beings thus depraved dwell in the presence of the infinitely holy God? Who can believe it possible? The gentleman has contradicted himself more than once, and is now involved in the gross absurdity of maintaining the doctrine of corporeal depravity!

I, therefore, again urge against him the unanswerable argument that his doctrine necessarily involves the damnation of all that die in infancy. The argument is a fair one—it is perfectly legitimate. It is what logicians call the *reductio ad absurdum*. He admits that the doctrine of infant damnation is both false and absurd. Consequently by proving that his doctrine necessarily involves this absurdity, I prove it untrue.

I will now bring forward some further Scripture evidence in favor of the doctrine of the special agency of the Spirit in conversion and sanctification, for I prefer to go by the Bible. I had supposed, from his former professions, that my friend, Mr. C., would do the same; but he has found it necessary to use a great deal of philosophy—quite an abundance of metaphysics. He seems to prefer these speculations to the Word of God.

I will read Ephesians ii. I: "And you hath he quickened, who were dead in trespasses and sins." The word "quickened," it is true, is not found in the original Greek, in the first verse; but it is in the fifth. "Even when we were dead in sins (God) hath quickened us together with Christ." The apostle represents men as dead in sin, and God as having quickened or made them alive. Did he quicken them with words and arguments? Did he reason with them, and exhort them to live? Surely this is not the meaning of the apostle. Jesus Christ stood at the grave of Lazarus, and said: "Lazarus, come forth." Did he raise Lazarus from the dead merely by the words uttered, or by an exertion of almighty power accompanying the word? Every one admits, at once, that Lazarus was quickened by an immediate exertion of divine power. Precisely similar language is used with regard to regeneration. Men are dead; and God quickens them.

The next passage I read is in the tenth verse of the same chapter, where the apostle proves that men are not saved by good works: "For we are his workmanship, created in Christ Jesus unto good works, which God hath before ordained that we should walk in them." Now observe how it came to pass that the Ephesian Christians performed good works. God created them anew unto good works; their good works were all the result of a new creation, of which God was the author. Was this a creation by arguments? A creation by words and motives? The apostle used the very strongest term in any language, without qualification. And when the inspired writers selected the strongest language to express their ideas, and used it without qualification, we must take their words in their obvious and undiminished meaning. What word in the English, Hebrew, or Greek language could be selected that would more unequivocally express the idea of a direct divine influence on the heart than the word "create"? God directs his servants to use the strongest expressions on this subject, evidently knowing that there was no danger of their being misunderstood. We are, then, obliged to understand by this language a special divine influence, distinct from words and arguments, on the hearts of men. The language is too plain to require the aid of criticism to elicit its meaning, or to be obscured by plausible interpretations. (Time expired.)

MR. CAMPBELL'S SIXTH ADDRESS.

Tuesday, November 28, 12 o'clock P.M.

Mr. President.—You perceive, sir, I doubt not, in common with this great assembly, that in the latitude and longitude of Mr. Rice's theory of response in debate, there is not a single point of theoretic or polemic theology that may not legitimately, or illegitimately, be brought into this discussion; and that, according to his interpretation of our rules of debate, we may touch at every point in the compass of the most extended ecclesiastic creed, in good keeping with the most strict construction of the proposition before us. Everything, it seems, can interest Mr. R. and call forth some attention except the arguments on which I rely, and to which I challenge special attention. It is exceedingly painful to me to have to occupy so much time in the mere statement of what has been done, or left undone, by my respondent. But to pass on, from argument to argument, without any reply or debate on the proper issue, and without a single notice of the failure or neglect on his part, would seem neither respectful to myself, nor to the audience. I exceedingly regret, sir, that I have so little to reply to, in the speech which we have just now heard. I have asked, not for the sake of asking a question with the appearance of something under it of great importance, as I have seen some persons do, but, sir, I have asked the gentleman for a single verse, Old Testament or New, that asserts regeneration by the Spirit alone. When adducing those of the most unambiguous and incontrovertible import, affirming regeneration through the instrumentality of the Word of God, I have not succeeded, either in getting such a text, or in obtaining a response to those which I have presented.

His assumed leading objection to our views on the proposition in discussion is, that we rather make void the necessity of spiritual influence in our teachings of the Christian religion, while our grand objection to his theory of spiritual influence in the work of conversion is, that it makes void the necessity of preaching the Gospel or reading the Bible. And while some affect to believe that we take too many into the church on our terms of discipleship, we are of opinion that the opposite theory takes in too many that ought not to be admitted, both adults and infants, and that it keeps out of the Christian profession a great mass of intelligent and virtuous persons, many of them more worthy than some in the church, who are waiting for some miracle, some special impulse divine, which may at once renovate and rouse them into spiritual life and action; in the absence of which they dare not presume upon making the Christian profession. To settle these matters, an appeal to the Scriptures, and to such reasonings as the Scriptures seem to sanction, has been instituted, and we have only to regret that it has not been followed up.

Notwithstanding the absurdity of the thing, there are not a few who still regard something like physical impulses operating upon the soul as a hammer in the hand of a smith operates upon the metal placed upon his anvil. Their notion, as far as we can gather it, is, that the spirit of God comes into a personal contact with the spirit of a man, and either new-molds, or attempers, or changes, or imbues it with something from himself, which is sometimes called the infusion of a holy principle. And this seed or principle remains immutably and forever in that person, according to one theory, without any possibility of a failure of eternal life, but according to others, it may be lost forever. This divine touch is sometimes compared to that which reanimated the body of Lazarus, or raised to life the dead body of Jesus. The other theory is, that the Word or Gospel of God is that type or medium through which it sheds abroad in the human heart the love of God to man in the gift of his Son, and thus renews him in the moral image of his Redeemer, through an inward revelation of his grace and mercy in the heart.

Mr. Rice is greatly indebted to my writings. They supply him with something to read and to say, and give him an opportunity to play upon words. Every man of observation, however, understands the policy; and, therefore, it fails, as he does, to establish any real discrepancy—and especially that he can not get me into a mere logomachy. But once more I will enter my protest against his manner of quoting my writings. It is neither magnanimous, nor is it generous, nor is it fair. A man with genius enough to be a mere quibbler, and that never had a very large capital, can figure away in great style in making Paul contradict James, and, worse still, in making Paul contradict himself. The master quibblers in the science of doubting are inimitably astute in the art. Paul, says one, affirmed that "a man was justified by faith without works"; and James says, "A man is justified by works, and not by faith." Reconcile your two inspired apostles, if you can! Again, continues he, Paul contradicted himself, for he said: "If you be circumcised Christ shall profit you nothing. Yet he took his son Timothy, a Christian man, who had been baptized also, and circumcised him, and sent him to preach Christ! What a consistent man was your Doctor Paul!

I could find a hundred instances of this sort in the Bible, and spend a month with a skeptic arguing them. See what a file of newspapers, pamphlets and Harbingers my friend has got around him! Does he dream of diverting me from the grand position into all these documents? I do not intend any such discussion. He may have that to himself, and I will attend to my business. I will give argument for argument, and document for document on the question before us; but these hundred and one other topics the gentleman will please reserve for some other more favorable opportunity. As the gentleman affirms regeneration without faith, he had better proceed to prove it by an induction of cases, and then I will examine them, if he can not respond to me.

He represented me as saying that all sin was in the body. I did not say so, nor anything so importing. I have only said that "Sin works in our members," and that "in the flesh dwelleth no good thing," and that there is "a law working in the flesh and warning against the law of the mind, and bringing it into captivity to the law of sin, which is in the body"—and that, therefore, the seeds of sin and the roots of transgression are in the passions, and that the spirit is brought into captivity to the flesh; but there are the "sinful desires of the mind," as well as of the flesh, in consequence of this captivity. I said that sin works through the body. Hence the greatest saint may, like Paul, long for the redemption of the body from sin and death. "Who shall deliver me from this body of sin and death? I thank God through Jesus Christ my Lord."

These reflections and associations led Paul to descant with great earnestness and grandeur upon the earnest expectation of the creature, and of the adoption, to wit: "The redemption of the body." I must take the pleasure of reading, with a passing remark, two or three sentences. Rom. viii. 19-21: "The earnest expectation" of our humbled body, "the creature, waiteth" in joyful hope "for the manifestation," the full development, "of the sons of God" in their pure, sinless and immortal bodies. "For the creature"—the mortal body—"was made subject to vanity"—dissolution—"not willingly," but it is reconciled to the grave "by reason of him who has subjected it, in hope that the creature"—the body—"itself shall be delivered from the bondage of corruption into the glorious liberty of the sons of God" at the resurrection. This is a portion of the glorious hope of every saint.

Now the dying infant is delivered from this body, sown with all these elements of sin, these "desires of the flesh," and the aged saint is also delivered from the same by death. This physical regeneration, the birth of the spirit, is essential to an entrance into the everlasting kingdom. But whence came this new designation, "elect infants"? It is not elect persons, nor elect men, but elect *infants*. There certainly were non-elect *infants*—not only non-elect men, but non-elect infants. Who taught this language? The creed and not the Bible. But we have been just now informed, by a revelation made from the upper world through Mr. Rice, that all infants that die are "elect infants." If we had only a miracle, we might believe in this new revelation. But what becomes of the non-elect infants? They become non-elect men. Why, then, call them non-elect infants, as none of that kind can die? All non-elect infants are immortal infants. As infants they can not die!! It is only above a year ago that this new revelation of elect infants being all dying infants, first reached my ears. The Scotch Presbyterians never have been favored with this new revelation. I must again read this remarkable passage.

"3. Elect infants, dying in infancy, are regenerated and saved by Christ through the Spirit, who worketh when, and where, and how he pleaseth. So also are all other elect persons, who are incapable of being outwardly called by the ministry of the Word."

The Westminster divines must have got into Mr. Rice's dilemma when they conceived this doctrine. They supposed but three conditions of the question. Infants dying were lost, or infants dying were saved; and if saved, they must be regenerated, because none can enter heaven but regenerate persons. They assumed the last, and made the doctrine to escape from the folly of the assumption! There are, then, three classes of elect persons to be regenerated by the Spirit without the Word. These are elect infants, elect pagans and elect idiots. Of four classes of mankind, but one are regenerated through the Word. My friend will have three subjects of physical regeneration for my one. Will the gentleman say that all these elect pagans are, like infants, in a state of irresponsibility? And if they are not, in what consists the parallelism? I heard of a lady who drank pretty deep into this new revelation. She became a monomaniac. She had a small family of infant children; and weary of the world herself, she thought it was best to make her own mind easy about her offspring, and to make their happiness secure. She accordingly rose up in the night and strangled them all. She gave this, on trial, as the only reason of her conduct. Of course, she was sent to the lunatic asylum.

I regret that my friend, Mr. Rice, could find so much time to discuss this matter rather than the question. I shall dismiss it with a single remark, viz., that it is but a flimsy and superficial covering for a very incredible and unchristian dogma. I would then advise its being expunged from the book altogether.

Because, among other reasons, it had been more rational to have made the non-elect infants die; for then there would have been much more mercy than in this scheme. The elect would have lost nothing by living seventy years, but rather gained much by their good works; and the non-elect would have gained much, too, in having no punishment to endure for actual transgressions; their only cause of regret would then be merely that they had been born. Thus dispose we of this branch of the philosophy of infant regeneration, without the Word.

The gentleman, in responding to my remarks upon the word "holy," quoted a passage highly complimentary to his philological skill in interpreting language. As a proof that God created Adam holy, he says, "God made man upright, but they have sought out many inventions." Now the question is, are "holy" and "upright" synonymous terms? Does "upright" and "holy" mean the same? Mr. Rice, by the force of the quotation, makes a holy man an upright man, and an upright man is a holy man—still, they are not at all equivalent. No man accustomed to criticism has ever argued that because two epithets are applied to one man, the epithets must be one and the same in sense. Holiness means separation from sin. Sin must, therefore, previously exist before the term "holiness" could come into use. *Hagiosune* is derived from *hagee*, and that is a compound of two words—*a*, privative, and *gee*, the earth. *Hagios*, "holy," therefore, means separate from the earth; no earth, no separation from it. There is, then, a contrast in the word itself—un-earthy, not earthy, separate from the earth. The very origin of the word "holy" intimates that there was something unclean before it, just as the word "un-earthy" indicates there was something earthy before it. It is, therefore, good sense to say that God made man perfect, or in his own image. But the Bible does not say that God made man holy, and therefore I object to it in such an argument as this; although, in common free conversational style, I have no objection to say that Adam was holy till he sinned.

The term "holy" is applied to the earth, to anything at all separated to God's service or presence. Moses, said God, "take off your shoes, for you stand on holy ground." The Lord was there; that spot was separated to the presence of God. There is no moral quality in the word "holy." It indicates no moral attribute. It can, therefore, be applied to an altar, a temple, a camp, a vessel, the earth, or anything sacred to the Lord. God is said to be holy, because he is separated from all impurity; infinitely separated from sin. "He is of purer eyes than to behold iniquity."

The argument, then, is, that God made Adam holy, and he makes an infant holy: the first by creation, the second by regeneration. And what means a holy infant? One regenerate, or one simply sanctified or separated to the Lord, as Samuel or John the Baptist was? If in that sense, the word is misapplied to regeneration; because these persons, like Jeremiah, are separated to the Lord or some special work. All persons and things called holy in the Bible were specially set apart and separated to God in some peculiar way, or for some very special purpose. To apply this word as Mr. Rice has done, is, therefore, to mystify its proper meaning in the Scriptures, to confuse the sacred dialect, and to mislead us in our conceptions of Adam and his offspring. It is, therefore, an innovation not to be tolerated, but rather repudiated by all sensible and reflecting men.

I shall fill out my time with a few remarks on his definition of regeneration. He has at last given us a definition of this important word. But he has not yet answered the great question whether regeneration is the cause or the effect of faith? Is regeneration the cause of faith or prior to faith, or is faith the effect of regeneration, or subsequent to it? Are they simultaneous? What connection between them? Is there any connection? and if any, what is it? I have brought up the subject in every form I can conceive of, to elicit from him such an expression as will facilitate our clear and satisfactory decision of this much and long-litigated case.

He has, indeed, vouchsafed the following definition of regeneration: "It is a change of heart from a love of sin to a love of holiness." Whether it be an act, a process, or an effect, is not distinctly stated. Nothing but the heart is changed in regeneration. No such regeneration is found in the Bible. Persons are there spoken of as regenerated after their hearts are changed. His is scholastic regeneration. Be it so. We now understand him. Regeneration is, then, a change of heart from one love to another love. Now I believe in such a change, though I do not believe in calling it regeneration: for certainly regeneration in the New Testament is not that thing. A regenerated person is *a new creature*.

It is, then, but a change of disposition: for love is no more than an affection or disposition of the mind. There must, then, be a prior disposition; for, unless there be a disposition existing already, there can be no change of it. This is self-evident. Now, a disposition always presupposes an object. No person can think of a disposition, without conceiving of something to which the mind is turned or disposed. No one can possibly be disposed to an object of which he knows nothing. He must see in the object something to call forth his attention—to allure, to attract, or some way draw out his affection or disposition towards it. Need I ask how a person can love an object, or hate an object, of which he is perfectly ignorant?

But regeneration is a change of one disposition for another. Consequently there must be a change of objects to the mind. The mind must have in contrast two sorts of objects. It must contemplate them clearly, compare them accurately, discover a difference, a superior beauty and loveliness, before the disposition leaves the one and cleaves to the other. Now, I ask, is an infant susceptible of all this discovery, contemplation, comparison, intelligence, preference and choice of objects? Can a child have any moral or immoral disposition, without an object? Can it have an object which it sees not, contemplates not, and can not apprehend? Can it abandon one object and prefer another, without perception, comparison, and conclusion—without the power of reasoning and the possession of previous knowledge? I repeat it, sir, the gentleman's definition is fatal to his cause. It is without fact, without philosophy, without the Bible, and therefore, can not be assented to by any one of thought and reflection, whose mind has been called to the rational examination of the subject. Have we not, then, from his own definition, given a requiem to his speculation, and forever sealed up his argument? When Mr. Rice disposes of this argument, we shall give him a few more. But, sir, he will never try. (Time expired.)

MR. RICE'S SIXTH REPLY.

Tuesday, November 28, 12:30 o'clock P.M.

Mr. President.—My friend calls on me to prove by the Scriptures that the Spirit ever operates in conversion and sanctification without the truth. He affirms, and has undertaken to prove, that the Spirit operates only through the truth. Has he produced a solitary passage that sustains his proposition? He has not, and he will not; for there is none such in the Bible. But he is in the affirmative. With what propriety, then, does he call on me to prove a negative? I might remain silent until he produces at least some show of argument from the Scriptures; for he professes to hold no article of faith for which he can not produce a "Thus saith the Lord." Where is his Scripture proof of the proposition now before us?

The Scriptures, as I have proved, speak of three agencies or influences, in the conversion and sanctification of men—the ministry, the Word, and the Holy Spirit. Mr. Campbell takes the ministry and the Word, but rejects the agency of the Spirit. I take all the three. This is the difference between us.

He say he did not assert that all depravity is in the body. Yet, to prove that it has its seat in the body, he read to us the language of Paul to the Romans, chap. vii. 23: "But I see another law in my members, warring against the law of my mind, and bringing me into captivity to the law of sin, which is in my members. Oh, wretched man that I am! who shall deliver me from the body of this death?" But by his members, and the body of death, Paul did not mean his own body, but the corrupt propensities of his nature. He represents his remaining corruption as a dead body, which, in all its loathsomeness, he was carrying about with him. He desired most earnestly to be delivered, not from his natural body, but from his indwelling corruption.

The audience will remember my argument on this subject. I proved that the gentleman's doctrine necessarily involves the damnation of infants, because they are depraved, and he denies that they can be sanctified without the truth. I then understood him to say that depravity is in the body, and, therefore, their souls might be saved. But now he has got the depravity back in the soul, and is involved in the old difficulty. The minds of infants, he admits, are depraved. How, then, can they be sanctified? Certainly not through the truth; and he denies that they can be sanctified by the Spirit, without the truth. Consequently, according to his doctrine, they die in their depravity, and are lost! There is no escape from the difficulty.

But Mr. C. says that I am very unfair in quoting his writings; that he could read the writings of Paul so as to make him apparently contradict himself. If any one attempts to prove that Paul contradicts himself, I am prepared to prove his perfect consistency. And if I have misrepresented Mr. Campbell, as he charges, he is the man, of all others, best qualified to correct the misrepresentation. Then let him do it. He is perfectly at liberty to produce his writings, and to prove, if he can, that I have misrepresented him. He conceded to me the right—as the correspondence will show—a right which I should have had without his consent—to read his writings in explanation of the proposition stated by himself; and now he is disposed to complain of me for doing it. I know it is distressing to him, but I can not help it. I can not possibly misunderstand his writings on this subject; for he states, with perfect clearness, that there are only two kinds of power—moral and physical. The former, which is exerted only by words and arguments, operating on mind; and the latter, on matter. In the book from which I read his views are presented with entire clearness. I only wish he had stated them as clearly in this discussion. If he had come out with an open and fair presentation of his views, we should have known just where to find him. As it is, they are involved in mist and darkness impenetrable. Yet he is a man of remarkably clear intellect; but he is singularly inconsistent. At one time he states his doctrines so clearly as to admit of no doubt concerning them; and at another, he is dark as midnight, and it is impossible to ascertain what he believes.

I am happy, however, to have his books, from which we are able to ascertain precisely what he has taught, and to repel his charges of misrepresentation. If a man should, in a public discussion with me, read from a book of mine, and should not read enough fairly to represent me, I would read the remainder of the connection. Let Mr. C. do so.

He quotes Paul, complaining that sin did work in his members, and that he carried about with him a body of death; and he tells us, the members are the corrupted passions seated in the body; and that Paul, when he came to die, needed a regeneration as much as do infants. I know of no system of philosophy that confines the passions to the body. We speak of the passion of hatred, or the passion of love. Some of the passions belong particularly to the body; others to the mind. These two classes Paul enumerates together, as the works of the flesh. (Gal. v. 19-21.) Anger, wrath, malice, hatred, envy, etc., belong to the mind. Paul found depravity in the mind. What he meant by the body of death, we may, perhaps, learn from chapter 6th, verse 6th, of the same epistle: "Knowing that our old man is crucified with him, that the body of sin might be destroyed, that henceforth we should not serve sin." The old man, or corrupt nature, is crucified; and the new man, or renewed nature, leads to a holy life. The same idea is conveyed, when he says, "They that are Christ's have crucified the flesh with the affections and lusts."

The gentleman is now placed in this predicament: he must maintain the absurd doctrine that depravity is only in the body, and not in the mind—and certainly his arguments look that way—and therefore infants, being pure when they leave the body, can go to heaven; or he must hold that they die in their moral corruption, and are forever lost! There is no way to escape from these absurdities, but by abandoning his theory concerning spiritual influence. I can not but believe it would be better to abandon his theory than meet the consequences.

But he seeks to shield himself by charging our Church with holding the doctrine of infant damnation. The expression, "elect infants," used in our Confession of Faith, teaches no such thing. The word "elect" signifies chosen from or out of; and infants are chosen from the world, the human family. But he says, as there can not be adults without infants, so there can not be elect infants without non-elect adults. I was not aware that there could not be adults without infants. I know there have been adults without infants, and possibly there might be again. It is not true that the word "elect," applied to infants dying in infancy, implies that there are non-elect infants! Though he can not prove the doctrine to be in our Confession, he tells us he has heard it preached in good old Scotland. I was never in Scotland, nor can I know what strange things he may have heard there; but I again call on him to produce one respectable Presbyterian author who has taught this doctrine. He has asserted that the Presbyterian Church holds the doctrine of infant damnation, and I demand the proof. Whenever I prefer a charge against his Church, the proof shall be forthcoming when called for, and when he makes charges against my Church, I shall certainly expect him to prove them. I hope he will not shrink from proving his assertions.

Concerning the doctrine of election, I will only remark, that I am not disposed to mingle together things which are entirely distinct; I am, however, prepared to discuss this doctrine with him, whenever he chooses to enter into it properly; but I do not intend to permit him to divert the attention of the audience from the subject under consideration.

That infants are depraved, he admits. That they can not be sanctified through the truth, we know. He denies that they can be sanctified without the truth. They must, therefore, die in sin, and be forever lost. I leave you, my friends, to determine whether a doctrine involving such consequences can be true.

Strangely enough, Mr. C. denies that God created man holy. I quoted the passage, "God made man upright." But now, for the first time in my life, I have heard it asserted that the word "holy" does not express moral quality. When the heavenly hosts exclaim, "Holy, holy, holy, Lord God Almighty," do not they express moral quality? But the gentleman says the word implies previous sinfulness. Angels are said to be holy, and God is holy. Does the word, in these cases, imply previous sin? If, however, the gentleman is disposed to be hypercritical about the word "holy" I will take the word "upright." "God made man upright." This word signifies, literally, standing erect or straight; and, as applied to denote moral qualities, it means conformity of God's law. He whose heart and life accord with that rule, is said to be an upright man.

The gentleman is now placed in the same difficulty from which he vainly sought to escape; for certain it is that God made man upright, and that he did it not by words and arguments. If, then, God did, at first, create him upright, not by words or arguments, who shall say he can not exert on his mind a divine influence, creating him anew unto good works? And if he can exert such an influence on the mind of an adult, who will deny that he can sanctify the infant?

He asks whether faith is the cause or the effect of regeneration. I am not disposed to be diverted from the proposition before us, to the discussion of other questions. The question now before us is, whether the Spirit of God operates only through the truth? Does the Bible say, the Spirit operates *only* through the truth? It does not. But it does plainly teach that infants must be regenerated, or born again. "For," said our Savior, "that which is born of the flesh is flesh, and that which is born of the Spirit is spirit." This is the reason why the new birth is absolutely necessary. But infants are born of the flesh; therefore they must be born of the Spirit. They can not be regenerated through the truth, consequently they must be regenerated without it. This passage, therefore, teaches clearly the doctrine that regeneration may be, and is, effected by the Spirit without the truth.

But the gentleman returns to the position that there can be no holiness without knowledge; and he asks, Can an infant love holiness or hate sin, when it knows nothing of either? And I ask, Can an infant love music before it has heard it? You say, No. But still there may be such a taste for music that the moment when it first hears it, it will be charmed and delighted. So the heart of an infant may be so purified that it will love and adore Jesus Christ so soon as it may be able to contemplate his character. Just here I will very briefly answer the gentleman's question concerning faith and regeneration, though I am under no obligation to do it. A dead man does not perform the acts which flow from life. He is first alive, and then he acts. Those who are spiritually dead do not put forth the acts of spiritual life. They are first quickened, then they exercise true faith and love. Spiritual acts flow from spiritual life. This I take to be the doctrine of God's Word.

Having now paid due attention to the gentleman's speculations and arguments, I will invite the attention of the audience to some further Scripture evidences in favor of the special agency of the Holy Spirit in conversion and sanctification. I prefer to establish the doctrine for which I contend by the clear testimony of the Bible.

I will read for your consideration Luke xxiv. 45: "Then opened he their understanding, that they might understand the Scriptures." The Savior, after his resurrection, appeared to his disciples, who as yet understood not the things concerning him which are taught in the Old Testament. It is not said that he opened their understandings *by* the Scriptures, but he opened their understandings, that they might understand the Scriptures. David felt his need of this divine illumination, when he prayed: "Open thou mine eyes, that

I may behold wonderful things out of thy law" (Psa. cxix. 18). There were wonderful things in God's Word; but because of his comparative blindness he did not see them in all their divine excellency. These passages clearly teach the doctrine of the agency of the Holy Spirit in enlightening the minds of men.

The next passage I read is in the epistle to Titus iii. 5: "Not by works of righteousness which we have done, but according to his mercy he saved us, by the washing of regeneration and renewing of the Holy Ghost, which he shed on us abundantly through Jesus Christ our Savior." We are saved by the renewing (making anew) of the Holy Spirit, which God shed on us. Does not this language teach with perfect clearness the doctrine of a direct divine influence on the heart? Or are we to understand by the Spirit being shed upon them, only their having the words and arguments contained in God's revelation? If such was the apostle's meaning, he certainly took a very singular method of expressing it. Let us compare with this the language employed in the Acts of the Apostles concerning the outpouring of the Spirit on the day of Pentecost: "I will pour out of my Spirit upon all flesh." Does not this language express an influence of the Spirit not exerted merely by words and arguments—a direct influence? All agree that it does. If, then, the pouring out of the Spirit expresses an influence distinct from mere words and arguments, does not the expression, "shed upon," mean the same thing? The expressions are very similar, and both evidently express a divine influence upon the minds of men, in addition to the truth, and distinct from it. Similar language is also used in regard to the descent of the Spirit on the family of Cornelius: "While Peter yet spake these words, the Holy Ghost fell on all them which heard the word" (Acts x. 44). Was not this a direct influence of the Spirit? All admit that it was. If, then, the expression "fell on" expresses a direct divine agency, not by word or argument, does not the expression "shed upon" also express a special divine agency? It will not do to say that one of these expressions has reference simply to the Word, and the other to an influence distinct from the Word. In employing this strong language without qualification, the apostles did not seem to fell the least apprehension that their language would be understood to teach the necessity of an immediate agency of the Spirit, in which they did not believe. We must, then, understand their language in its obvious sense.

I will now invite your attention to 1 Cor. ii. 14. I am acquainted with Mr. C.'s mode of commenting on this passage, and I bring it forward now, that he may have an opportunity of defending his interpretation of it, if he can. "But the natural man receiveth not the things of the Spirit of God; for they are foolishness unto him; neither can he know them, because they are spiritually discerned." The first question in order to ascertain the meaning of this passage, is concerning the expression, "natural man." I understand the natural man to be man as he is by nature unsanctified. That this is the correct explanation of the expression is evident from the other instances in which the word "natural" is employed in the New Testament. Thus in 1 Cor. xv. 44, 45, "It is sown a natural body, it is raised a spiritual body. There is a natural body, and there is a spiritual body." The natural body here evidently is the body in its natural state, unchanged. The spiritual body is the body as it will be changed and refined at the resurrection. So the natural man means man as he is by nature unrenewed. The word translated "natural" is also used by James iii. 15: "This wisdom descendeth not from above, but it is earthly, sensual (Greek—natural), devilish." Here the word "sensual" or "natural" evidently denotes moral corruption. The word is again found in the 19th verse of the epistle of Jude: "These be they who separate themselves, sensual (Greek—natural), having not the Spirit." The apostle is here speaking of "mockers in the last time, who should walk after their own ungodly lusts"; and he says they are natural, having not the Spirit.

These are all the instances in which the word translated "natural" is used in the New Testament; and it is a fact that in every instance where it is employed, with reference to moral character, it is used in a bad sense. When used with reference to the body, it denotes its natural state. It is, then, clear from the usage of the word, that by the "natural man" Paul means man as he is by nature, sinful. The correctness of this interpretation is rendered certain by the connection. The natural man does not receive the things of the Spirit. Why? Because "they are foolishness to him." The meaning of this expression is made perfectly clear by the eighteenth verse of the first chapter: "For the preaching of the cross is to them that perish, foolishness; but unto us which are saved, it is the power of God." That is, they that perish see in the preaching of the cross no wisdom, no adaptation of the plan of salvation to their condition, nothing attractive. It appears to them foolishness. So the natural man, like those who perish, receives not the Gospel, the truths revealed by the Spirit; for they appear to him unmeaning, unwise, unlovely.

But if, as Mr. C. supposes, the natural man were simply a pagan, ignorant of divine revelation, the apostle would have said: "The natural man receiveth not the things of the Spirit; for they are *not revealed* to him." But when he says they are foolishness to him, we are compelled to understand that they have been presented to his mind, and that he sees in them no wisdom, nothing lovely or attractive to him; and therefore he rejects them; for a thing of which a man has never heard can not be said to be foolishness to him; and especially can it not be said that he does not receive what was never presented to him, because it is foolishness to him.

By the natural man, then, we are to understand the unrenewed man, man as he is by nature. All such reject the gospel of Christ, "the things of the Spirit." Consequently the gospel alone is not sufficient to effect their conversion. They do not receive it—can not understand it. Hence the absolute necessity of an agency of the Spirit, additional to the Truth, and distinct from it. They must experience such a change as will cause them to see wisdom, adaptation to their condition, beauty and attractiveness in the gospel. The spiritual or regenerated man, enlightened from above, admires and embraces the truths of divine revelation.

The next passage of Scripture to which I call your attention, is 1 Cor. i. 22-24: "For the Jews require a sign, and the Greeks seek after wisdom; but we preach Christ crucified, unto the Jews a stumbling-block, and unto the Greeks foolishness; but unto them which are called, both Jews and Greeks, Christ the power of God and the wisdom of God." Here you will observe the gospel was preached indiscriminately to Jews and Greeks, and both rejected it. There was, however, a third class, composed of both Jews and Greeks, to whom it was the power of God unto salvation. Those who received the gospel, and were converted and saved, are mentioned by the apostles as "Them which are called." By this language he can not mean the call of the Word, for all had this indiscriminately. It must be, then, an additional influence, an influence effectual in securing their conversion; for, to all such, the gospel was the power of God to salvation. By this call, then, we must understand the special agency of the Holy Spirit, not simply by words and arguments, calling them "out of darkness into his marvelous light." This passage establishes beyond controversy the doctrine for which we contend. That I have given the correct interpretation of it would appear still more manifest by comparing it with other passages in which the same apostle uses the word "called."

I have time only to read one other passage in Heb. viii. 10: "For this is the covenant that I will make with the house of Israel after those days, saith the Lord; I will put my laws into their mind, and write them in their hearts: and I will be to them a God, and they shall be to me a people." This is a prophecy quoted by the apostle from Jeremiah. What does God promise to do? "I will put my laws into their mind, and write them in their hearts." Are we to understand by this that he would influence them simply by words and arguments? They, at that time, had the Word of God before their minds—"line upon line, and precept upon precept." Inspired men were sent to reform, exhort, and warn them; but God declares his purpose, at a future day, to teach them effectually, to write his laws upon their hearts, and to cause all to know him, from the least to the greatest, and to walk in his statutes and do them. Does not this language most clearly and conclusively establish the doctrine that, in conversion and sanctification, the Spirit exerts on the human mind an influence in addition to that of the Word, and more powerful and efficacious? It is this agency only that can subdue the rebellious dispositions of men, melt their obdurate hearts, and cause them to love and serve Jesus Christ in sincerity and in truth. (Time expired.)

MR. CAMPBELL'S SEVENTH ADDRESS.

Tuesday, November 28, 1 o'clock P.M.

Mr. President.—The gentleman has finally complied with my request. He has given an answer to so much of the question as concerns the priority of faith, or regeneration. He has clearly committed himself by avowing his conviction that regeneration, or a change of heart, is previous to faith. This is a point which I desired to elicit at an earlier period of this discussion. It would have saved time. We, however, thankfully accept it at this late hour. The gentleman backed it well with a liberal collection of Scriptures. The only exception to his quotations is, that they happen not at all to pertain to the subject. He tries to show that the Spirit operates through the Word. But that is not the question. We both professedly agree in that point. That the Spirit operates is agreed on both sides. I hope the gentleman will not attempt to make another false issue here. He also admits that the Spirit sometimes operates through the Word. That is not the point to be proved. What, then, must I again ask, is the proposition? Is it not that "In conversion and sanctification the Spirit of God operates *only* through the Word?" He has proved that it operates through the Word. This I affirm. Has he come over? Or does he mean to use the Scriptures that prove his operation *through* the Word, to prove his operation *without* the Word! All Scriptures, then, that prove that the Spirit of God operates through the Word are irrelevant to his position, but relevant to mine, unless he comes fully over and affirms that it operates only through the Word.

I do not, indeed, think that the gentleman understands those portions of Scripture right, else he could not have so quoted them. But it is not necessary now to make a commentary upon them. You will all understand that a passage of Scripture that proves the Holy Spirit operates *through* the Word, does not prove that he operates *without* the Word, or independent of it. It is with him, then, essentially necessary that a change of heart should precede faith. All men are dead. They must be quickened. True, all living men are dead to something.

And a pagan man, or a Jewish man, may be alive to his own theory, and dead to another. But the sophism seems to be, what rhetoricians sometimes call "killing the metaphor, or running it mad." Now a man that is metaphysically dead to one thing, is not literally dead to everything else. There is still something alive in him, through which truth may find its way to his heart. His reason and conscience are not dead, although his heart may be. Paul says of a certain person: "She that liveth in pleasure is dead while she lives." All this I have shewn in my opening speech, to which the gentleman has yet paid so little attention. Whenever any point or portion of Scripture is so interpreted, as to make another void, I set it down that it is most certainly misconstrued. Any theory, or view, of any passage which makes the preaching of the Gospel of no use, that makes faith vain, or the Bible useless to that particular end, I hold to be infallibly wrong.

It is no new development. I have read it from the days of Thomas Boston till now. I presume the gentleman would make regeneration a miracle, a positive immediate act of Omnipotence, without any instrumentality at all. And I have drawn him out as large as life on that topic. A change of heart is therefore before belief, because the throng of the old modern school of self-ycleped orthodoxy stands in need of it. Whatever is before anything is without it. The cause may be without the effect, in one sense of the word "cause," but the effect can in no sense be without the cause.

I say again, my voice never could have been raised upon the subject of spiritual influence, had not I seen in these extravagant forms, as I judge, it making void the Word of God, and the preaching of the Gospel. I yet remember the singular impressions that sometimes accompanied my early readings of modern revivals. Many years since I read of a singular outpouring of the Spirit in New York. In a certain neighborhood there were a thousand converts reported, as the result of a great outpouring of the Spirit. Of these thousand converts about one-third went to each of the three leading denominations in that neighborhood—Presbyterians, Methodists, Baptists. The first impression was, Did the Spirit of God thus at one outpouring make three hundred Presbyterians, Methodists, Baptists? Strange operation! In old times he made them all Christians, and of one heart and soul. I concluded there was some delusion in the affair; that man's spirit had likely as much to do in it as the Spirit of God. Since that time I have been an observer of such occasions and reports, and suffice it to say, twenty-five years' observation has greatly confirmed the first impression. Men and parties often make revivals, and now we have got a class of preachers, known by the title of "Revivalists," men well disciplined in the art and mystery of obtaining outpourings of the Spirit.

But my standing proof of the great amount of deception practiced on such occasions is the lamentable fact that after the excitement ceases, and reason resumes her wonted dominion, the converts are about as unenlightened in the religion of the volume of God's own inspiration as before. Their feelings were moved, and their hearts quailed, or their affections were overcome by the scenes around them; yet still their minds were not enlightened, their spirits were not more elevated, nor their faith enlarged. In most instances the converts are as ignorant of God and Christ, after, as before. Persons so converted, too, rarely love the Bible. They believe more in excitement than in the twelve apostles; and would rather listen to exciting speeches than keep the commandments of God. Children love their proper parents more than others. Hence those born of great excitement, love them—born in storms and tempests of the soul, they have a great attachment to them. They feel more in debt to the revivalist than to the Bible; and they love him more ardently, and will obey him more joyfully and faithfully. They soon learn a few texts, and by these they prove everything. A universal favorite is, "The Spirit bears witness with our spirits that we are the children of God." They reason from that within to prove that without, rather than from that without to prove that within. They prove the doctrine to be true by their feelings, and then they prove their feelings to be true by the doctrine. They reason in a most fallacious circle; and multitudes, it is to be feared, are deluded into fatal mistakes.

I heard the other day, indeed since the discussion commenced, that a preacher of some pretensions, and of some notoriety in this State—a man fond of conspicuity—in a recent discourse undertook to prove the resurrection of Christ to his audience by their feelings. He was himself suddenly transported into an ecstacy at the discovery of the new proof. He was, with Archimedes, ready to say, *Eureka*—I have found, I have found. He said, My friends, I have never heard it uttered, I have never read it in a book. It is to me a perfectly original argument, but really it appears to me the best I have ever heard. It is simple, and you can all apply it. Paul says, "If Christ be not risen faith is vain, preaching is vain; you are yet in your sins." Now follows it not, that when sins are pardoned, preaching is proved to be not in vain, and faith is demonstrated not to be in vain, and, consequently, Christ is risen from the dead? Now, brethren, I feel that my sins are pardoned, and you feel that your sins are pardoned; surely, then, neither our faith nor our preaching is vain. Hence we are infallibly certain, from our own hearts, that Jesus Christ rose from the dead! But suppose this sense, or feeling of forgiveness, is a delusion, what comes of the argument?

In one word, if a spiritual illumination makes a Methodist, and a spiritual illumination makes a Baptist and a Congregationalist, it is not only a new light, a modern illumination, but it makes these parties of divine authority; and thus the Spirit is at war with itself in these different denominations. Here is A preaching against the Baptists by divine illumination, here is B preaching against the Methodists by divine illumination, and here is C preaching against them both, and in favor of old-fashioned Presbyterianism, by the same divine illumination. Well, there are different ways to London, they say; and so there are to heaven, they argue!

But I will submit another case to these learned doctors. Of the numerous converts that joined a certain church, many have gone over to infidelity. They told of raptures, felt ecstacies, had their visions, and rejoiced in the assurance of pardoned sins. But now the Bible and religion are with them a mere delusion. They affirm it all to be a hoax. What now has become of their former illuminations? their visions and their ecstacies? They are all abandoned as a mere delusion. It is not denied that they once had those feelings, emotions, and transporting views. They still admit the fact of their former actual existence; but they were the results of a delusion? With their faith in the Bible, those pleasant dreams and fancies fled. No more light, nor spirit, nor inward witness. Now does not this prove that there is no real foundation of confidence, no true hope in God, no real love of the truth, nor of the God of truth, in these phantoms! Had they been solid, substantial evidences, would not their faith in them have remained when their faith in the testimony of prophets and apostles failed?

For these reasons, and not from any aversion to the doctrine of spiritual influence, do we repudiate the popular notions of getting religion, and of enjoying religion. We rejoice in the belief of the influence of the Spirit of God in the great work of our salvation from sin. We pray for larger measures of these divine influences. We desire them for the union of Christians, and as an end to all these vain wranglings and controversies. No greater proof of the enjoyment of God's spirit can be given, than an ardent devotion to all his oracles, and to the keeping of his commandments.

To return again to regeneration. Mr. R. has got the heart purified without faith, if I rightly understand him. The heart is renewed, changed, regenerated by the Spirit before faith; consequently faith is not necessary to the purification of the heart. There is much difference between our two systems. Mr. Rice has the heart purified before faith; I have the heart purified through faith. My reason for so believing is found in the fact that Peter said God made no difference between Jew and Gentile, in that "he purified their hearts by faith."

We are accustomed to regard the purification of the heart as the greatest of all things in religion. If, then, that be accomplished without faith, of what essential use is faith afterwards? If the greatest of all events is achieved without it, why may not the effects of that change be accomplished without it? Why do we preach the gospel to convert men, if, before they believe the gospel, and without the gospel, men are renewed and regenerated by the direct and immediate influence of God's Spirit? I would conclude that if a man may be born of the Spirit without faith, he may also be saved without faith; and thus faith, from being the primary principle in religion, is anticipated and set aside by the Holy Spirit in the capital point of the renewal of the heart.

In the case of adults, for, with Mr. Rice regeneration is the same in all cases, we have a regenerated unbeliever; and if we could suppose an interval between regeneration and faith, as must be the case in all infants, then we have not only a regenerated unbeliever, but also the possibility, in the case of death, of such a one being saved without faith. Again, in the case of infants, the interval between regeneration and faith may be an interval of years, for anything known to the contrary, and then we have the extraordinary case of an infant being a child of God, and living in the world without the knowledge of God, without Christ, and without hope!

I hope Mr. Rice will throw some light on this knotty subject, and, if possible, reconcile these views of his Church with those of the Bible, and the experiences and observations of a Christian community. He has certainly been driven to a very high latitude, by adverse winds, when he has to assume that regeneration is wholly independent of faith, and always anterior to it, and thus, by one bold assumption, make void all the means of grace, and the utility of a Christian ministry. But we shall wait for his expositions.

The gentleman, in his disquisitions upon holiness, still compares it to a taste. This is his only escape from the difficulties propounded in my last address. According to his Church, holiness is set forth as the supreme love of God, or, "he is said to be holy who loves the Lord with all his heart, and soul, and mind, and strength." A regenerated child possesses not this holiness—himself being judge. Neither has it a disposition towards God, for it has no knowledge of him. These concessions Mr. R. is obliged to make. The common sense of community requires them at his hand. But will it satisfy the intelligent, after having defined regeneration to be a change of heart, from the love of sin to the love of holiness, to be informed, that, instead of having this love of holiness, and hatred of sin, an infant has an undeveloped taste for them—something like a taste for music?! But even this taste is an assumption. However, the gentleman does not even say it *has*, but a child "*might have* a taste for music." Still, this *might have* and *having* are different things. And inasmuch as the gentleman has not yet produced any child, nor any well-authenticated fact of any child having a taste for holiness, as having been charmed, as with music, on the first presentation of the subject, we must put it down as a complete failure on his part, to sustain his infant regeneration. He has truly toiled hard in this case, but certainly has not made out either the theory or the fact of instinctive holiness.

We have also had another dissertation on the word "holiness." Anything but the question on hand. Well, now, must I repeat that this term indicates no real substantial attribute, or virtue, but mere separation from all impurity?—or, if any one prefers it—it is purity itself. The tabernacle, and afterwards the temple, and all its functions, were holy. God's presence on earth or in heaven, makes all things holy, as did his presence in the mount with Moses. And even Mount Tabor, where Moses and Elias appeared to Jesus, is called the "Holy Mount" by Peter. The angels incessantly repeat this adorable conception of God; and thus represent him as infinitely, eternally and perfectly pure—removed from all contaminations. They say, "Holy, holy, holy, is the Lord God Almighty!" But with them this is not merely a single attribute, but an ineffable conception of his infinite, awful, and glorious purity. In their eyes it is his superlative beauty and loveliness. He is said to be of purer eyes than to behold iniquity; and the very heavens are represented as not clean in his sight.

But we are reminded that holiness is a substantive requisite from Christians, and that Jesus, the Messiah, is made unto us by God—"wisdom, righteousness, holiness and redemption." It is, therefore, important to understand it well, inasmuch as "without holiness, no man shall enjoy God." Jesus is not imputed to us for wisdom, righteousness, etc., but he is the author of these perfections in us. These terms comprehend much, and are indicative of very distinct conceptions and excellencies. Justice, or righteousness, has respect to positive duties and obligations to society. Holiness, or sanctification, a hatred of, and separation from, all impurities; and redemption expresses our deliverance from death and the grave. We may, indeed, suppose it, as this term indicates, the consummation of salvation—that as it is the ultimate goal of man's aspirations, ("Be you holy, for I am holy,") it must indicate the supreme of moral grandeur, and the perfection of moral excellence. But, in discussing the term philologically, it intimates no more than simple separation from sin, or any kind of legal or moral impurity. But we shall now proceed to a new argument on the modus operandi, or means of sanctification, which we shall call our ninth argument.

IX. It shall be based on the special commission given to Paul, as explained by that given to the Messiah himself. And, therefore, we shall read that to the Messiah, as introductory to that presented to the Apostle Paul. "I give thee," says Jehovah, "for a covenant of the people; for a light of the Gentiles; to open the blind eyes; to bring out the prisoners from the prison, and them that sit in darkness out of the prison-house." "The Spirit of the Lord God is upon me; because the Lord has anointed me to preach good tidings to the meek; he hath sent me to bind up the broken-hearted, to proclaim liberty to the captives, and the opening of the prison to them that are bound; to proclaim the acceptable year of the Lord, and the day of vengeance of our God; to comfort all that mourn." Isaiah xlii. 6, 7; lxi. I, 2. We shall now hear Paul relate his own, as he had it from the mouth of the Lord: "I have appeared unto thee for this purpose, to make thee a minister and a witness both of these things which thou hast seen, and of those things in the which I will appear unto thee. Delivering thee from the people and from the Gentiles, unto whom now I send thee—to open their eyes, to turn them from darkness to light, and from the power of Satan unto God, that they may receive forgiveness of sins, and inheritance among them which are sanctified by faith, that is in me." Here, then, we have a full development in these grand commissions, of the manner and means employed in the wisdom and grace of God in converting and sanctifying the nations of the earth, through the mediation of the Messiah. The most conspicuous point, or the chief means stated, is, that God would use light, knowledge, the gospel, and that he would open the eyes of men—turning them from darkness to light, and from the kingdom and power of Satan to God. God, then, who commanded light to arise out of darkness, has used moral light—that is, revelation, the gospel—as the means of conversion and sanctification. Illumination is, therefore, an essential prerequisite to conversion and holiness. Without light there is no beauty; for in the dark beauty and deformity are undistinguishable. Without light there is nothing amiable, because amiability requires the aid of light for its exposition, as much as beauty. The power of Satan is in darkness; the power of God is in light. God, therefore, works by light; and Satan by darkness. Hence, in Paul's commission, it reads, "Turn them from darkness to light"; and the consequence will be, "From the power of Satan to God"; and the ultimate effect will be remission of sins, and an inheritance among the sanctified. After the study of these, and many such similar documents, found in the Bible, I confess I am wholly unable to conceive of a religion without knowledge, without faith, without an apprehension, an intellectual, as well as a cordial reception, of the gospel of Christ. I repudiate, therefore, with my whole heart, this notion of infant, idiot and pagan regeneration—this speculative conversion, without light, knowledge, faith, hope or love. It makes void the whole moral machinery of the Bible, the Christian ministry, and the commission of the Holy Spirit. It is no advocate of Christ; it is no comforter of the soul, on the hypothesis of infant, and pagan, and idiot regeneration.

But again, what is orthodoxy worth on Mr. Rice's hypothesis? What is it better than heterodoxy? In not one single point. Persons are regenerated without any doctrine, good, bad, or indifferent. It is a work that depends on nothing but the special, direct, and immediate impulse, or impression of the Spirit upon the naked soul of an infant, a pagan, or a gospel hearer. This rage for orthodoxy is madness upon his hypothesis. Why this crusade against us on the part of my friend? We can do no harm, if his theory of conversion and sanctification be true! All that the Spirit regenerates live forever according to him! Consequently they can not be injured; and none else can be saved. In what a singular attitude stands he before this community and the universe, if his notions of regeneration are worth anything! The gentleman will not, because he can not, explain his zeal for orthodoxy on his principles. If the Spirit descends from heaven on a person, and by a direct touch regenerates him without faith, without knowledge, or preparation of any sort, what can sound doctrine and sound preaching avail? Mr. Rice's theory is a moral paralysis to the tongue and to the heart of a preacher. It is to the hearers a moral stupor, a spiritual lethargy.

There are no means of regeneration at all on his assumption. I wish I could say, with an emphasis that would seal it upon the heart forever, if Mr. Rice's theory be anything but a mental hallucination, there are no means of conversion or sanctification—no means whatever of regeneration. I ask him what are the means? Can he name them? He can not. Prayer, preaching, reading, all ordinances, are useless. Man, with him, is born again before he believes. He is as passive in the new birth as in the first birth. There were no motives, no volitions, no previous impulses of the soul in his first; nor are there any in his second birth. He runs the two metaphors of birth and death into a fatal paralysis.

Are you prepared, fellow-citizens of the nineteenth century, are you prepared to receive a doctrine of regeneration that at one fell swoop annihilates all means of grace whatsoever?—that makes faith, preaching, praying, reading, etc., altogether vain! This has been, in my esteem, for many years the most false delusion. I saw the doctrine of metaphysical and romantic regeneration leading just to this point. This is its natural Ultima Thule issue. If it always ends not here with you, it is only because you can not, or do not understand it. Well did the Messiah say, of certain Rabbis, You make void the Word of God by your traditions.

I do, sir, most sincerely regard the Spirit of God as the author of every spiritual and noble desire in the human heart; the author of every pious affection, of every holy aspiration of our souls. His mysterious but certain power is in and with the gospel, and he makes it the power of God to salvation to every one that believes it. He sanctifies us through the truth. He works in us by it to will and do of his good pleasure. He is the Spirit of grace, because he is the Spirit of truth.

Much has been said, and whispered, and gossiped, concerning my heterodoxy. But, sir, allow me to compliment myself—I am, in all the great and weighty matters of religion, more orthodox than any of my impugners. I speak it not boastingly, sir, but in declaration of my general views of all gospel truths. I do not believe, sir, most sincerely, that there is any of those gentlemen that oppose us, more radically and universally orthodox on all these great subjects of evangelical faith, piety, and morality, than we.—Time expired.

MR. RICE'S SEVENTH REPLY.

Tuesday, November 28, 1:30 o'clock P.M.

Mr. President.—I do not remember ever to have seen a man who pretended to religion of any kind, who did not consider himself rather more orthodox than others. This is a common weakness of human nature. It displays itself everywhere, and especially in men who imagine themselves to be great reformers, and believe all but themselves in serious error. If it be true, as my friend evidently thinks, that of all the world he only, and those who agree with him, are in the light, whilst all Christendom gropes in midnight darkness, it follows, as a necessary consequence, that he is one of the most orthodox men! There can be no doubt about it.

We might, perhaps, excuse the other remarks the gentleman has so repeatedly made, concerning the doctrine of Presbyterians, which he professes perfectly to understand; but when he charges our Church with holding the doctrine of infant damnation, we have the right to expect him to produce at least one Presbyterian author who has taught it. I have challenged him to produce even one, and he has not done it; nor has he been able to prove that it is countenanced by our Confession of Faith. I deny that our Church holds the doctrine. He has made the charge, and once more I demand the proof. I had supposed him to be a man who had so much experience in public discussions that he would be prepared at once, when he stated facts, to prove them. But it is not so. Very far otherwise.

I will now proceed to respond to his remarks and arguments, if, indeed, he has offered arguments, to prove the proposition he affirms. Let me ask you, my friends, has he produced one passage of Scripture that says the Spirit operates in conversion and sanctification only through the truth? What passage has he quoted? Do you remember one? I certainly did not hear one quoted. Yet the gentleman boasts that he, more than all other men, confines his faith within the lids of the Bible.

He says: "I have been proving only that the Spirit does operate," and this he admits. Such, however, is not the fact. I have been proving that the Spirit does not operate only through the truth, but that in conversion and sanctification there is an influence of the Spirit, an addition to the Word, and distinct from it. This doctrine he, in his writings and discussions, has positively denied. I like to see a man march up boldly and fearlessly to the defense of his published principles, or openly and candidly retract them. He has very repeatedly taught and published that only moral power can be exerted on mind, and moral power can be exerted only by words and arguments, addressed to the eye or ear. Yet from what we have heard from him on this occasion, no one would imagine that he had ever believed such a doctrine. I do desire to see him come up and openly defend his published doctrines, or retract them. I have been proving that in the conversion and sanctification of adults, there is, first, the instrumentality of the Word, and second, a distinct agency of the Holy Spirit, for which the pious are accustomed to pray—an influence effectually renewing and sanctifying the soul. This latter agency Mr. C. denies. This is the most important point in regard to which we differ; and I am resolved to keep it prominently before the audience.

The gentleman has asserted that a number of his arguments remain unnoticed. If there are such, I have entirely missed them; and I do not know how it could have happened, for I have taken full notes of his speeches. If there are any that remain unanswered, I hope he will mention them.

He has informed us how he was led to adopt his present views. He heard of the Spirit being poured out in divers places, and the result was, that so many Baptists, so many Methodists, and so many Presbyterians were made; and he concluded that if all this had been the work of the Spirit, it would have been more unique. Really, I had supposed that he professed to have been led to the adoption of his views simply by a calm and unprejudiced examination of the Bible; but it appears that I was mistaken. He now informs us that his faith in the special agency of the Spirit was shaken, if not destroyed, by hearing that the Spirit was poured out in this, that, and the other place. Verily, I see nothing in this to shake the faith of a believer in the truth of the Scriptures. What is the language of the Bible on this subject? On the day of Pentecost the prophecy of Joel began to be fulfilled, in which he said: "It shall come to pass in the last days, saith God, I will pour out of my Spirit upon all flesh," etc. And Paul says:

"God saves us 'by the washing of regeneration and renewing of the Holy Ghost, which be shed on us abundantly, through Jesus Christ.'" I can not envy the feelings of the man who can speak slightingly of the very language of the Bible. If Paul, and Peter, and Joel, were in error, I am willing to err with them.

But, he says, if the Spirit had converted all those Baptists, Presbyterians, and Methodists, they would all have been alike. I see no absurdity or inconsistency in believing that the Spirit of God may renew the hearts of several hundred persons, and that some of them might become Baptists, others Presbyterians, and others Methodists. I believe that in all these, and other evangelical denominations, there are vast numbers who, with garments washed in the blood of the Lamb, will stand in the presence of God, where there is fullness of joy forever. I have never taken the ground that the Presbyterian Church constitutes the whole family of God on earth, and that all other Churches are synagogues of Satan! The gentleman can not believe that the Spirit of God would make Methodists, Episcopalians, Baptists and Presbyterians. But, I ask, has he not repeatedly published his belief that there are Christians among "the sects"; Christians, of course, converted by the Holy Spirit?

But, he says, the work, if it were the work of the Spirit, would be more unique; those converted would be in their views more alike. Is the work unique in his own Church, where he holds that disciples are made on principles truly apostolic? Do he and his brethren agree with each other in their views? I can point to a preacher of high standing in his Church, who, for a length of time after joining his Church and being recognized as a minister, believed in the doctrine of universal salvation! I can point to another prominent preacher in his Church who denies that man has a soul, and contends most zealously that in the Scriptures the word "soul" means "breath"! Why is not the work of the Spirit unique in his Church? If this be a fair test of the work of God, and Mr. C. professes to think it is, his Church is the very last place in this wide world where we could expect to find it; for in it, as he himself has informed us, all sorts of doctrines have been preached by all sorts of men! If the uniqueness of the work be the ground on which we are to form a judgment of its character, he would better have said nothing on the subject.

He has told you an anecdote illustrative of the fanaticism to which our doctrine leads, and I like to hear anecdotes occasionally. He told you of a certain preacher who adopted a very singular method of proving the doctrine of the Resurrection; and he argues, even gravely, that those who are said to have experienced the special influences of the Spirit, are quite as ignorant of the Word of God as before. Well, I must tell an anecdote to match his. I hope my "laughing committee" are all present. [Laughing.] A young man not far from Lexington had been immersed into the Church of my friend, where, we are to suppose, converts are made in the right way. After his immersion he, as is rather common in certain quarters, was somewhat wise in his own conceit, and anxious to make converts to his new views. He soon got into a discussion with some persons older and better informed than himself, who quoted against his doctrine a passage from the Old Testament. Not being quite prepared to meet the argument, he replied: "I care nothing about that; the Old Testament was written before the flood." [A laugh.] I doubt whether he was even so well taught as the gentleman's preacher. Indeed, it admits of very serious doubt, whether, as a general thing, his people, in the knowledge of the Scriptures, can justly claim any superiority over others.

But, as further evidence that the doctrine for which we contend is not true, Mr. C. tells you that he has known many who professed to be converted by the Spirit, who afterwards apostatized and became infidels. Does he know whether, in the days of the apostles, there were any cases of the kind? Were there not many who seemed to run well for a time, and then turned to the beggarly elements of the world? Perhaps the apostles did not preach as they should. Certainly they employed language very much like that we use on this subject. This circumstance may, perhaps, account for the fact that many apostatized! I should like to inquire of my friend, whether any who have become members of his Church, and who appeared zealous for a time, have afterwards apostatized? I think he will admit that many such cases have occurred, and that they became worse than before their professed conversion. One of his preachers, as I remarked several days since, stated that he knew churches to which, some little time since, large accessions had been made, that were now almost dead. It is not wise in my friend to use arguments that, if at all sound, will ruin his own cause. The same class of arguments might be urged with equal conclusiveness against Christianity itself. At any rate, his argument, if it proves anything, affords conclusive evidence that he himself preaches false doctrine.

But it is a principle universally acknowledged, that the abuse of a doctrine is no valid argument against it. If men delude themselves, or are deluded by others into the belief that they have experienced a change of heart, when in truth they have not, is this to be urged against the fact that all true conversions are effected by the special agency of the Spirit? Another objection urged by Mr. C. is, that according to our doctrine regeneration precedes faith. Suppose the matter to be just as he has represented it, he is reasoning as decidedly against the apostle John as against us. John says: "Whosoever believeth that Jesus is the Christ, is born of God" (I John v. I). According to the apostle, every believer is born of God, is regenerated. Regeneration is the cause of which faith is an effect. The fact that an individual believes is proof that he is regenerated. Paul, too, represents men as "dead in trespasses and sins," and God as quickening them. (Eph. ii. 1-5.) If my friend had lived in those days, and had entertained his present views, I can not but think he would have disapproved of Paul's theology. For certainly a dead man can not put forth acts, as one who is alive. And he would have exposed the ridiculous absurdity of preaching to men who are dead! Faith is certainly the act of a being who is spiritually alive, and he must be quickened before he exercises faith.

But, says Mr. C., this doctrine makes faith and the preaching of the Word wholly unnecessary and useless. There is a passage in Paul's defense before Agrippa, that completely refutes this objection. "King Agrippa," exclaimed Paul, "believest thou the prophets? I know that thou believest" (Acts xxvi. 27). Was Agrippa a pious man? Had he the faith that overcomes the world? He had faith, but not the faith that secures salvation. He believed the truth of divine revelation; but he did not approve and embrace it. In this sense multitudes believe. They doubt not the inspiration of the Scriptures, nor that they teach the great and essential doctrines and duties of Christianity; but they do not love and embrace the Gospel. Evangelical faith works by love, and leads to good works.

The kind of faith exercised by Agrippa, though it could not secure justification and eternal life, is not useless. It induces men to hear the Word, to read it, to think of it; and God may, through the truth, renew and sanctify them. This faith precedes regeneration; but the faith that works by love and overcomes the world, is consequent upon regeneration. He who is induced to embrace fundamental error is not likely ever to be converted; for God does not sanctify through error. But he who theoretically believes the truth, may be converted and sanctified by the Spirit through the truth.

As to the objection that this doctrine makes the preaching of the Word unnecessary, it has not the least foundation. God is pleased to work by means, when they can be employed. And not only does he employ means where they are wholly inefficient without the exertion of his power, but he has employed such means as had not the least tendency to produce the desired effect. Our Savior used clay and spittle in opening the eyes of a blind man. According to the logic of Mr. C., it was wholly unnecessary and unwise to use such means. He would ask, why use means that will not produce the effect? God has been pleased to say that he will convert and sanctify the heart through the truth, though the truth alone can not convert and sanctify; and who shall say it is unwise? The gentleman's whole difficulty arises from an entire misapprehension of our views.

He tells us he has known persons who professed to have been regenerated one day, and yet they did not believe for many days afterwards. I am obliged to admit that he has found more singular people in this world than any man I have ever known! I, of course, can not dispute the truth of his statement, but I have never heard of persons entertaining such notions. Just as rationally might you talk of a man being alive several days without breathing. The moment when there is life there are the actions that flow from it. Lazarus was no sooner made alive than he breathed. So soon as there is in the soul spiritual life, it manifests itself by spiritual acts. He who is regenerated believes, loves, and obeys God. Such is the simple truth on this subject. It is God's truth.

The gentleman tells you that I have reduced holiness to mere instinct. And he asks, how can there be holiness, which is love to God, where there is no knowledge of God? How can an infant be holy, when it can not know God? In reply, I say, everything possesses what we call nature. Our Savior said: "A good man out of the good treasure of the heart bringeth forth good things; and an evil man out of the evil treasure bringeth forth evil things" (Matt. xii. 35). Here the heart or moral nature of man is represented as a treasure, fountain or source from which flow all his good and all his evil actions. If the heart be impure, it will prompt to conduct of the same character. There is something in the fruit tree which we call its nature, which causes it to produce fruit of a particular kind. Two trees may grow in the same soil, be watered by the same stream, and warmed by the same sun; and yet they will produce different kinds of fruit. Common sense leads us to ascribe these different effects to causes equally different. The circumstances being the same, we conclude that the causes are in the trees, and we say, they have different natures. The chemist can not analyze the trees, and point out what we call their nature; yet common sense forces us to admit its existence.

No less certain is it, that men may and do possess a nature or disposition prior to their acts and choices, which is sinful or holy. It was in illustration of this very principle that our Savior said: "Make the tree good, and his fruit good; or else make the tree corrupt and his fruit corrupt; for the tree is known by his fruit" (Matt. xii. 33). Of two men, who are living under the government of the same God, and enjoying the same gospel privileges, one loves, adores, and serves God; and the other knowingly, willfully, and deliberately rebels against him. You call the one a good man, a holy man; and the other an unholy, wicked man. Common sense compels us to believe that the actions of the one flow from a pure source—a holy nature, and those of the other, from an unholy nature. The cause exists before the effect; and these different natures or dispositions exist before the actions to which they prompt. There may, then, be in the mind of an infant the disposition which will induce it to love and serve God, or the opposite disposition, which will induce it to rebel against him, so soon as capable of knowing him. There is in this nothing more unphilosophical than that there should be a disposition to love music. If I were to assert that there can be no such thing before the person has heard music, how could he prove the contrary? He asserts that there can be no disposition to love God where there is no knowledge of him. To prove this he can produce no acknowledged principle of philosophy; and, as I have proved, it is directly contradictory of the Bible. I will not give up plain and positive declarations of the Word of God for his unphilosophical speculations.

In reply to the gentleman's charge that our Church holds the doctrine of infant damnation, I gave the common interpretation of the language of our Confession of Faith. This interpretation, he says, he never heard until recently. Well, I verily believe there are a great many things in this world of which he has never heard; for it is a notorious fact that the interpretation I gave of the language of our book, is the one universally given by Presbyterians.

All the gentleman's learned criticisms on the word "holy," even if they were correct, could not help him out of the difficulty, arising from his limiting the power of God over the human mind. The word "holy," he says, does not express moral quality. Suppose we admit it. I have proved that God originally made man upright; and all we desire is to have him made upright again. If God made him upright once, he is able to make him so again. Mr. C. says God can not exert on the human mind any moral power, except by words; I say he can.

The word "holy," when applied to moral character, as it is constantly in the Bible, does not mean simply separation from all impurity. A log of wood might be separated from all impurity; but it would still not be holy. The word expresses most clearly moral purity. But I will not spend time in such criticisms.

My friend has brought forward one more passage of Scripture to sustain his doctrine. We occasionally induce him to leave his metaphysics and enter the Bible. He quotes Acts xxvi. 18, where we are told that God sent Paul to the Gentiles, "To open their eyes, and to turn them from darkness to light, and from the power of Satan unto God." But here a very important question arises, viz.: Was Paul sent to do this work by the Word only? The passage does not say so. Paul had certain work to do. He was sent to preach the unsearchable riches of Christ. But God had also a work to do. So Paul taught the Ephesians. They were dead in trespasses and in sins, and God quickened them. (Eph. ii. 1-5.) I should like to hear the gentleman explain that passage, so as to make it consistent with his faith. He has brought forward several passages; but, unfortunately, they all, when properly understood, refute his doctrine, and establish ours.

He says he can not conceive of a religion that begins in darkness, in mere blind feeling. Neither can I. But I can conceive that God may "call men out of darkness into his marvelous light" (1 Pet. ii. 9), that he may open their eyes and renew their hearts, causing them to love the light; for, our Savior said, "This is the condemnation, that light is come into the world; and men love darkness more than light." For this pure light David prayed: "Open mine eyes, that I may behold wonderful things out of thy law." The Word was before his mind, but he prayed that God would grant him more purity of heart, that he might better understand it, and appreciate more fully its glorious truths. Such is the religion in which we believe.

I have now gone through the whole catalogue of my friend's arguments. I do not consider them very strong. I believe he quoted but one text of Scripture. I will now very briefly present one more argument, in proof of the doctrine that the Spirit operates not through the truth only. The Scriptures teach that God gives repentance. Christ was exalted a prince and a Savior, "For to give repentance unto Israel, and remission of sins," (Acts v. 31). Can any one believe that God gives both remission and repentance, merely by the preaching of the Word? The obvious meaning of the apostle is, that he inclines men by his blessed Spirit, to repent, that he may grant to them remission of sins." So again, in Acts xi. 18: "Then hath God also to the Gentiles granted repentance unto life." Now, what is meant but that God granted the Gentiles the gracious influence of his Holy Spirit, and thus induced them to repent? The grace of God brought them to repentance; but going to God brought them also to repentance. I have one more passage—2 Tim. ii. 25, 26: "In meekness instructing those that oppose themselves; if God peradventure will give them repentance to the acknowledging of the truth; and that they may recover themselves out of the snare of the devil, who are taken captive by him at his will." The truth is before them. They have heard it; but will not receive it. Now, here God is said to give them repentance, or a change of mind, to the acknowledgment of the truth. I ask any man if this language does not mean something additional to the mere influence of the Word? They had heard the truth, but it failed to lead them to repentance; and now God exerts in their minds a more effectual agency. We do not see how it was possible for the Savior and the apostles to have taught more plainly the doctrine of a special agency of the Spirit, in addition to the Word? I defy any one to teach it in stronger language. If the Bible does not teach the operation of the Spirit, distinct from the Word, I defy mortal man to teach it by any language. When the apostles used the strongest language, without qualification, did they not wish it to be understood according to its obvious import? It is, then, clear that they taught that the Spirit operates not only through the Truth, but in addition to it. They all taught it, and took delight in it. It is one of the chief pillars in the Temple of Truth; and he who denies it, leaves man to perish without hope. But I will close for the present. (Time expired.)

MR. CAMPBELL'S EIGHTH ADDRESS.

WEDNESDAY, NOVEMBER 29, 10 A.M.

Mr. President.—It is all-important in every debate, especially in this one, that the proper issue be kept distinctly and definitely before the minds of the debatants and of the auditors. There is no question of more sublime comprehension, of more awful grandeur, or of more transcendent importance, than the question of spiritual and divine influence. Like the vital principle, however, it is the most sublimated, and in its naked and abstract form, the most unapproachable of all the entities of creation. It is, indeed, the vital principle of religion, and therefore, the most incomprehensible, though the most real and substantive existence in the universe. The question before us involves the value of the Bible, and all its ordinances—the gospel, its ministry, and all that mortals have comprehended under that most precious conception called the means of grace. I feel that I am discussing the value of the Bible, the gospel, the church, the ministry, while endeavoring to know what the converting and sanctifying power and influence of God's Spirit is. Let us, then, fix our minds upon the precise points expressed in the proposition before us. "In conversion and sanctification the Spirit of God operates on persons only through the truth."

There is no debate upon spiritual operations. They are of an abstract nature and quality. It is not possible for a man to conceive of spiritual operations. The fact of the operation is as evident as gravity, but who can explain it? No man can form a single conception of any spiritual influence or operation. Who can grasp the idea of a spirit? Who can apprehend its nature, its identity, its form, its person, or its modes of living, moving, and operating! We can neither have a consistent idea of a spirit nor of any of its operations. That the spirit of God operates on the human understanding and heart is just as certain as that man has an understanding and affections. Our spirit is allied to the spiritual system, to the Great Spirit. God can commune, and does commune with man, and man with God.

It is the glory of our religion that it is spiritual and divine, and that as man has both a body and a spirit, his religion also has both. This question has respect rather to the means and to the effect of the operation, and not to the operation itself. Times without number have I declared that the Scriptures are but an instrument, an embodiment in speech of spiritual power, and like all other instruments, this instrument is adapted to some end. Without that instrument the end proposed by it can not be obtained.

Now, does the Spirit operate through the instrument, or without it, in the ordinary work of conversion and sanctification? This is the question in its present form. This question involves various other questions. No question either in nature, religion, or society, is properly insular. These are all perfect systems, and, therefore, there is not one insular or independent truth in any one, nor all of them. Not a particle of the universe, not an atom of our planet is independent of other atoms and principles. Nor is there an isolated verse, nor an independent period in the Bible. Those atoms of the universe, those particles of our planet, and those verses of our Bible, are to be contemplated with reference to the whole. Little minds sport with particles, great minds with systems.

Mr. Rice has quoted some passages of Scripture. But have they been quoted as proverbs, or as parts of great contexts? I do not believe that any one passage, read you by my friend, has anything specially to do with the question before us. I might throw into a speech thirty verses, and make thirty assertions, and prove nothing, only that I intended to employ some one else, some other mind than my own, for not one of the thirty may come within a thousand miles of the real issue. My manner is to notice everything relied upon as proof of the proposition on hand; not everything, however, that may be offered on various other matters. That would be the work of months, and not of weeks. I will, so far as I have recollection or memoranda, allude to some of the proofs offered, to show that the Spirit operates in conversion without the Word. These are supposed to be against my views. I have proved that it operates through the Word, and my proofs are in the main unassailed. Mr. R.'s plan is to prove a proposition the contrary of our stipulated proposition. He seeks to prove that the Spirit operates without the Word from such passages as the following: Luke xxiv. 45: "Then opened he their understanding, that they might understand the Scriptures." In the first place it is irrelevant, because this has no respect to regeneration nor conversion; nor does it speak particularly of sanctification. Again, it was Jesus and not the Spirit. They were disciples, and not sinners. "To open the understanding" is also explained in the context, verse 32. Thus the subject of the operation is explained in these words: "Did not our hearts burn within us, while he talked with us, and while he opened to us the Scriptures?" To open the Scriptures to the understanding, is the meaning of the Hebraistic phrase, "open the understanding to understand the Scriptures." Their hearts burned not by the abstract spirit, but through the talk—"while he talked with us." So dispose we of this passage. Was the opening previous to, and independent of, the speaking of the Word?

Another proof text was 1 Cor. ii. 14: "The natural man receiveth not the things of the Spirit of God, for they are foolishness to him; neither can he know them, because they are spiritually discerned." The natural man is here contrasted with the spiritual man. The word is sometimes rendered physical, natural, animal, sensual. Natural is the most common. It is four times natural, and twice sensual in the common version. McKnight prefers the animal man, and he is high authority in Scotland, and I learn, of high authority in the theological school at Princeton. Some of the professors there, I am told, speak of him in much admiration. The animal man, then, in the context, means the "wise man according to the flesh,"—in contrast with the spiritual man, wise according to the Spirit.

A sensual man is a man merely of sense; but it has come to signify one enslaved to sense. Now such a man, who has no other guide than sense, can not receive the things of the Spirit of God. "The things of the Spirit" can only be discerned by him that is spiritual—one that is enlightened by the Spirit. But the things of the Spirit are revealed things—and, therefore, the discernment of revealed things is very different from the discernment of nothing—as in the case of infants, pagans, idiots, etc., supposed to be regenerated without having the things of the Spirit discerned at all. The text, therefore, comes not within a thousand miles of the subject on hand.

I object, however, altogether to the theological appropriation of this term. Our gospel-hearers are not Paul's natural men and, therefore, it is the sophism of equivocation, or of an ambiguous term, of which all are guilty, who use this word as equivalent, to the citizens of Kentucky who read the Bible. We have no natural men in that sense, nor in the proper sense of that word. Adam was a natural man; we, as his mere offspring, are preternatural men, and under Christ we hope to rise to be supernatural men.

I object to much of the nomenclature of modern theology. We have drawn too much on the paganized vocabulary of Rome. Neither Jewish, Christian, nor Pagan, but a mongrel dialect, is the jargon of the present age. Nature and grace are from the same God—twin sisters of the same divine family. But man has strayed away from God and nature, and has become a preternatural being. From this miserable condition God proposes, in his glorious philanthropy, to redeem man and to make him supernatural through Christ, the second Adam, the Lord from heaven. God made man upright, and while he remained in nature,—that is, in his natural or original state,—he had not a passion, appetite, or instinct which he might not most religiously gratify. But now his soul is harassed with the tumult of a thousand passions, lusts, appetites, and elements that war against his soul. If there were no sin in human nature, there could be none in obeying all its passions. Skeptics are deceived always deceived, and fatally deceived, in their reasonings from Mr. Rice's premises. Like him, they suppose man to be in the state of nature; and, therefore, think it no crime to gratify their passions. Their reasoning is just, but their premises are false, and their conclusion is a fatal error.

We have had numerous allusions and references to Titus iii. 5. The gentleman can find in the phrase "renewing of the Holy Spirit," no proof of a proposition contrary to mine. The renewing of the Holy Spirit is in the second birth connected with other means. He has saved us through the washing of the new birth, and the renewing of the Holy Spirit. This renewing of the Spirit is not immediate, nor exclusive of other means; it being associated with a washing, and a shedding forth of the Spirit through Jesus Christ our Savior.

The gentleman has more than once called upon me to read something from some of my books contrary to what he has read. Being here in person, I prefer speaking on these subjects viva voce, to reading my views already published. Besides, I have no time to debate a hundred questions, growing out of his designs, of which I am now apprized. The gentleman may read from them when he is hard pressed for matter. I perceive this is his principal use of them. For me, when my present resources are exhausted, I may turn in and debate with him on those writings. I have another reason: I do not find just such passages as suit all the topics that occur. Yet, as a matter of complaisance, I will furnish the gentleman with one or two extracts, if he will ask me for no more (Christian System, p. 66):

"Some will ask, Has not this gift been conferred on us to make us Christians? True, indeed, no man can say that Jesus is Lord but by the Holy Spirit. As observed in its proper place, the Spirit of God is the perfecter and finisher of all divine works. 'The Spirit of God moved upon the waters'; 'the hand of the Lord has made me; the Spirit of the Almighty has given me life'; 'by his Spirit he has garnished the heavens; his hand has formed the crooked serpent'—the milky way; 'the Spirit descended upon him'; 'God himself bare the apostles witness, by divers miracles and gifts of the Holy Spirit, according to his will'; 'holy men of old spake as they were moved by the Holy Spirit'; 'when the Spirit of truth, the Advocate, is come, he will convict the world of sin, because they believe not on me, and of justification, because I go to my Father'; 'God was manifest in the flesh, and justified by the Spirit.'

"Now we can not separate the Spirit and Word of God, and ascribe so much power to the one and so much to the other: for so did not the apostles. Whatever the Word does, the Spirit does; and whatever the Spirit does in the work of converting men, the Word does. We neither believe nor teach abstract Spirit, nor abstract Word; but Word and Spirit, and Spirit and Word." Again (pp. 277, 278):

"'He has saved us,' says the apostle Paul, 'by the bath of regeneration, and the renewing of the Holy Spirit, which he poured on us richly through Jesus Christ our Savior; that being justified by his favor (in the bath of regeneration), we might be made heirs according to the hope of eternal life.' Thus, and not by works of righteousness, he has saved us. Consequently, being born of the Spirit, or the renewing of the Holy Spirit, is as necessary as the bath of regeneration to the salvation of the soul, and to the enjoyment of the hope of heaven, of which the apostle speaks. In the kingdom of which we are born of water, the Holy Spirit is as the atmosphere in the kingdom of nature: we mean, that the influences of the Holy Spirit are as necessary to the new life, as the atmosphere is to our animal life in the kingdom of nature. All that is done in us before regeneration, God our Father effects by the Word, or the Gospel as dictated or confirmed by his Holy Spirit. But after we are thus begotten and born by the Spirit of God—after our new birth, the Holy Spirit is shed on us richly through Jesus Christ our Savior, of which the peace of mind, the love, the joy, and the hope of the regenerate is full proof: for these are amongst the fruits of that Holy Spirit of promise of which we speak."

Many other such passages might be read from our numerous writings on this subject. But this, as a specimen, may perhaps suffice to gratify my friend.

The gentleman also relies upon the new covenant in proof of his proposition. Of the four provisions of the new institution only one of them applies to this subject. The first is: "I will put my laws into their mind, and write them upon their hearts." Now, in every covenant there are parties—the covenanter and the covenantees. God is the covenanter, and Christians the covenantees. "With the house of Israel, (not according to the flesh, but according to the Spirit,) I will make a new covenant." Now, what bearing has this on the question before us? Were the covenantees infants, pagans, idiots, unconverted men? If not, the passage is wholly misapplied, because brought to prove a subject wholly different from that in the mind of the Spirit. We are debating about the work of the Spirit on conversion, and in that discussion a question has arisen about regeneration, and the question on that subject is—are persons regenerated by the Spirit without the Word? This position the gentleman is now seeking to prove, and this is one of his proofs. Having shown its entire impertinence to the subject, we shall attend to another point.

Mr. Rice, from some remarks made in some of my essays, in illustration of the converting power in the divine Word, on the influence which the writings of Demosthenes and Cicero have exerted upon the world, has sought to institute a comparison for me—to make me say, that, as all the moral or argumentative power of Demosthenes and Cicero is in their writings, so all God's moral power is in his Word. So far so good; but the gentleman goes a little farther, and would not allow the case to terminate there, but supposed me to assign no other power or presence to the Spirit of God than to the spirit and personal influence of those ancient orators. I am prepared to say, that, so far as moral power is concerned, the arguments and motives of the Spirit of God are all set forth in the New Institution, in all their perfection; and that this power can not be increased. Nay, I argue, that if the Spirit of God were again to descend, as on Pentecost, and in the person of a new legate from heaven, should plead with the human race, touching their condition and destiny under God's philanthropy and active benevolence; when he had set forth, in all their amplitude, all the facts and promises in the universe on this subject, he would then, at the close of the effort, have not increased one grain the amount of the moral momentum and influence of the Gospel. He would not then have increased, in the least, its converting power. For if the story is all told now, and if God veraciously and sincerely asks, what more could be done than what I have done for my vineyard, then there is no possibility of accumulating the power by any other means; but whether the ever-living and ever-present Spirit of our God may not through that truth, in ways unknown to mortals, affect the soul of man, by fixing the attention upon it, or removing, providentially, obstructions, etc., is neither affirmed nor denied in that comparison, nor in the circumstances that called it forth. And this having been spoken with special reference to the fanaticism and wild enthusiasm of the age, in certain cases of pretended new light and new-converting power, ought to have been construed accordingly. But this method of torturing men's words by putting them on the partisan rack, and dislocating every joint, works as pervertingly on them as on the Word of God. Whenever all the gospel argument is comprehended, all the moral power of God is exhausted; for beyond that he has never displayed any to any man, and he that hears not Moses and the prophets, Christ and his apostles, would not be persuaded though one rose from the dead.

The gentleman has more than once asked me for proof that the Spirit operates only through the Word; and avows that unless I shew him some text that exactly affirms that, he will not believe. Well, I gave him, in my proposition on the design of baptism, the very words in the book, with the mere supplement past, to which he did not demur, and then he would not believe. And I verily believe if I gave him every word in one verse, he would be for construing it in a different sense. But this is a new mode of argumentation, by which he could not prove one article in his creed; for not one of them is found in the identical words of the book. Nor could we prove any proposition not found verbatim in the Bible. But I have proved *only* through the Word. By shewing, first, that the Spirit does regenerate and sanctify through the Word, and, in the same place, by that great law of the physical and moral universe, that whatever is necessary to any given result, is always necessary. Also, by various other considerations and arguments, yet unnoticed by him. Did I not, on yesterday, demonstrate on his own definition of regeneration, the utter impossibility of infant regeneration? and yet he has neither retracted nor defended the definition. Surely, he ought to do the one or the other.

At the commencement of this discussion he clearly stated that the Spirit does sometimes operate through the Word. Had it not been for idiots, pagans, and infants, he would, no doubt, have said only through the Word. He has since admitted that on adults he operates generally through the Word. It was some time before he gave us a definition of regeneration; and still longer before he informed us whether faith or regeneration were prior, or which was the cause of the other. Finally, he informed us that regeneration preceded faith, therefore both infants and adults are regenerated without faith, and prior to faith. Without perceiving, and, I am confident, without intending it, he has thus indisputably proved my fourth argument, which, you will remember, says: "Whatever is essential to regeneration in one case, is essential in all cases." For having been brought to concede namely, that regeneration is prior to faith, thus making adults the subject of regeneration without belief, and infants, as a matter of course, because incapable of belief, we have obtained from him the admission of my fourth argument. Again, we have proved to his own satisfaction that the Spirit generally operates through the Word on adults, and in some cases only through the Word; follows it not, then, that according to our fourth argument, regeneration must be through the Word, and therefore infant regeneration is impossible? In any view of the matter, then, I may say, without fear of successful contradiction from any quarter, that Mr. Rice has given us the data for his own refutation, and now stands self-refuted for the reasons now assigned. This subject is still susceptible of farther illustration, but my time being almost expired, I shall only add a few words on the plan of the Bible as developing its theory of regeneration.

The Old and New Testaments are arranged upon the same grand plan. They present a record of facts well documented and proved. The first five books of both Testaments are historical. The historical and the didactic go together. The fact first, the testimony concerning it, and then the development of it. There is one grand arrangement of revelation, adapted to the constitution and philosophy of man. The order of things is simple, because it is rational. The connection is first, fact; next, testimony concerning that fact—that something said or done; then faith, or the belief of that testimony; after that, feeling—in harmony with whatever is believed—joyful or sorrowful, good or bad; and in the last place, action—a course of conduct corresponding with that feeling. This is not only the rational, but it is the fixed and necessary and immutable arrangement of things producing faith and growing out of it. It is no arbitrary division, no conventional arrangement. It must be so while man is a being that walks by faith, and while faith is the belief of testimony. These five words—fact, testimony, faith, feeling, action—set forth the economy of the Bible, and are the grand links in that divine chain that give to the facts of revelation their influence on the soul of man. The thing done or spoken by God, or man, called the fact, passes into the testimony, and the testimony passes into faith, and the fact, in that faith, passes into corresponding feeling, and then it is made living and efficient in the action. Now this being the immutable order of things, and regeneration being the offspring of the Word of God believed, it is impossible that any one, incapable of understanding the fact, of believing the testimony, of exercising faith, of possessing moral feeling, and of correspondent action, can be regenerated. (Time expired.)

MR. RICE'S EIGHTH REPLY.

WEDNESDAY, NOVEMBER 29, 10:30 A.M.

Mr. President.—I intend that, throughout this discussion, the precise points in debate shall be kept distinctly in view. Mr. C. says he admits that in conversion and sanctification the Spirit does operate, and that the Word is only the instrument. I inquired of him, on yesterday, what he meant by this language? Whether he holds that there is any operation of the Spirit distinct from the Word, or whether he believes only that the Spirit dictated the Word and confirmed it by miracle, and now the Word converts and sanctifies? To this important question I received no answer. If he believes the Spirit to be the agent in this work, he must put forth some power; for there can not be an agent without an action. If, then, his language means anything, it must be that at the moment when the soul is converted the Spirit of God exerts converting power, performs an act which produces this result. I wished to be informed whether he believes that the Spirit exerts an influence distinct from the Word, but he would not answer the question.

He told us, also, that the Spirit is always present with the Word. I asked him what he meant by this language, but I received no answer. I discover plainly that the audience are not to see the real point at issue, unless I constantly keep it before them, and this I am resolved to do.

The great question is not, whether ordinarily the Spirit operates through the truth, but whether the only influence exerted in conversion and sanctification is that of words and arguments; whether the Spirit of God operates on the hearts of men only as Mr. C.'s spirit operates on the minds of this audience. This is the question—I use the gentleman's own illustration. We are not debating the question by what instrumentality the Spirit converts and sanctifies men, but what is the work which the Spirit does. We hold that in the case of infants and idiots, inasmuch as instrumentality can not be employed, sanctification takes place without the truth. In the case of adults we hold that there is not only the influence of words and arguments, but a distinct influence of the Spirit, opening the eyes and purifying the heart. This Mr. C. denies.

The gentleman has a clear head. I wonder at the confusion in which he keeps his real sentiments. On some subjects he delivers himself with great clearness, and on the one before us he has written clearly. Yet this is the third day we have been on this proposition, and I must say that more fog and mist I never did see thrown around any subject!

Let me now give you a specimen of the manner in which my Biblical friend expounds Scripture. He professes to be a very Biblical man. In proof of a divine influence, in addition to the Word, I quoted Luke xxiv. 45: "Then opened he their understandings, that they might understand the Scriptures." The inspired writer, you observe, does not say he opened their understandings in order that they might understand the Scriptures. What is the gentleman's reply? He turns to the 27th verse: "And beginning at Moses and all the prophets, he expounded unto them in all the Scriptures, the things concerning himself." Now, according to his principles of interpretation, expounding the Scriptures and opening their understandings that they might understand them, are the same thing! Why, you might expound the Scriptures to persons by the hour, and yet they might have no correct understanding of them; but if you had power to open their understandings, the whole difficulty would be at once removed. Remove the causes of their blindness, and they will see clearly. So did David pray: "Open thou mine eyes, that I may behold wondrous things out of thy law." Did he not pray for a divine influence on his mind, opening his understanding? It is vain to attempt to evade the force of language so perfectly plain. It will not do to say that to open the understanding, and to open the Scriptures, are phrases meaning the same thing.

To prove the necessity of the special work of the Spirit on the heart, I quoted 1 Cor. ii. 14: "The natural man receiveth not the things of the Spirit, for they are foolishness to him: neither can he know them, because they are spiritually discerned." The gentleman appeals to McKnight, who translates the phrase "animal man." And he tells us he has somewhere heard that the professors in the Princeton Theological Seminary have placed McKnight at the head of critical commentators. This may be true, but I should prefer to have some proof of the fact. But let us take his translation. Now, the question is, who is the animal man? Mr. C. says he is the pagan without a divine revelation to guide him. But the fact is, the word translated "natural" or "animal has not this meaning in one instance in the New Testament. It is used in 1 Cor. xv. 44, 45, to distinguish the natural body from the spiritual body. The natural body, we know, means the body as it is by nature, unchanged. "It is sown (or buried) a natural body." The spiritual body means the body as it will be changed at the resurrection. So the natural man means man as he is by nature—depraved; and the spiritual man is the man renewed by the Holy Spirit.

The same word, as I have already stated, is used by James, who describes the wisdom which is not from above, as "earthly, sensual, (Gr., natural,) devilish." In this passage the word is used with reference to moral character, and it certainly expresses the idea of depravity. It is also used by Jude (vs. 19), where he describes the wicked thus: "These be they who separate themselves, sensual, (Gr., natural,) having not the Spirit." The wicked, who have not the Spirit, are described as natural or sensual. On the use of the word in these passages, the gentleman forgot to make even a passing remark. The usage of the New Testament, in regard to this word, leaves no room to doubt what is its meaning. The natural man certainly is man in his native depravity. Mr. C. objects to the use of the word "natural," as applied to man in his depravity, because by nature he was not depraved. He, therefore, uses the word "preternatural." But he seems not to remember that in making this objection he is finding fault with the language of inspiration. In the epistle to the Ephesians, Paul says men are by nature the children of wrath" (chap. ii. 3). The word here used is *phusis*, the literal and uniform meaning of which is "nature." If Paul thus uses the word "nature," I may be excused for following his example.

But Mr. C. was careful not to notice the succeeding part of the verse under discussion. Why does not the natural man receive the things of the Spirit? Because, says Paul, "they are foolishness unto him." The meaning of this language, as I proved, is made perfectly clear by Chapter i. 18: "The preaching of the cross is to them that perish, foolishness; but unto us which are saved, it is the power of God." That is, when they hear the Gospel preached it is to them foolishness; they see in it no wisdom, no adaptation to their condition, nothing attractive; and therefore they reject it. So to "the natural man" the things of the Spirit, the truths, of the Gospel, are foolishness, and he rejects them. But if Mr. C.'s interpretation be correct, the passage should read thus: "The animal man receiveth not the things of the Spirit, for they are not revealed to him."

It is now perfectly clear that "the natural man" is the unrenewed man; and since unrenewed men do not receive, but uniformly reject the Gospel, it follows, inevitably, that the special influence of the Holy Spirit, in addition to the Word, is absolutely necessary to their conversion and sanctification. Consequently, in every case of conversion, such a divine influence is actually exerted.

To show you how much I have misrepresented him, the gentleman read a paragraph or two from his "Christian System." I am pleased to see him read his publications, and I am quite disposed to aid him in presenting them before you. On page 66 he read as follows: "Some will ask, Has not this gift [of the Spirit] been conferred on us to make us Christians? True indeed, no man can say that Jesus is Lord, but by the Holy Spirit. As observed in its proper place, the Spirit of God is the perfecter and finisher of all divine works. 'The Spirit moved upon the waters,'" etc. But the difficulty is, that in this whole paragraph he says not one word concerning an influence of the Spirit upon the heart, in conversion! He quotes several passages, as follows: "The hand of the Lord has made me, the Spirit of the Almighty has given me life"; "By his Spirit he has garnished the heavens, his hand has formed the crooked serpent"; "The Spirit descended upon him; God himself bore the apostles witness, by divers miracles and gifts of the Holy Spirit, according to his will." Not one of these passages, nor any one quoted by him, has the slightest reference to a change of the heart by the Holy Spirit.

He also read on the next page: "Now we can not separate the Spirit and the Word of God, and ascribe so much power to the one and so much to the other; for so did not the apostles. Whatever the Word does, the Spirit does; and whatever the Spirit does, in the work of converting men, the Word does. We neither believe nor teach abstract Spirit nor abstract Word, but Word and Spirit, and Spirit and Word." All this is perfectly ambiguous. For if the Spirit dictated and confirmed the Word, and the Word converts and sanctifies men, it is true, in a sense, that the Spirit does the work. But does Mr. C. hold to an influence of the Spirit in conversion, distinct from the Word? On this point these paragraphs give us no light. Let me read on the 277th page of his "Christianity Restored." Perhaps we shall here gain some information. He says:

"But this pouring out of the influences, this renewing of the Holy Spirit, is as necessary as the bath of regeneration to the salvation of the soul, and to the enjoyment of the hope of heaven, of which the apostle speaks. In the kingdom into which we are born of water, the Holy Spirit is as the atmosphere in the kingdom of nature: we mean, that the influences of the Holy Spirit are as necessary to the new life as the atmosphere is to our animal life in the kingdom of nature. All that is done in us before regeneration, God our Father effects by the Word, or the Gospel, as dictated and confirmed by his Holy Spirit. But after we are thus begotten and born by the Spirit of God—after our new birth, the Holy Spirit is shed on us richly through Jesus Christ our Savior; of which the peace of mind, the love, the joy, and the hope of the regenerate is full proof: for these are amongst the fruits of that Holy Spirit of promise, of which we speak."

On this passage I make two or three remarks: 1. "This pouring out of the influences, this renewing of the Holy Spirit," he says, "is as necessary as the birth of regeneration (immersion) to the salvation of the soul, and to the enjoyment of the hope of heaven." The influences of the Spirit only as necessary to salvation, as immersion—not more so!!! 2. Observe, he says, "All that is done in us before regeneration (immersion) God our Father effects by the Word, or the Gospel as dictated and confirmed by his Holy Spirit." Here we have a denial as clear and as strong as language can make it, of any influence in conversion, except that of the Word as dictated and confirmed by the Spirit. This is the most important point about which we differ, and which I desire the audience not to lose sight of. 3. As my friend is fond of asking questions, I wish to ask him, What kind of influence does the Spirit exert on the minds of immersed believers? This is a very important question. He has said in his publications, that there are but two kinds of power—moral and physical. He has also said, that the only power that can be exerted on mind is moral power; and he has said, that "every spirit puts forth its moral power in words"; that "all the power it has over the views, habits, manners or actions of men is in the meaning and arrangement of its ideas expressed in words; or in significant signs addressed to the eye or ear." Now I am particularly anxious to know what kind of influence the Spirit does exert on the minds of believers, after they are immersed. Is it physical power? My friend will say No. Is it spiritual power—neither physical nor moral? He will say No. Is it a moral influence which sanctifies the heart? If so, it must be an influence simply and only of the Word. Will the gentleman enlighten us on this subject? We wish to know something about this influence which is not physical, nor moral, nor anything else!

I was pleased to hear him, for once, come out and express with some clearness his real sentiments. The Spirit of God, he tells us, produces moral effects only by arguments; that when all his arguments and motives are brought to bear on the mind, his moral power is exhausted. This is precisely what I read on yesterday from his "Christianity Restored." What moral power could Demosthenes or Cicero exert on their hearers or readers, after they had put forth all their arguments? So it appears, according to this doctrine, that the Holy Spirit has no more power over the minds and hearts of men than had those ancient orators, except that he may reason more powerfully!!! So he teaches in his "Christianity Restored" (pp. 348, 349):

"Because arguments are addressed to the understanding, will, and affections of men, they are called moral, inasmuch as their tendency is to form or change the habits, manners, or actions of men. Every spirit puts forth its moral power in words; that is, all the power it has over the views, habits, manners, or actions of men, is in the meaning and arrangement of its ideas expressed in words, or in significant signs addressed to the eye or ear. All the moral power of Cicero and Demosthenes was in their orations when spoken, and in the circumstances which gave them meaning; and whatever power these men have exercised over Greece and Rome since their death, is in their writings. * * *

"From such premises we may say, that all the moral power which can be exerted on human beings, is, and must of necessity be in the arguments addressed to them. No other power than moral power can operate on minds; and this power must always be clothed in words, addressed to the eye or ear. Thus we reason when revelation is altogether out of view. And when we think of the power of the Spirit of God exerted upon minds or human spirits, it is impossible for us to imagine that that power can consist in anything else but words or arguments. Thus, in the nature of things, we are prepared to expect verbal communications from the Spirit of God, if that Spirit operates at all upon our spirits. As the moral power of every man is in his arguments, so is the moral power of the Spirit of God in his arguments."

This limiting of the power of God, I have said, is both unscriptural and unreasonable. God originally created man upright. He exerted on him an influence, not by words and arguments, which made him holy. Who shall venture, in view of this fact, to say he can not now exert an influence which will renew his sinful nature?

The gentleman asks, What can the Spirit do, after all his arguments have been put forth? Will he inform us how the devil tempts men to sin? He acknowledges that the devil has access to the minds of men, and exerts a moral influence, not by words and arguments addressed to the eye or ear; yet he can not tell us how that influence is exerted. If, then, we do not know how good or evil spirits can exert an influence on our minds, is it not most presumptuous in any man to assert that the Holy Spirit can not exert a moral or spiritual influence except by words and arguments addressed to the eye or ear? Shall we venture to say that the devil has more power over the human mind than God?

Let all this false philosophy go to the winds, and give us the Bible. The gentleman is attempting to prove that in conversion and sanctification the Spirit operates on persons only through the truth. If there is a passage in the Bible that expresses such a sentiment, let us have it. I desire to see the passage, if it is in the Bible. If it is not, he would better abandon his doctrine.

But he says the proposition he affirmed on the design of baptism was, with the exception of one word, precisely the language of the Bible, and yet I was not satisfied with it. The difficulty was, that I was not satisfied with his interpretation of the language of the Bible, because it flatly contradicted many of the plainest declarations of Christ and the Apostles! The gentleman has a remarkable tact at representing all men who differ from him as fighting against the Scriptures. I verily do not believe that he is infallible; and believing him fallible, I must venture to differ from him.

He has given you, my friends, some important information this morning, viz., that on yesterday I gave up the whole question! I venture to say that not an individual in the house, except himself, discovered that I had done so. It was, therefore, particularly important that he should make the announcement! But how did I give up the question? By admitting that generally the Spirit operates through the truth. So says Mr. C. Let me repeat the substance of my remarks on this point, and the audience will judge whether I gave it up. I stated distinctly that the Scriptures speak of two kinds of faith, very different in their character. King Agrippa had the one, and Paul had the other. Paul, in his defense, thus addressed the king: "King Agrippa, believest thou the prophets? I know that thou believest." Yet Agrippa was not a Christian, but only almost persuaded to be a Christian. It is evident to every man's common sense, that you may believe a thing to be true, and yet be perfectly indifferent concerning it. "Gallio cared for none of these things." You may be constrained by clear evidence to believe the truth, and yet most earnestly wish it were not a truth. Thousands believe the Bible to be a divine revelation, and yet are wholly indifferent to its sublime truths. Their minds are occupied with other subjects, and their time employed in worldly pursuits. One goes to his farm, another to his merchandise; and each says, "I pray thee, have me excused." There are others who are constrained to admit the truth of the Bible, but are deeply averse to its doctrines and precepts. "The devils believe and tremble."

This faith, though it leads the soul not immediately to Christ, is yet important; because it causes men to hear and to think, that their consciences may be reached, and that God may regenerate and sanctify them through the truth. Thus they may be induced to embrace the Gospel, which before they both believed and hated; or to the appeals of which they were indifferent. The faith of Agrippa is the faith which precedes regeneration; and the faith of Paul is the effect of it. The faith of Paul worked by love, and overcame the world. This is the faith of which John speaks, as an effect of the new birth: "Whosoever believeth that Jesus is the Christ, is born of God." I should be pleased to know whether Mr. C. ascribes to faith any moral quality; or whether he supposes that men believe in Christ, just as they believe that there was such a man as Caesar, and as they believe what he relates of his wars. Is not faith the cordial reception of Christ as our Savior? I did not give up the question.

I have offered a considerable number of arguments, to which my friend has attempted no reply. He has pursued his usual course. He says they are irrelevant. This is the easiest way in the world to answer arguments. If a man finds them unanswerable, he can say they are all irrelevant! To prove that in conversion and sanctification there is an agency of the Spirit, distinct from the

Word, I quoted such passages as the following: "I will pour out my Spirit upon thy seed." "A new heart also will I give you, and a new spirit will I put within you." "I will give them one heart and one mind," etc. They are all irrelevant, says the gentleman. Such is his answer, though every one can see that they bear directly and most conclusively on the point at issue, for they teach in the clearest manner that men repent and believe, because God sheds upon them his Holy Spirit.

My time is so nearly out that I will not now introduce another argument. (Time expired.)

MR. CAMPBELL'S NINTH ADDRESS.

WEDNESDAY, NOV. 29, 11 o'clock A.M.

Mr. President.—More than half the time occupied by my friend has been devoted to the consideration of passages of Scripture more or less animadverted on before. He deems them of great importance, and I am willing that he should think so. But as I deem them no way relevant to our position in the question, I shall hasten, in the first place, to state some other arguments, reserving for further notice of these to circumstances. His remarks on spiritual operations, when further explained, may, perhaps, be comprehended. As yet, however, to me they are not comprehensible. I will answer his interrogations when they are more definitely set forth. Let him explain his distinct power. I can not comprehend his theory of an abstract power. If he say superadded power, I wish to know of what character it is—physical or moral? I can readily conceive of various means being employed to secure the attention of persons to impress the subject on the mind, and of means used providentially to remove obstructions; but, to talk of superadded power, of a distinct power, without any definition of the nature and character of it, seems not in the least to enlighten us. If I see a man take an ax and fell a tree, I call the ax the instrument, and I say, whatever power he puts forth in felling the tree is put forth through the ax. Not one chip is removed without it. This illustrates so much of the subject as pertains to instrumentality. I am at a loss to understand his additional power. I see but the man and the ax, and the tree falls. That the Spirit operates through the instrumentality of the Word I doubt not; but if asked to explain the *modus operandi*, I confess my inability. The fact of the power I admit, but the how it works I presume not to comprehend. If Mr. Rice will set it forth, I will cheerfully avow my assent or dissent, as the case may be; for I keep no secrets on that subject, or any other, connected with man's salvation. I candidly consider that the gentleman has, however, conceded the real issue. He has got a regeneration without true faith, but now seems to have need of a pretended faith, or some sort of an indescribable, partial, imperfect faith as a pre-requisite. He has a faith before, and a faith after regeneration. But this seems not to meet the case, nor relieve him from the dilemma. His indefinable, previous faith is just no faith at all; and, therefore, his true doctrine is regeneration without faith, and consequently without any human instrumentality. A faith that does not renew the heart is a species of infidelity. His infant and adult, his pagan and idiot, regeneration are therefore all of one sort; all special miracles without any instrumentality whatever. He has, indeed, as before shown, admitted my fourth argument; and, according to it, as regeneration is in one case, it is in all cases. Whatever means are necessary to produce one ear of corn, are necessary to the production of every other ear of corn. So in all well-regulated States, whatever is necessary to constitute one foreigner a citizen, is necessary to the naturalization of every other foreigner. We shall, then, till otherwise informed, regard this case as settled.

On my side of this question, I have only to prove that the seed is essential to the fruit, and on this, I presume, amplification is not called for. When, however, Mr. Rice again brings up this same view, I may amplify still further. Till then I will not spend time in expatiating on principles so well established, so universally admitted. Neither need I dwell upon the peculiar arrangement of the Scriptures, on the principle submitted at the close of my last address. It is true, that I intend it to be the basis of a branch of the evidence adduced, in confirmation of the views given. Our feelings are properly called our active powers. Now, in religion, they are properly dependent on our faith—no true faith, no true feeling. That again depends not merely upon the testimony being good and valid, but upon our appreciation of it. No one can believe testimony which he does not understand; hence, if either the testimony of God, or the facts contained in the Bible, have anything to do with renewing or purifying the heart, there can be no renewal without a previous belief.

But I hasten to state another argument, which shall obtain the rank of my tenth argument, in proof of the proposition. It is expressed in the following words:

X.—Whatever influence is ascribed to the Word of God in the Sacred Scriptures, is also ascribed to the Spirit of God; or, in other words, what the Spirit of God is at one time, and in one place, said to do, is at some other time or in some other place ascribed to the Word of God. Hence, I argue that they do not operate separately, but in all cases conjointly. We shall give an induction of a number of cases in exemplification of the fact. Are we said to be enlightened by the Spirit of God? We are told in another place, "The commandment of the Lord is pure, enlightening the eyes." Again, "The entrance of thy Word giveth light, and makes the simple wise." Are we said to be converted by the Spirit of God? We hear the prophet David say, "The law of the Lord is perfect, converting the soul." Are we said to be sanctified through the Spirit of God? We hear our Lord praying to his Father, "Sanctify them through thy truth, thy Word is the truth? Are we said to be quickened by the Spirit of God? The same is ascribed to the Word of God. David says, "Thy Word, O Lord, hath quickened me," "Stay me with thy precepts, thy statutes quicken me." This is one of the strongest expressions.

In other forms of speech, the same effects and influence are ascribed to both. Paul, in one context, says, "Be filled with the Spirit"; and when again speaking of the same subject, in another, he says, "Let the Word of Christ dwell in you richly." In both cases the precepts are to be fulfilled in the same way, "teaching and admonishing one another in psalms and hymns and spiritual songs, making melody in your hearts to the Lord." "The Spirit," says Paul to Timothy, "speaketh expressly that in the latter day some shall depart from the faith. Again, "Know ye, in the last days perilous times shall come." Again, Paul says he has sanctified the church and cleansed it with "a bath of water and the Word." In another instance he says, he hath saved us "with the washing of regeneration and renewal of the Holy Spirit." Are we said to be "born of the Spirit"? We are also said to be born again, or "regenerated by the Word of God." I might trace this matter much further, but I presume, as we have touched upon the most important items, we have found such an induction as will satisfy the most scrupulous. Unless questioned, I shall then affirm it as a conclusion fairly drawn, that whatever effects or influences connected with conversion and sanctification are, in one portion of the Scripture, assigned to the Word, are ascribed also to the Spirit; and so interchangeably throughout both Testaments. Whence we conclude, that the Spirit and Word of God are not separate and distinct kinds of power—the one superadded to the other, but both acting conjointly and simultaneously in the work of sanctification and salvation.

As Mr. Rice would seem to argue for two substantive powers, essentially distinct from each other, I do hope he will be at pains to explain to us the peculiar discriminating characteristics or attributes of each.

XI.—My eleventh argument is deduced from the important fact, that resisting the Word of God and resisting the Spirit of God, are shown to be the same thing, by very clear and explicit testimonies, such as Stephen, the proto-martyr, when filled with the Holy Spirit, and, indeed, speaking as the Holy Spirit gave him utterance, in the presence of the sanhedrin, said, "You uncircumcised in heart and ears, as your fathers did, so do you. You do always resist the Holy Spirit." What proof does he allege? He adds, "As your fathers did, so do you" (resist). "Which of the prophets did they not persecute?" This, then, is his proof. In persecuting the prophets, they resisted the Holy Spirit; because the words spoken by the prophets were suggested by the Spirit. We are said to resist a person when we resist his word. When, then, any one resists the words of the prophets or the apostles, he is said by inspired men to resist the Holy Spirit. This important fact should be more frequently insisted on than it is. Men should be taught that in resisting the words spoken by apostles and prophets, they are, in truth, resisting the Holy Spirit, by whom they uttered those words. May we not, then, consistently say, with Stephen, that when men resist the prophets and apostles in their writings, and will not submit to their teachings, they are resisting the Holy Spirit? This being admitted, follows it not again, that the Spirit of God operates through the truth; and that we are not to suppose that in conversion and sanctification, they do not act separately and distinctly from each other?

A still more impressive instance of this kind we find in the book of Nehemiah. In his admirable prayer, preserved in the ninth chapter, he has two very remarkable expressions; one in the 20th and one in the 29th verse. In the former, when speaking of the instructions given the Jews by Moses, he said, "Thou gavest also thy good Spirit to instruct them"; and in the latter, he says, "Many years didst thou forbear them, and testifiedst against them by thy Spirit in thy prophets, yet would they not hear." Here, then, we are taught that God, by his Spirit in Moses, instructed the Jews by his good Spirit, and that in testifying to them by the prophets, God was testifying to them by his Holy Spirit. We are, then, still more fully confirmed in the conclusion that the Spirit of God operates through his Word, and only through his Word, in conversion and sanctification; and that the Word and Spirit of God, in those spiritual and moral changes and influences of which we now speak, are never to be regarded as operating apart; that whatever is done by the Word of God, is done by the Spirit of God; and whatever is done by the Spirit, is done through the Truth—and certainly he can through that instrument operate most powerfully on the spirit of man, as all Christians experience, and the saints of all time exhibit.

Notwithstanding the pains taken in my opening speech on this subject, to indicate the different offices assigned to the Father, and the Son, and the Holy Spirit, in the work of salvation, it seems, from some of the quotations offered by Mr. Rice, that he indiscriminately assigns to any one of them the work peculiarly and exclusively assigned to another. Seeing this so often done by others, and presuming that it might occur here, I remonstrated against it as both illogical and unscriptural. How often is the passage, Matt. xvi. 17, "Flesh and blood hath not revealed this to you, Peter, but my Father, who is in heaven," quoted, with a special reference to the work of the Holy Spirit. The system-makers and system-mongers, almost to a man, press this passage into their service. They prove by it a special revelation to Peter by the Holy Spirit: to all of which I have no objection whatever, so far as either the possibility or practicability of making original suggestions to Peter, on this or any other subject, is concerned. But I plead for the proper application and interpretation of the Scriptures, much more than for the particular import of a single text, however important that text may be.

It was the Father, and not the Spirit, of whom Jesus here speaks. It was "my Father who is in heaven," that revealed this fact to you, Peter, that I am the Son of God, and the Christ of God. The fact, as stated, too, is very plain. God spake out, from heaven, after the Messiah's baptism, and revealed who he was. He also indicated him by the Spirit descending in the form of a dove, and lighting upon his head. This being done very publicly, and reported in Jerusalem, as we learn from John, Chapter v., "Peter must have heard and believed," whether at the Jordan, when it happened, or not. Thus it was that the Father revealed, and in person introduced, his Son. Peter, in common with some others, believed it.

I said in the commencement of this discussion, that I did not affirm or deny as to any other operations of the Spirit, save in conversion and sanctification. What he may do in the way of suggestions or impressions, by direct communication of original ideas, or in bringing things to remembrance long since forgotten, I presume not to discuss. I believe he has exerted, and can exert, such influences. Nor do I say what influence he may exert, or cause to be exerted, in bringing man's minds to consider these matters; but I confine my reasonings and proofs to conversion and sanctification. I wish, Mr. Rice, when he next quotes John iii. 5, would give us the predicate of "So is every one born of the Spirit." What means the word "so"?

XII.—My twelfth argument is deduced from the fact that God created nothing without his Word. "He said, Let there be light, and there was light." "By faith," says Paul, "we know that the worlds were framed by the Word of God." All the details of the six days show that "God made all things by the Word of his power." Of course, then, we have no idea of any new creation or regeneration without the Word of God. Mr. Rice has taken it for granted, that God made man holy at first without his Word. But this is a mere assumption. It is an overwhelming fact, that God does nothing in creation nor redemption without his Word. His creative power has always been embodied in that sublime instrument. Nay, it is the sword of the Spirit. Still, there was through that Word an almighty power put forth, and still there is both in conversion and sanctification. God works mightily in the human heart by his Word. The heart of the King's enemies are mightily broken by it. Hence, faith comes by hearing, and hearing by the Word of God.

Indeed, there is much of this wisdom of God apparent in the fact that he has chosen the term *Logos* to represent the author and founder of the Christian faith in his antecedent state of existence. And hence, John represents Jesus Christ himself as the Word of God incarnate. "Now the Word was made flesh," or became flesh, "and dwelt among us." This is a mysterious name. He had a name given him which no one can comprehend. His name is the Word of God. Now, as Jesus Christ was "once God manifest in Word," and now God manifest in flesh, we have reason to regard the Word of God as an embodiment of his wisdom and power. This, however, is spoken with a reference to the Gospel Word; for Jesus Christ is both the wisdom and the power of God, and so is his Gospel, because containing this development. It is the wisdom and power of God unto salvation, to every one that believes it.

It was not, however, in creating light alone that God employed his Word. Every work of creation is represented as the product of his Word. He said, "Let there be a firmament in the midst of the waters," and it was so. Again, "Let the dry land appear," and it was so. "Let the earth bring forth grass," and it was so. And last of all, "Let us make man in our image, after our likeness, and let them have dominion. So God created man." God, therefore, made man in his own image by his Word, and he now restores him to that same image, by his Word of power. Thus we have all the authority of the Bible with us in our views of spiritual and divine influence. A spiritual, or moral, or creative power, without the Word of God, is a phantom, a mere speculation. It receives no countenance from the Bible.

The gentleman said something about false premises. It will come up in its own time. If he would follow my argument in the usual way of response, it would prevent many such assertions. These matters would then come up in their proper place, as well as in their proper time.

The Lord has embodied his will in his Word. Now the will of God is another form of his power. Divine volition is divine power. The Word of God is the fiat of God. "Let there be" is a mere volition expressed. Indeed, we may go further, and say that the Word of the Lord is the Lord himself. The word of a king is the king himself, so far as authority or power is considered. As the Lord Jesus is the Word of God incarnate, so is his Word an embodiment of his power. For, as Solomon says, "Where the word of a king is, there is power"; there is the power of the king himself. The Word of God is, then, the actual power of God. God is a consuming fire, and his "Word is as fire, and as a hammer that breaketh the rock to pieces." It should not, therefore, be thought strange, that the Word of God, and the Spirit of God, are sometimes represented as equi-potent—as equivalent. Indeed, in all those passages that represent the Word and Spirit of God as being the causes of the same effects, this equivalency is clearly implied. Hence, while Peter says, "By the Word of God the heavens were of old, Job says, "By his Spirit he has garnished the heavens."

Can any one imagine what power could have been superadded to the Word of God, that created light, that made the heavens and the earth, that made man upright or holy, as Mr. R. says! Let him explain what that power could have been, which was distinct from, and attached to, or that accompanied that word by which all things were created and made. Explain that accompanying power, and I will explain the accompanying spiritual or superadded power in the case of regeneration! You can not break a man down by physical power. You can not soften and subdue the heart, as you grind a rock to pieces. A superadded power beyond motive is inconceivable to any mind accustomed to think accurately upon spiritual and mental operations. The heart of man is to be subdued, melted, purified from all its hatred of God and enmity, by love, by developments of grace, and not by any conceivable influence of a different nature. His love is poured out into our hearts, says Paul, by the Holy Spirit that is given to us.

Men had better be careful how they speak of, and how they treat, the Word of God. It will stand forever. Till the heavens pass away, not one word shall fail. Mountains, by the wasting hand of time, may crumble down to dust; oceans may recede from their ancient limits; the heavens and the earth may pass away—but God's Word shall never, never pass away. It is God's mighty moral lever, by which he raises man from earth to heaven. It is his almighty, awful, sublime and gracious will, embodied in such a medium as can enter the secret chambers of the human heart and conscience, and there stand up for God, and confound the sinner in his presence. The love of God is all enveloped in it, and that is the great secret of its charm—the mystery of its power to save. It is love, and love alone, that can reconcile the heart of man to God. Now love is a matter of intelligence—a matter that is to be told, heard, believed, and received by faith. "The power of God to salvation" is the persuasive power of infinite and eternal love, and not the compulsive and subduing power of any force superadded to it. The promise of eternal life is itself a power of mighty magnitude. So are all the promises that enter into the Christian hope. These are almighty impulses, when understood and believed, upon the veracity and faithfulness of God.

But there yet remains another argument, of the inductive kind, which adapts itself to all minds, which I may, in my next address, offer to your consideration. We shall have an examination of every case of conversion reported in the Bible history of the primitive Church, down to the end of the inspired record. Meantime, I must attend to some texts of Scripture advanced by Mr. Rice, to show that repentance is the gift of God. But who denies it? He has quoted three texts upon this subject. Two of the three speak of the grant of repentance and remission of sins, in the sense of the Gospel. And one of them, the last, speaks of one opposing the truth. They are the following: "He," the Messiah, "is exalted a Prince and a Savior, to grant repentance to Israel, and the forgiveness of sins"—a dispensation of mercy. The second is, "Then has God also granted unto the Gentiles repentance unto life." He has also extended salvation to the Gentiles upon the same principles of repentance given to the Jews. And, in the case of an opponent, says Paul, "Instruct him meekly"; that if he have not hardened himself against the truth, God may, peradventure, extend to him the advantage of repentance. (Time expired.)

MR. RICE'S NINTH REPLY.

WEDNESDAY, NOV. 29, 11:30 o'clock A.M.

Mr. President.—I was very much gratified to hear the illustration of the work of the Spirit introduced by the gentleman at the commencement of his last argument. It is this: An individual takes an axe and cuts down a tree. All the power he exerts is through the axe. Now I wish to know, whether the man does not, at the time he is cutting the tree, put forth power? Is this not the fact? Then if the illustration be appropriate, it follows, that at the time when a man is converted, the Spirit of God must put forth power in some form— by some direct act; and that is precisely what my friend denies. For he contends, as I proved in my last speech, that before immersion no other influence is exerted on the mind, but that of the Word. To make the illustration suit his doctrine, the axe must cut the tree till it is almost ready to fall, and then the man must take hold of it, and complete the work! I think I can give a much more correct and striking illustration of his doctrine than the one he has given. A certain man made and tempered the axe; the axe cut the tree; and therefore the maker of the axe might be said to have cut it. So the Spirit of God dictated and confirmed the Word; the Word converts men; and in this sense the Spirit converts them. Just as the man who made and tempered the axe might be said to do what the axe does, so the Spirit who dictated and confirmed the Word, may be said to do what the Word does. Or, a certain man made a gun; and the gun, in the hands of some other person, shot a man. Then the maker of the gun is chargeable with having killed the person who was shot with it. These illustrations are precisely in point, and if my friend can gain anything to his cause by them he shall be welcome to them. But in the cutting of the tree there must be an agency distinct from the axe, which is the instrument. The man who employs the axe as the instrument, must, at the time, put forth power, or the instrument can accomplish absolutely nothing. Now, the question before us is, whether conversion is effected by the truth alone; or whether the Spirit puts forth its power in addition to the influence of the Word? The gentleman's illustration proves our doctrine conclusively.

I have not admitted, nor will I admit, that in regeneration, or conversion, God's mode of proceeding is, in all cases, the same. The Bible does not teach that God always produces this change by the same instrumentality. Mr. C. has not produced a passage which sustains his assertion. I have said, and I repeat it, where God has not limited himself, no man dares attempt to limit him. Ordinarily, he works by means; but he has not said that he will never work without means. When his people were journeying in the wilderness, where food could not be procured by means, he gave them manna for food; and if he fed the bodies of the children of Israel without means, may he not save the souls of infants without means?

There is not a text in the whole Bible which says that the Lord can not sanctify the heart without the intervention of the Word. Nor is there one which says he will not. Yet my friend has ventured to say that he will not, and that he can not! In his *Christianity Restored* he says, if all the reasons and arguments by which men can be converted, are contained in the Old and New Testaments, the power of the Holy, Spirit is spent—that he will not, and that he can not do more. The Bible says neither one nor the other. And if it be true, either that he can not, or that he will not, exert a sanctifying agency in any case without the truth, all infants must go to perdition. The argument is one that can not be answered.

The gentleman has repeatedly contradicted himself since this subject has been before us. You will remember that on the first day of this discussion he told us that nothing more is necessary to secure the salvation of infants than the atonement of Christ. I replied that the atonement can not change the heart. On yesterday he told us that depravity was seated in the body, not in the mind, and therefore infants need no change to fit them for heaven, but the separation of the soul from the body. Now he seems to have it in the mind. So he is still involved in the old difficulty, and has left infants and idiots without the possibility of being saved!

The gentleman excuses himself for having been so constantly involved in the mists of metaphysics by telling you that he is following me. Did you hear his first speech? It was one of the most metaphysical discourses I ever heard. There was scarcely a passage of Scripture in it. Now he is following me! I did not introduce these philosophical or unphilosophical speculations. He introduced them, and I followed him partially. On this, as on all other religious subjects, I am perfectly satisfied with the plain instructions of the Bible—a book which I love infinitely more than his philosophy.

In his last speech he gave us what he considers the philosophy of the Bible concerning conversion and sanctification. It is this: First, fact; then testimony; then faith; then feeling; then action. Now, there is a very serious difficulty about this philosophy. For when a fact is proved, and the people are constrained to believe it true, their feelings are of different and even opposite characters. One approves, another disapproves; one loves, another hates. So it is in regard to the Bible. All men by nature are opposed to it. When convinced that it is a revelation from God, and informed concerning its contents, they do not approve and embrace them; nor will they, until their hearts are renewed. And if ever they are to be induced to love God, the Spirit must so purify their hearts that they will no longer love darkness more than light; that they will see the odiousness of sin, the beauty of holiness, and the glory of the divine perfections. There must be a radical change, for no human being ever loved a moral character which is the opposite of his own. This difficulty completely overturns all the gentleman's philosophy. It will answer him no purpose. His fact, his testimony, his faith, may all exist, and yet the right kind of feeling—the great thing, after all—may be wanting.

I will now briefly reply to his arguments drawn from the Scriptures. He says, whatever influence is ascribed to the Spirit, in the Bible, is also ascribed to the Word. If the Spirit enlightens, the Word also enlightens; if the Spirit converts, the Word converts. By this argument he expects to prove that when the Scriptures speak of the operations of the Spirit, the written Word is meant—that when the Word operates on the heart, the Spirit is said to operate. By this mode of reasoning, I could establish some very singular propositions. I could prove that, when the Lord Jesus opened the eyes of the blind man, the light caused him to see. What would you think if I should thence infer that he opened his eyes by means of light? It is true, the psalmist says, "The entrance of thy Word giveth light"; but if my eyes are diseased, the light can not heal them. This is the work of the great Physician. When he put forth his power and healed the eyes of the blind man, then the light broke in, and he could see. In one sense it is true that the light caused him to see. In another and most important sense, the Savior, and not the light, gave him vision. There was a divine power exerted, which was entirely distinct from the light. So in one sense it is true that the Word of God causes the spiritually blind to see; but in another and most important sense, the Holy Spirit opens their eyes, effects their conversion.

In the Acts of the Apostles (chapter xxvi.) it is said that Paul was sent to open the eyes of the blind. Now, by adopting the logic of Mr. Campbell, I could prove by this passage, that whatever influence is ascribed to the Word is ascribed also to Paul, and from this fact I would reach the conclusion that in conversion and sanctification the Spirit operates only through human instrumentality! I could also prove conclusively that if conversion is ascribed to the Spirit, it is also ascribed to Paul and other preachers of the Gospel; for James the apostle says, "Brethren, if any of you do err from the truth, and one convert him, let him know, that he which converteth the sinner from the error of his way shall save a soul from death," etc. Now, does the Spirit of God convert sinners? So does Paul; so do other preachers. Therefore (and the conclusion is precisely as legitimate as that by which the gentleman proved that the Spirit operates only through the truth)—therefore, in conversion and sanctification the Spirit never operates, except through a preacher. Such is the reasoning of my worthy friend.

The truth is, that conversion and sanctification are commonly effected by three distinct agencies: the agency of the Word; the agency of the man who presents it, and the agency of the Spirit, which is taught as distinctly as the others, and is represented as more important, causing men to receive the truth in the love of it, and to obey it. I believe in all the three. God does not confine the operations of his grace in converting men to the instrumentality of the living preacher. My friend will agree that some have been converted by reading the Word, without a preacher. Sometimes all the three are employed—the preacher, the Word, and the Spirit; sometimes only two; and sometimes only one, as in the case of infants, where it is impossible that either the Word or the ministry can be employed.

The fact that the Word is said to convert men does not prove that the Spirit does not sanctify infants without the Word; nor that conversion is ever effected simply by the influence of the Word. I might say with truth, that the blowing of the rams' horns prostrated the walls of Jericho; for they would not have fallen if the horns had not been blown. But it would be folly to say that the blowing of the horns was the power by which alone they were made to fall. Christ opened the eyes of the man born blind by the use of spittle and clay, but if I were to affirm that his eyes were opened only by spittle and clay, I should speak most unwisely. So the gentleman's argument will not bear one moment's careful examination. It is absolutely worthless.

Mr. C. told us, a few days ago, that according to a correct principle of language the definition of a word, if substituted for it, will make good sense. Now let us try his doctrine by this principle. He says that when the agency of the Spirit is spoken of, the Word is meant. Let us try it: "He saved us by the washing of regeneration and renewing of his Word, which he shed on us abundantly," etc. Now, did the apostle mean that he shed his Word on men abundantly through Jesus Christ? Again: "I will pour out my Word upon your seed!" Is this the idea the prophet intended to convey? Again: "I will take away the stony heart out of your flesh." That is, I will reason, talk, argue with you! Is this the meaning of the prophet? The fact is, there are passages of Scripture which teach that conversion and sanctification are effected by the instrumentality of the Word, but not by the Word only. There are others that recognize the agency of man, but not his agency only. The agency of the Spirit is the only agency which is declared to be absolutely necessary in all cases. The ministry is sometimes necessary, and so is the Word; because God has appointed these as the ordinary means through which the blessings of his salvation shall be conveyed to men. But neither of these is always necessary. The agency of the Spirit is absolutely essential in all cases; because, as all men and all infants are "born of the flesh," and are, therefore, carnal, so all must be born of the Spirit.

Great errors, the gentleman seems to think, grow out of systems of theology; and he would have you believe that he is quite opposed to system-making. Do you see that book? [Pointing to the *Christian System*.] Who is the author of it? My friend. If he is not a system-maker, he has not told the truth; for he calls this book "*The Christian System*," and he says those who make systems are system-makers. I think he is in very good company; but I hope he does not claim the exclusive privilege of making systems. Certainly he should allow others to make systems, at least occasionally. "*Christianity Restored*" was his first system, and the "*Christian System*" his second. If he can make two systems, he should, at least, permit us to make one.

Another argument urged by Mr. C. is, that God never made anything without a word, and he tells us that God created the world by a word. But I assert that he never created anything only by a word. If we were to admit that in the work of creation he did literally speak words, this would only prove that when he spoke he exerted Almighty power to produce the result. So the Word of God is used ordinarily in conversion. But there is also a divine influence exerted on the heart, in addition to the Word, and distinct from it.

But what is the truth in regard to creation by words? The inspired writers, to express most strikingly the infinite ease with which God created all things, represented him as speaking, and it was done—as commanding, and it stood fast. He had but to speak and the universe sprang into being at his bidding! But will the gentleman say that he created all things by words and arguments? Has he not told us that words and arguments could only exert a moral power? Did God create the soul of man by arguments? He is confounding things as dissimilar as light and darkness. What connection is there between creation and argument? If he will prove that God created man by argument and motive, I will admit that the same influence may renew him in the image of God. Christ raised Lazarus from the dead by words, but not by words only. When he said, "Lazarus, come forth," he exerted an omnipotent power.

In the original creation of man, God exerted immediate power. He created nothing by words. So in creating man anew, in restoring his divine image to his soul, there is an agency of the Spirit, in addition to the Word, and distinct from it. How absurd, then, the gentleman's argument from the works of creation, to prove that in conversion and sanctification the Spirit operates on the mind simply by words and motives! Strange logic indeed!

My friend will alarm us, if he can not convince us. He says, men had better take care how they trifle with the Word of God. And I would say, that he had better take care how he speaks of the Holy Spirit. In the *Millennial Harbinger* (Vol. II., p. 211,) he uses this language: "Some Holy Ghost is the soul of every popular sermon, and the essential point in every evangelical creed." I must confess I was shocked when I cast my eye on this sentence. I know the gentleman does not admire the English word "Ghost," but he is perfectly aware that these words are used as the name of the third person in the adorable Trinity. I have heard similar language from men less intelligent, but I could not have supposed that he would allow himself to utter, or to write, such an expression. Since he has done so, I can not help thinking that the warning he has given, does not come well from him. I have never heard any professor of religion speak of the Word of God as he has spoken of the Holy Spirit.

I will now proceed to offer some additional arguments against the doctrine taught by Mr. Campbell. The first that I will offer is this: His doctrine makes it both useless and improper to pray for the conversion of men. I know he will not deny that it is the duty and the privilege of Christians to pray, that God would convert sinners; for we have both precept and example authorizing and requiring it. Paul said concerning himself: "My heart's desire and prayer to God for Israel is, that they might be saved" (Rom. x. 1). And he directed that "supplications, prayers, intercessions, and giving of thanks, be made for all men" (1 Tim. ii. 1). But whilst the duty is perfectly clear, if we regard either precept or precedent, or both, the doctrine of Mr. C. makes it wholly unnecessary, if not improper. This objection did not originate with me, or perhaps it might be supposed to be founded in a misconception of his views. It has occurred to his own friends and followers, as a very serious difficulty. I will read part of a letter written to him by a gentleman who is a member of his church, and published in the *Millennial Harbinger* (Vol. II., p. 469,) in which the objection is strongly stated:

"Without any further preface or apology, I will come at once to the object I had in addressing you at this time, and that is, to ask your opinion whether it be lawful, according to the will of God as revealed to us, to pray for our unconverted friends—that is, to, ask God to convert them to the Christian religion? If it be true, as you affirm, (and which I am not prepared to controvert,) that the righteousness of a Christian is a righteousness by faith in Jesus as the Messiah; that that faith comes alone by hearing or reading the testimony concerning Jesus; and that we have no right to expect any influence superinducing the mind to faith, or even causing the sinner to examine this testimony, or place himself in circumstances for the light of divine truth to shine upon his mind; I say, upon the supposition that these things are so, what right has any one to expect that God will answer his prayers in the behalf of his unconverted friends? Ever since I have felt the importance of divine things, I have felt the most anxious solicitude for many of my relatives and friends who on their part manifested the greatest indifference to these matters, and have often tried to pray for them, too, that God would cause them to submit themselves to Jesus as the only Savior of sinners; but whether these prayers were in accordance to the Word of our Divine Master, I confess I am somewhat at a loss to say. When we pray, we are told to pray in faith; and in order that we may pray in faith, as I understand, we should pray for such things as our Heavenly Father has authorized us to expect at his hands, and no other. Now if the Divine Being exercises no other influence over the minds of men than that influence which is derived to them through the words he has spoken to men, and we can not prevail upon wicked men to give attention to those words, the question is, are we authorized to expect that God will answer our requests in the behalf of such a one? Here is my difficulty, and it has long been a difficulty with me; and I find it is no less so with many of my friends and your friends. If you have opportunity to write me a private letter on this subject, I will esteem it as a singular favor; or if you consider the subject of enough importance, you can, if you please, furnish us an essay upon it through the *Harbinger*. Very affectionately,

Will. Z. Thompson."

The difficulty, it appears, had presented itself, not to the mind of some one individual of a speculative character, but to many of Mr. C.'s friends, who were familiar with his writings. In view of his denial of the agency of the Spirit in conversion, they ask, whether it is right that they should pray to God to convert their unbelieving friends, and whether they have any right to expect God to answer such prayers? In his reply to this letter Mr. C. gave not the slightest intimation that the writer had misconceived his views of the agency of the Spirit, and yet he states them precisely as I have stated them.

Now, if this doctrine be true, I ask emphatically, where is the propriety of praying for the unconverted? Have we a promise from God, that he will answer such prayers? If this doctrine be true, we have not; for the Spirit has dictated and confirmed the Word of Truth, and no influence will or can be exerted, in addition to the Word, to cause the wicked to turn to God. If, then, no special divine influence is promised, or can be exerted to cause men to repent and believe, why should we pray for it? And how can we pray in faith?

This I regard as a most important matter; for it is as truly a part of the plan of Infinite Wisdom to convert men in answer to prayer, as by the instrumentality of the preached Gospel. It is, moreover, one of the consolations of many an afflicted father and mother, that they can pray in faith for the conversion of their children, when far away, exposed to the temptation and unhallowed influences of a wicked world. Could you approach their closet, where they have retired to commune with God, and to pour the desires and the sorrows of their hearts into his ear, you might hear them plead with an irresistible eloquence, that by his Holy Spirit he would convince their children of sin, of righteousness and of judgment; that he would turn their feet from the paths of folly and sin unto his testimonies. How many ten thousand such prayers are incessantly ascending from the hearts of God's faithful children for those who are dear to them, and for a sin-ruined world! But if this doctrine be true, those prayers are all in vain. Not one of them ever was, or ever can be heard. We must bid the weeping father and mother, and the heart-broken wife, to pray no more for those whose salvation is almost as dear to them as their own. Then let all prayers for the unconverted cease. Let it be known that God has done for them all he will do, or can do; and if they are not converted by reading or hearing the Word, they must perish! If this doctrine be true, why did the apostles give themselves to prayer and the preaching of the Word? Why did Paul pray that Israel might be saved? Why should we pray for the success of the Gospel? Shall we bow down and implore God to do what we believe he never will do?

The difficulty stops not here. It makes prayer for believers equally vain—at least so far as regards their sanctification. For, although the gentleman says the Spirit is poured out on those who are immersed, it does not exert a sanctifying influence. In the proposition under discussion the ground is taken, that in sanctification, as well as in conversion, the Spirit operates only through the truth. Why, then, should Christians pray for themselves and for each other, that they may be sanctified? Paul prayed for the Philippian Christians, because he was confident that he who had begun a good work in them would perform it until the day of Jesus Christ. (Philip. i. 6.) He prayed for the Ephesians, that they might be strengthened with might by his Spirit in the inner man. The apostles once prayed to the Savior, "Lord, increase our faith." Did they desire an additional revelation or other miracles? Or did they desire that he would take away the cause of their unbelief—their depravity? A certain man came and desired the Savior to heal his son. He asked him, "Believest thou that I can do this?" He answered, with tears, "Lord, I believe; help thou mine unbelief." He also said to Peter, on a certain occasion, "Simon, Satan hath desired to have thee, that he may sift thee as wheat; but I have prayed for thee, that thy faith fail not." Here we have examples of prayers offered, for a divine influence to strengthen faith and to sanctify the heart.

I turn your attention to one more example of this kind. David, under a deep sense of the corruption of his heart, prayed: "Create in me a clean heart, O God, and renew a right spirit within me" (Psa. li. 10). Now, I ask, would not every unprejudiced mind understand the Psalmist to pray, that God would exert a purifying influence on his heart? Did he believe that all the converting and sanctifying power of the Spirit is in the Word? Multitudes of similar passages are found in the Scriptures. I have brought forward several where prayer was offered and answered for a supernatural influence to be exerted on the hearts of the wicked. In a word, the Scriptures teach with perfect clearness, from Genesis to Revelation, that the Spirit of God can and does exert a controlling, converting, enlightening, and sanctifying influence on the hearts of men, not by words and arguments simply, but more powerful and efficacious. (Time expired.)

MR. CAMPBELL'S TENTH ADDRESS.

WEDNESDAY, NOV. 29, 12 o'clock P.M

Mr. President.—I am now so well acquainted with my friend, Mr. R., as to know when he feels himself grievously pressed and oppressed. He has not responded to any of those all-important questions and difficulties, propounded to him as growing out of his assumptions. What light has been thrown upon the subject of that power, abstract and superadded, of which he speaks so much? Has he not passed the matter in perfect silence? May I not with propriety say it is an indescribable power—wholly unintelligible—since the gentleman himself can give no account of it? I repeat once more, that whenever the gentleman describes his metaphysical abstract power, superadded to the Word, I will affirm, or deny, in the most definite manner. I believe in a substantive influence of the Spirit of God through the truth, upon the conscience, the understanding and the affections.

He appears to approve of the figure of the wood-chopper and his axe. But in his remarks, he seems to have forgotten that, on his theory, the wood-chopper has to cut the tree down without the axe. Or, if he should use the axe in any case at all, he must superadd some power without the axe, beyond the axe, and wholly extra its instrumentality! Figures are not to be used for any other purpose than they are proposed. I do not make this one represent the Word of God in any other particular than its mere instrumentality. He had no time to explain how his infant is cut off the stock of depravity, without one stroke of the axe. But he had time to hold up this book (*The Christian System*) as my Confession of Faith. He ought, in these precious moments, to avoid things extraneous, and refer that subject to the creed question. I shall then show who makes creeds, and binds them, as heavy burdens, upon men's shoulders.

His dissertation upon power is inapplicable to the subject before us. I might, on his own principles, ask him why he prays for the salvation of any person, seeing he believes and teaches that the number of the elect is so definite and fixed that it can neither be increased nor diminished one single individual! Is that not, by his own showing, labor in vain? The means and the end are both so foreordained, that without the one, the other can not be, either in salvation or condemnation. Hence, all the powers of the universe can not add one to either the saved, or the condemned.

Fellow-citizens, from all the premises before my mind, I conclude that the Spirit of Truth—that omnipresent, animating Spirit of our God—whose sword or instrument this Book is, is always present in the work of conversion, and through this truth changes the sinner's affections, and draws out his soul to God. It is, therefore, doing us an act of the greatest injustice to represent us as comparing the Bible to the writings of any dead or absent man, in this point of comparison. In some points of view, all books are alike; but in other points of view, they are exceedingly dissimilar. In comparison of all other books, the Bible is superlatively a book *sui generis*. Its author not only ever lives, but is ever present in it, and with it, operating through it, by it, and with it, upon saints and sinners. The gentleman talks upon themes he does not comprehend. Abstract spiritual operations in nature, and in redemption, are wholly beyond his ken. Were he to speak to the day of eternity, he can not communicate one distinct idea on the subject.

The singular course of my opponent has constrained me to quote and comment on numerous passages of Scripture no way connected with our topics of discussion. But he will have it so, and therefore we must occasionally launch into matters somewhat remote and recondite. He relies much upon such passages as "The wind bloweth where it listeth; and thou hearest the sound thereof, but canst not tell whence it cometh, or whither it goeth. So is every one that is born of the Spirit." He seems to glory in the mystery of his regeneration, because he can not explain it. His main argument is, it is a mystery, and we can not understand it; therefore, my doctrine is true! I asked him to explain the predicate of the last proposition. The words were: "So is every one that is born of the Spirit." But has he done it? No. He can not, I predict, explain the word "so." The subject of the proposition is, "Every one that is born of the Spirit"—is compared to what? So what? That is the question he can not answer! He has mistaken the point of comparison. To him, indeed, it is a mystery. I call for the predicate of the proposition, and then we shall canvass the whole matter.

When I sat down I was expatiating on some other of my respondent's proof-texts—the passages concerning the grant of repentance to Jews and Gentiles, by him that is exalted a Prince and a Savior. I shall illustrate the view, which I partially expressed at the close of my last address. Suppose the people of any country had all been destitute of the right of suffrage—living under an absolute despotism, in consequence of some great political disaster. Meantime, some great prince interposes in their behalf, invades the country, overcomes the tyrant, and, when in authority over the people, grants to the whole State the right of suffrage—would it be just to say that he had, by some special, personal, direct approach to every man, constrained or specially induced him to go to the polls and vote? That, indeed, he might do. But the question is, not whether he might, or might not do so, but whether the language imports that he does so! True, Jesus Christ has been exalted a Prince and a Savior, to grant to Israel, and afterwards to the Gentiles, repentance unto life and remission of sins. Does that mean he makes a personal appeal to every one, or to any one in particular?—or, that he has opened a way in which all, if they please, may obtain the benefits of repentance and remission of sins? I do not say that other Scriptures may teach this doctrine. But the question is, do the passages Mr. Rice has quoted prove that point at all? I affirm the clear conviction they do not. But let every man judge for himself. It is one thing indeed to confer a right upon a people, but whether they shall use it is quite another question. An opponent may so oppose the truth as to make it questionable whether, on repentance, God would forgive him—whether God would grant him the benefits of repentance. Thus says Paul, in meekness instructing them that oppose themselves, if God peradventure might grant them repentance (the advantages of repentance), to eternal life. I am not controverting the fact, but I am controverting the appositeness of the gentleman's quotations, and that extreme latitudinarianism in which he indulges. To grant a right, and to compel to use it, are very different ideas. God confers the rights, and thus opens the way for our voluntary acceptance of them. We rejoice in the glorious fact that God has granted repentance unto life to the whole Gentile world. Philology peremptorily forbids any other interpretation of this passage. It is not to believing Gentiles, or to a few Gentiles, but in contrast with the Jews. They said: "Then hath God also to the Gentiles granted repentance unto life." Repentance unto life is, then, bestowed on all the nations to which the Gospel is preached; and whosoever will, may come and possess its advantages. To interpret this according to my opponent's scheme—that is, to make it respect a few individuals, specially called and constrained to come in, is to rob the Gentile world of one of the richest charters ever expressed in human speech. I thank my God that Jesus Christ has been exalted a Prince and a Savior, to grant repentance unto life, not unto Israel only, but to the Gentiles also. Mr. Rice's freedom with this statute robs us of our rights, for the sake of a speculative assumption.

As great injustice is done me by Mr. Rice, in sometimes changing this position of *only* in the proposition, I do not maintain that a person is converted by the Word only. I say that "in conversion," etc., the Spirit operates only through the Word; not that a person is converted by the Word only. The latter excludes the Spirit altogether, which is directly in contradiction of the ground assumed in my opening speech. We are only converted through the Word; only we are converted through the Word; and we are converted through the Word only, are three very different propositions. The gentleman ought to place the word "only" where it stands in the proposition.

The gentleman has again introduced the subject of infant damnation. I am sorry to spend so much time on such an ungracious theme; but as my reputation is somewhat involved in what was said yesterday, I must show that I have not misconstrued the doctrines preached, and interpretations of Scripture given on this subject, by the good old Scotch Presbyterians. I am indeed pleased to see that Mr. Rice is ashamed of it, and has taxed his ingenuity to find a new way of expounding the elect infants of the creed. His interpretation is ingenious—apparently so, however, because it does not read elect persons, but elect infants.

All infants that die are elect infants! A happy conception truly! But a fair construction of the Confession will not authorize it. I first heard the gloss last year. But neither the founders of Calvinism on the continent, nor the Westminster divines, so understood this matter, as my reading and recollection fully justify. I shall read a few passages on this subject, and, first, one from Calvin's Institutes. I have both the Latin original and Calvin's own French translation of the passage. I wonder not that Calvin, to quote his own words, calls it *Decretum quidem horribile, fateor*, which Professor Norton renders as follows: "I ask again, how it has come to pass, that the fall of Adam has involved so many nations with their infant children in eternal death, and this without remedy, but because such was the will of God? It is a dreadful decree, I confess." Knowing that Allen has translated it, softening it down, I give the following from other authorities:

[Translated from the Latin]:—"I ask, again, whence has it happened, that the fall of Adam has involved so many nations together with their infant children, in eternal death, without remedy, unless that it has so pleased God?—A horrible decree indeed, I confess."

[From the French]:—"I ask them again, whence it has come to pass, that the fall of Adam has involved with him so many nations with their infants, unless that it has thus pleased God?—I confess that this decree ought to shock us."

But Calvin, besides this passage quoted from his Institutes, (Lib. 3, c. 23, sec. 7,) in speaking of the errors of Servetus, says: "In the meantime, certain salvation is said (by Servetus) to await all at the final judgment, except those who have brought upon themselves the punishment of eternal death, by their personal sins; (*propriis scelerribus;*) from which it is also inferred that all who are taken from life while infants and young children, are exempt from eternal death, although they are elsewhere called accursed," (*Tract. Theo. Refut. Error. Mich. Serveti.*) This was one of Servetus' errors, according to Calvin. Servetus would have all infants saved that died; but Calvin thought this a great error, because there were of these some infants called accursed. Augustine, in condemning the doctrine of Pelagius, says, "We affirm that they (infants) will not be saved and have eternal life, except they be baptized in Christ"; and much more to the same effect.

Turretin, the chief of Calvinistic writers, teaches the same doctrine in the clearest manner. He is of high authority at Princeton, and has stood on my shelf for thirty years. He says:

"The ancient Pelagians, who, having followed as their master Pelagius the Briton, denied original sin in all its parts, contending that the sin of Adam hurt nobody but himself, or if it should be said to have injured anybody else, that it was through example or imitation, not by propagation. Not unlike them are the Remonstrants, who in their apology pronounced certain, whatever Augustine and others may have determined to the contrary, that God will appoint, and that he, on account of original sin, so called with justice can appoint no eternal torments to infants, of whatever lot or descent, dying without actual and personal sins; holding that their opinion, viz., that any infants will be appointed to eternal torments is opposed to divine goodness and right reason; nay, that it is uncertain whether the preponderance is in favor of the absurdity or its cruelty.

Here, then, is an explicit declaration from a Calvinist of the highest authority, that God can, in justice, appoint infants to eternal torments. Indeed, I can quote distinguished Calvinists in considerable numbers, in proof that infant damnation on account of original sin, was the doctrine of a portion of the Protestant Reformation, of the Synod of Dort, and of the Westminster Assembly. But I am sorry to have been compelled to bring up a doctrine of this sort on this occasion; and certainly would not, had Mr. Rice not compelled me to it. But when I undertake to prove anything, I do prove it, and can prove it.

One man may be said to convert another, as Paul begat the Corinthians, through the gospel, and was spiritually their father. But Mr. Rice says, then they may be said to do all other things akin to conversion—quicken, save, etc. That is not a fair inference. It is so far-fetched and so gross as not to entangle any one—no one can believe it. But it seems I committed a great sin in his eyes, in speaking of the Holy Ghosts of several systems—the alleged chimeras of modern theories. Be it understood, then, that I never use the words "Holy Ghost" with disrespect, although I think the term ought to be changed into "Holy Spirit." Time was when it was a very proper term. I have shown somewhere within the last seven years that our Saxon forefathers used the word "ghost" as equivalent to our word "guest," and properly enough called our spirits guests, while in our bodies—regarding the body as a house or tabernacle, and the spirit as a guest or ghost. I was, some years since, much struck with the fact that we have not in the common English Bible the words "Holy Ghost" in the Old Testament at all, but "Holy Spirit"; and, in the same version, we have "Holy Ghost" most frequently, though not exclusively, in the New. Tyndale, I presume, was the cause of this, in the New Testament; for in many points, nay, in most points, Tyndale was followed by James' translators. The question arose in my mind, why Tyndale did so, and the answer occurred in this way: the Spirit of God was promised in the Old Testament to be the *guest* of the Christian church—that, as in a temple, it was to reside in it; hence, the Spirit of the Old Testament having become the guest of the New, Tyndale introduced "Holy Ghost" for the "Holy Spirit" of the previous age. With us, however, "ghost" has degenerated into the representative of a disembodied spirit, the spirit of a dead man. Hence, I think it is bad taste to call the living Spirit of the living God a "Holy Ghost," according to our modern usage.

While, then, the new theories of modern times about spiritual influence is, indeed, more ghostly than spiritual, they may, with more propriety than we, use the term "Holy Ghost"; and as all parties have not one theory, more than one faith, I see no more impropriety in speaking of Holy Ghosts, more than of two faiths, two Lords, two Spirits, two baptisms, which I believe are universally tolerated. Still, if I am, by so doing, chargeable with disrespect for either the name or the persons that use it, I should not patronize it at all. For my own part I prefer, and almost universally use, the name "Holy Spirit."

The theories of spiritual influence are as variable as the winds, and fires, and floods of the earth. With some it is the baptism of fire, with others it is a mighty rushing wind, and with some it is water. Some read "born of the Spirit, even born of the water"—thereby making water and Spirit identical. The sin against the Holy Spirit, as explained by our Savior, consists in speaking against the works of the Spirit, ascribing his miracles to satanic influence—a sin which can not, in this, his view, be committed now. It was not a sin of thought, a general action; but a sin of the tongue, accompanied with a cordial malice.

Mr. R. would make me almost, if not altogether, guilty of the sin and error of Manicheism, because of my remarks upon the law of sin in the fleshly members. I must now, according to him, have translated all sin from the mind into the flesh. Hence he quotes envy, and hatred, and pride, etc., as antagonizing with my views. And yet, while I give to the mind sinful views and desires, may I not ask him whence come envy, and pride, and hatred? Do they not generally come from the flesh? Do they not spring from our worldly and fleshly associations, from our carnal and temporal interests? The mind is enslaved to the body. Our intellectual powers are all placed under tribute to some fleshly and earthly objects. Hence hatred, variance, strife, emulation, fraud, etc., come almost exclusively from our competitions about securing so much of earth's and time's favors, as gratify our fleshly lusts and pleasures. Whence, then, come these sinful desires but from the flesh? Still, I am very far from saying that sin is wholly and exclusively confined to the flesh. But all the elements of sin are there. Through "this body of sin and death," as Paul calls it, sin "works in our members to bring forth fruit unto death." The mind is, indeed, made to participate in all these fleshly lusts that war against our souls; "for the flesh lusteth against the Spirit, and the Spirit against the flesh, so that we can not do the things that we would."

We must also revert to the word "holy." I objected merely to his use of the word, and not to the word, nor the thing. He represented the heart as being made holy by an immediate fiat. God made man holy as he created him. Today he has added "not by the word only." Did I say, in my speech, "by the word only"? That is a wrong issue. His argument was, that God made man without a word. Mine was, that he did not. He has changed his position, and got up a new issue. I argue that God created nothing without a word. But it was so inapplicable! In his view, I presume it was, because fatal to his assumption. No one can form a single conception of naked power. It is bad philosophy to descant upon it, as well as bad theology.

Still, holiness is not of the nature of a distinct, separate and substantive attribute, as wisdom, power, goodness. And yet it is not an attribute of God, as eternity, infinity, immutability, because it is relative to impurity. It is an attribute, or perfection, in contrast with sin and impurity. In classifying the divine perfections, I usually destribute them into four classes: three which nature develops—wisdom, power, and goodness; three which the law develops—justice, truth, and holiness; three which the gospel develops—mercy, condescension, and love; and three attributes of all these, viz., eternity, immutability, and infinity. These apply to all the others. Hence God our Father is eternally, immutably, and infinitely just, wise, good, powerful, etc. These three last are perfections of perfections. Purity has been preferred to holiness by some writers, because a more clear and distinct conception to most minds than the term "holiness." It is indeed, as before observed, the supreme excellence and majesty of God; and in the esteem of the higher order of intelligence, it is a generic exponent of all his adorable perfections. Hence, in their most sublime anthems and ecstacies, this word is a consecrated symbol of their highest admiration.

I now proceed to the argument proposed at the close of my last speech. It is to be deduced from that inestimable document called the "Acts of the

Apostles"—a document of the highest value to the Church. It is worth all the ecclesiastic histories of all nations and languages, because it is authentic and authoritative; and because it gives just such a development of things as reveals Christianity to us in all its practical details. We see the apostles in the field of labor, carrying out their commission; and also the particular lessons Christ and the Holy Spirit taught them! I have much use for the Scriptures of truth in this argument, and will use them very freely.

The argument I now propose is simply this: I will show that all the reported conversions, detailed in that book as occurring for some thirty years after the ascension, are represented as having been through what the persons saw performed, and heard said, from the original witnesses and heralds of the resurrection of the Messiah. I wish to adduce every case on record, and show from them all, that these conversions were in accordance with our proposition. And certainly, if Mr. Rice can not produce a single case in which conversion was accomplished without the Word, or Gospel testimony being presented and heard, he will have most signally failed in sustaining his negation of this proposition. (Time expired.)

MR. RICE'S TENTH REPLY.

WEDNESDAY, NOV. 20, 12:30 o'clock P.M.

Mr. President.—I shall be prepared to pay due attention to my friend, when he comes to speak of making systems and binding them upon the consciences of men; and I expect to prove that he is quite as liable to the charge as are those whom he denounces. I am truly anxious to reach that subject.

The gentleman has failed to make any answer whatever to my argument against this doctrine, that it makes prayer, especially for unbelievers, unnecessary and improper. Does he deny it, or attempt to prove, that the objection is not valid? Not a word of it. He makes no attempt to prove that his doctrine is at all consistent with prayer. But he says I am in the same predicament, because I believe in the doctrine of election of election. Suppose this were true; would he be the better for having me in company with him in his errors? If the doctrine of election were the subject under discussion, I would promptly meet and refute his charge, not by showing that he is involved in the same difficulty, but by proving the objection not to be well founded. I should have no fears in meeting the gentleman on that subject. If we were discussing the doctrine of election, I would turn to his *Christian System*, and prove that he himself teaches that the purposes of God are eternal, and that "the whole affair of man's redemption, even to the preparation of the eternal abodes of the righteous, was arranged ere time was born." This might pass for tolerable Calvinism.

He tells us, the Spirit of God is always present with his Word. I have asked, and now ask again, what does he mean by this language? It is easy, and not uncommon for men to use expressions which convey no definite idea either to their own minds or to those of their hearers. In his writings he has so clearly stated and illustrated his views, as to leave no room to doubt what he really believes. He has said distinctly that no power but moral power can be exerted on minds; and that moral power can be exerted only by words and arguments. He has declared his belief that when the Spirit of God had dictated and confirmed the Scriptures, all his converting and sanctifying power was spent. Perhaps I can explain in what sense he supposes the Spirit to be present and to operate with the Word. As Mr. Campbell's spirit is present with the ideas he has published in his *Harbinger*, operating on the minds of his readers, so in the same sense the Spirit of God is present with the Scriptures. I use his own illustration. Such being his meaning, does he believe in any other agency in conversion and sanctification, than that of the Word dictated and confirmed by the Holy Spirit?

It is not necessary for me now to enter into any discussion of the passage in John iii.—"The wind bloweth where it listeth," etc. I quoted it while we were discussing the design of baptism, and since simply to prove that the new birth is, in some sense, mysterious. I was proving the erroneousness of Mr. C.'s doctrine by showing that, according to the Bible, there is a mystery connected with the new birth; but according to his views there was no mystery about it.

How the Spirit operates on the heart in conversion and sanctification I profess not to understand. And since Mr. C. can not explain how Satan exerts an influence on the human mind, I am certainly not bound to explain how the Spirit operates in conversion. Indeed, we can not explain the how of any one fact in nature. No wonder, then, if the agency of the Spirit is mysterious.

The gentleman has made an attempt to answer some of my arguments. I am gratified that he made the effort. I wish to see him march up to the question boldly, and expose my arguments, if he can. I proved the doctrine of the special influence of the Spirit by the fact that God is said to give repentance. Paul directs Timothy in meekness to "Instruct those that oppose themselves; if God peradventure will give them repentance to the acknowledging of the truth" (2 Tim. ii. 25). This argument the gentleman attempts to answer by an illustration. Suppose, says he, certain persons for a time deprived of the right of suffrage, and again having this right restored, he who restored the right would be said to give them the right of suffrage, but would not force them to exercise it. This is indeed a most singular illustration. Did Paul say, Instruct those who oppose themselves, if peradventure God will give them the right, the privilege to repent? Does Luke say, Christ is exalted a Prince and a Savior to give men the right to repent? Really, I was not aware that any human being had ever been deprived of the right to repent! Nor did

I know that God had ever refused to look with compassion on the broken heart and contrite spirit. Men have always had the right, and it has always been their duty to repent. Consequently we find nothing in the Scriptures about granting men the right, the privilege! This is one of the many absurdities into which the gentleman's erroneous doctrines force him. The language of inspiration is: "Then hath God also to the Gentiles granted repentance [not the right to repent] unto life" (Acts xi. 18). Instruct them, "if peradventure God will grant them repentance to the acknowledging of the truth." But to make these passages accord with Mr. C.'s theology we must allow him to introduce the word *right* or *privilege* before repentance! If I may be permitted thus to interpolate or expunge words from the Bible, I can make it teach anything, even the greatest absurdity. But the Scriptures declare that God does grant unto men repentance to the acknowledging of the truth, repentance unto life—that he does exert upon their minds a divine influence, leading them to repent and turn from sin to God.

I proved the doctrine of a special divine influence also by Luke xxiv. 45: "Then opened he their understandings, that they might understand the Scriptures." The gentleman replied that this passage is irrelevant, because Christ, not the Holy Spirit, opened their understandings. Strange reply! Christ is represented as working many miracles, and he is said to have wrought them by the Spirit of God. (Matt. xii. 28.) The Spirit is said to be shed on us abundantly through Jesus Christ. (Tit. iii. 5.) It is by virtue of his atoning sacrifice and intercession that the Holy Spirit is poured out upon the hearts of men. By his blessed Spirit, therefore, he opened the understandings of his disciples, that they might understand the Scriptures.

The gentleman makes a criticism on the difference between the phrases "through the Word only," and only through the Word." I am not concerned to answer it. I was not pleased, as he knows, with the proposition as it is worded, because I believed it left room for quibbling; and I would not have consented to debate it, but with the distinct and express understanding that I should interpret it by his publications on the subject. I have proved that in his *Christianity Restored* he says there are only two kinds of power, moral and physical; that only moral power can operate on the human mind; and that all moral power is in words and arguments. Let the gentleman either come out candidly and say that he was in error when he wrote the books from which I have quoted, or come up to the defense of his published doctrines. It does not look well for a man to attempt to conceal the truth in this way.

He seems to regret the necessity that is laid upon him to speak of the doctrine of infant damnation, as held by Presbyterians! I am truly glad that the subject has been brought up on this occasion, for Mr. C. is the very man to prove upon us this stale charge, if it can be proved. On yesterday he professed to find it in our Confession of Faith. He now acknowledges that it is not there, but he says Calvin taught it. I deny that Calvin ever taught it. If he did, I have failed to find it in his writings.

Now, what is the doctrine taught by Calvin in the passage quoted? Does he teach that infants are actually lost? He does not. He contends that in consequence of the fall of Adam, all his posterity, infants and adults, are in a state of condemnation, and are exposed to the wrath of God; and that, had no remedy been provided, all must have perished. He does not say that any infant actually perishes, but that all are exposed to ruin in consequence of the fall, and must have perished had no remedy been provided. The gentleman might have proved, with equal conclusiveness, that according to Calvin, all nations, adults as well as infants, do actually perish forever; for he speaks not of infants only, but of both adults and infants—of the whole race.

Is it true that the gentleman's reformation can not sustain itself without such caricatures and gross misrepresentations of the doctrines of others? No man has more frequently complained of being misrepresented than Mr. C., and no man living has done greater injustice to others, living and dead.

Calvin did not teach the doctrine he has charged upon him. But he quotes Augustine as teaching it. Was Augustine a Presbyterian? The gentleman is attempting to prove that the Presbyterian Church holds the doctrine of infant damnation, and, to establish the charge, he quotes Augustine! But he quotes Turretin, too. Was Turretin a member of the Presbyterian Church? But I will subscribe to the doctrine of Turretin. He opposes the sentiments of those who say that it would be unjust in God to exclude infants from heaven—that he is bound in justice to save them. He holds, not that infants are actually lost, but that their salvation is of grace, not of justice. Zanchius was also quoted. Was he a Presbyterian? This author, in speaking of infants, uses the Latin word *damno*; but Mr. C. certainly knows that this word means simply to condemn. The doctrine of Zanchius, as that of Calvin and Turretin, seems clearly to be, that all the human race, in consequence of the sin of Adam, are involved in a common condemnation, from which they can be saved only by the grace of God in Christ.

But this doctrine, as Mr. C. ought to know, is not peculiar to those who are called Calvinists. It is taught with great clearness and force by Rev. Richard Watson, in his Theological Institutes; which, if I mistake not, is regarded as a kind of text book by our Methodist brethren. He, as well as Presbyterians, teaches that in consequence of the sin of Adam, the human race are all, old and young, justly exposed to the wrath of God, and that all who are saved, are saved by grace. The gentleman has repeatedly boasted of his thorough acquaintance with Presbyterianism. I will not charge him with willful misrepresentation of the doctrines of the Presbyterian Church, but I will say that you can scarcely find an old Presbyterian lady who does not know that our Church never did teach or hold the doctrine he has charged upon her. Charity, then, requires us to suppose that his knowledge of Presbyterianism is very limited. He certainly is not half so well informed concerning these matters as he professes to be.

He attempted to prove that the Spirit operates in conversion and sanctification only through the truth, by the fact that whatever the Spirit is represented as doing, the Word is also said to do—that if the Spirit converts men, the Word converts them. I replied, that by the same logic I could prove that the Spirit operates only through human instrumentality, because Paul was sent to convert the Gentiles, and ministers of the Gospel are said to convert men. The argument, therefore, would prove as conclusively that the Spirit never converted a person without human instrumentality—that he operates only through the living minister, as that he never converts and sanctifies without the truth, or that he operates only through the truth. But the gentleman seeks to escape from the difficulty by saving Paul was not sent to quicken men. Paul was to open their eyes and to turn them from darkness to light, and from the power of Satan to God. Could this be done without their being quickened or made spiritually alive? Paul said to the Corinthians: "In Christ Jesus I have begotten you through the gospel" (1 Cor. iv. 15). Can a person be begotten, and not quickened? There is no way in which he can escape. His argument proves as conclusively that the Spirit operates only through human instrumentality, as that he operates only through the truth.

I think it unnecessary to press the gentleman much further with the absurdity of locating all depravity in man's animal nature. It is perfectly certain, without argument, that anger, wrath, malice, hatred, are passions which belong to the mind; that have no necessary connection with the body. The mind can hate as malignantly out of the body as in it. There is no truth in his philosophy. It is profoundly absurd. Nor is there one word in the Bible to countenance it.

I see neither pertinency nor meaning in all the gentleman has said about the word "holy." On yesterday he told us, strangely enough, that it did not express moral quality. I did not choose, because it was wholly unnecessary, to spend time disputing about a word. I therefore quoted the passage, "God made man upright." The word "upright" is admitted to express moral quality. If, then, God originally made man upright, not by words and arguments, it follows that he can do it again; that his power over the human mind is not confined to mere motives. But, says Mr. C., God did not make man upright without a word, but he said, "Let us make man," etc. Were these words addressed to man? Did they create him in whole or in part? Did they exert even the slightest influence? No; man was created in the image of God by an immediate exertion of his omnipotent power. A word never created anything. If, then, God did originally exert on man such a power, as made him holy or upright, not by words, who shall dare say he can not restore his image to the soul, either through the Word or without it? The Word of God is not able, of itself, to overcome the enmity of the human heart, and to inspire it with supreme love to God.

I wish now to present the remaining arguments which I had proposed to offer, and then to give a brief and condensed view of the ground over which we have passed. I have said that Mr. C.'s doctrine prescribes to the power of God an unreasonable and unscriptural limitation; and this I have proved by the facts, that originally God created man holy, and that he does exert a controlling influence over his moral conduct, not merely or chiefly by words and arguments. I will now prove that God can, and that he does, exert on the human mind a converting and sanctifying power, distinct from the Word, by the inspired accounts of the first revivals. In the second chapter of the Acts of the Apostles, we learn, that on the day of Pentecost three thousand souls were converted. Men who went to the temple in all their pride, unbelief, love of sin, and hatred of the truth, were on that day converted, became penitent believers, were filled with hatred of sin and love to God, and were added to the church. This was a most remarkable event. The change wrought in their minds was sudden. They went to the temple loving sin and hating the truth. They left it hating sin and rejoicing in Christ. The change was radical and thorough. The things they hated one hour before they now supremely loved. They beheld in the Savior a beauty and a glory they had never before discovered; and in the plan of salvation they saw an adaptation to their condition and necessities which they had never discovered. They trusted, loved, praised, and worshiped the Redeemer of men. The change was permanent. From that hour to the hour of their death they proved by their lives, that they were new creatures. Through reproach and persecutions, even unto death, they held out faithfully. They counted not their lives dear. They suffered joyfully the spoiling of their goods, knowing that through Christ they had the assurance of a heavenly inheritance.

Now let me ask any reflecting man, how do you account for this sudden, radical, permanent change in the hearts and lives of those persons? Was it effected by the miracles they witnessed? Miracles, Mr. C. admits, can not convert men. They can only arrest their attention, and convince them of the truth; but they can not change the heart. The question is, what caused these wicked men so suddenly and so ardently to love the truth which they had hated? What caused them to see in sin an odiousness they had not before seen, and in holiness a beauty they had never before perceived? Why did they now find their highest happiness in that service from which hitherto they had turned with aversion and disgust? Was this astonishing revolution in their dispositions, views and feelings effected by Peter's arguments? Many of them had doubtless heard the preaching of Him who spake as never man spake; and they were not thus affected. Thousands had heard the gracious words which constantly fell from his lips; but no discourse of his ever produced effects such as we are now contemplating. Besides, it is a fact, proved by universal observation, that if the characters of bad men are changed by arguments and motives, the change is very gradual. They do not readily subdue passions long indulged, and attain to the possession of opposite virtues. Such changes, even if effected merely by motives, are the work of months, if not of years. But the work we are now contemplating, was effected in a day, even in an hour; for when the Lord works, a moment is as good as a year. Suddenly the three thousand had new hearts, new views, new feelings, new sorrows, new joys. They were new creatures. Old things had passed away, and, behold, all things were new!

Here we learn why it was that the apostle's preaching was attended with so much greater success than that of the Savior. He wrought stupendous miracles, and spake with an eloquence which no human orator could ever rival; but the Holy Spirit was not so abundantly poured out before his ascension to heaven as after. Can any one, not blinded by false theory, doubt that on the day of Pentecost the Holy Spirit exerted on the minds and hearts of the three thousand a power distinct from the Word, and more efficacious?

Another argument in favor of the doctrine of a special agency of the Spirit, an argument which, as it appears to me, has great weight, is this: The contrary doctrine leaves man in a hopeless condition. Heaven is a holy place. An infinitely holy God reigns there; and holy angels bow around his throne. God has taught us that nothing impure can enter into the holy city; that none from earth but "the spirits of just men made perfect" can approach his presence. Men are deeply depraved. Even the most godly groan under indwelling corruption. Tell them that they must, by their own exertions, in view of the motives of the gospel, prepare themselves to see God, and they will be down and weep in despair. A man is suddenly called to die, and appear before his Judge. He may be a pious man, but he is conscious of being very imperfect. What assurance can he have that he is pure enough to be admitted to stand in the presence of God? What distressing apprehensions must fill his mind. How gloomy must be his future prospects. But let him hear the language of Paul: "Being confident of this very thing, that he which hath begun a good work in you will perform it until the day of Jesus Christ" (Phil. i. 6). Cheered by such a promise, the humble believer, though conscious of great imperfection, feels his fears subside, and his hopes rise. If God has undertaken the work, it will be well done. He is assured that Christ will present his happy spirit before his Father, "without spot or wrinkle. He knows he will soon behold his face in righteousness. Never will I give up this soul-cheering doctrine, and those great and precious promises founded upon it. Living and dying, I hope to experience their fulfillment.

This doctrine is the hope of our guilty and polluted race. God will pour out his Spirit on all flesh. In answer to the prayers of the faithful, it shall descend as showers on the thirsty earth, and shall cause the wilderness and the solitary place to be glad, and the desert to blossom as the rose.

I must present one more argument. It is this: The great mass, the overwhelming majority of the readers of the Bible, in all ages, have understood it to teach the doctrine for which I am contending. This fact can not be denied. Now Mr. C. agrees with me, that on all important points of faith and duty the Bible is a plain book, easily understood. It was designed to be read and understood by the unlearned as well as the wise. Ask all who have made that blessed book their study, how they understand it on this subject, and with wonderful unanimity they declare their firm belief that it teaches that in conversion and sanctification there is a divine and efficacious influence of the Spirit, distinct from the Word. This influence, in connection with the cross of Christ, is the ground of their hope. For it they pray day and night, and in the witness of the Spirit that they are the children of God they rejoice.

If the doctrine of Mr. C. is indeed true, the fact I have just stated is most unaccountable. How shall we account for the fact that the whole Christian world have misunderstood the Bible on this vital point? Is its teaching plain? and yet almost all have misunderstood it! If Mr. C. so thinks, he of all men should, in consistency, believe most firmly in the doctrine of total depravity. How else can he account for the amazing blindness of almost all the readers of the Bible? Indeed, I know not whether we should more wonder at the blindness and stupidity of all Christendom, or at the superior illumination of Mr. C. and those who agree with him! How it has happened that they, whilst denying all supernatural illumination, have gained so much greater light than all others, I can not comprehend.

I trust the time will never come when I shall feel myself constrained to differ in regard to any fundamental doctrine of Christianity, from the overwhelming majority of the wise and the good. Were I to entertain such views, I should greatly suspect myself of being under some blinding influence. We need not, however, appeal to the views of even the wisest and best. On this vital subject, the language of inspiration is clear and full. It leaves no room to doubt that God has promised to save us, by the washing of regeneration and renewing of the Holy Ghost, shed upon us abundantly through Jesus Christ.

I have now offered as many arguments as I designed to present on this topic—not all that I could offer. It is not my plan to confuse your minds by a great multiplicity of arguments, but to present a few that are clear, striking, and conclusive.

I will now commence a brief review of the ground over which I have traveled. What have been the precise points in debate? I have said that my opponent and myself agree that the Holy Spirit dictated and confirmed the Scriptures. We agree, also, that ordinarily the Spirit operates, in some sense, through the Word.

Mr. C. contends that the Spirit never operates without the truth. I contend that in the case of infants and idiots, he does. Mr. C. believes that in the conversion and sanctification of adults the Spirit operates only through the truth; that he dictated and confirmed the Word, and the Word converts and sanctifies. I maintain that, in addition to the Word, and distinct from it, there is an influence of the Spirit on the heart, without which the Word would never convert and sanctify any human being.

Let me repeat a few explanations, that I may not be misunderstood. I do not hold that in regeneration there is a change of the physical nature of the mind, but a change of the dispositions and affections of the heart. Nor do I hold that in regeneration any new revelation is made, any new ideas given which are not taught in the Scriptures; but such a change of heart as enables the renewed soul to see the beauty and excellency of the things there revealed. "Open mine eyes" prayed David, "that I may read wonderful things out of thy law."

Again. The *modus operandi*, the manner in which the Spirit operates on the heart, I do not profess to understand. The fact that he does operate is clear; the mode is mysterious. That God created man is certain; how he created him is mysterious. How spirits communicate their thoughts to each other, or to the mind of man, I do not comprehend. We pry not into things beyond our comprehension.

The necessity of the special influence of the Spirit I have said does not arise from any lack of evidence that the Scriptures are true; for the evidence is convincing and overwhelming. Nor does it arise from any obscurity in the manner of presenting the truths taught in the Bible; for they are presented with remarkable simplicity and clearness. Nor does it arlse from the fact that men are not perfectly free agents; for they are. The necessity of the divine influence arises from the deep, the total depravity of human nature; the aversion of the unsanctified heart to the holy character of God, to his pure law, and his soul-humbling gospel. "This is the condemnation," said our Savior, "that light is come into the world; and men loved darkness more than light, because their deeds were evil." The Word of God alone can not change their hearts, so that they will hate darkness and love light—turn from sin and follow holiness.

The effects of this depravity are, that the affections of men are placed on forbidden objects; their minds are preoccupied with worldly plans and des1res; and they refuse to hear the Word; or, hearing, they reject or pervert its divine teachings and become infidels or heretics; or, being speculative believers, they live without Christ and without God in the world. (Time expired.)

MR. CAMPBELL'S CLOSING ADDRESS.

WEDNESDAY, NOV. 29, 1 o'clock P.M.

Mr. President.—I have but thirty minutes to close the argument, unless I should be indulged with a few more. I am sorry to see Mr. Rice so positive in his assertions and contradictions respecting the readings and comments on Calvin. He has not given a correct translation of Calvin's Latin, according to the copy now before me. I have read other translations of it, besides my own, and I have also read Calvin's own French translation of the passage in dispute. I will read an interpretation of it by Jeremiah Taylor:

"If we are guilty of Adam's sin by the decree of God, by his choice and constitution that it should be so, as Mr. Calvin and Dr. Twiss (that I may name no more for that side) do expressly teach, it follows that God is the author of our sin, so that I may use Mr. Calvin's words: 'How is it that so many nations with their children should be involved in the fall without remedy, but because God would have it so; and if that be the matter, then to God, as the cause, must that sin and that condemnation be ascribed."—*Jere. Taylor's Works*, Heb. ed., vol. ix., p. 322; quoted by the *Christian Examiner*, Boston, 1828.

Now, if the gentleman desires to contest the matter farther, I now inform him that I shall be forthcoming under the next question of creeds. At present we must, close this present argument, and reserve what we have farther to say on the "horrible decree" till the next question, under which it will be quite as suitable as here. I will sustain the ground which I occupy by ample authority.

His allusions to repentance unto life and remission are more for appearance than from any new ideas or new arguments. I have shown it to be not individual and personal, but commensurate with the Gentile world—a rich and glorious tender to all the nations of the earth. A matter alike unexpected by Jew or Gentile. The question stands as I left it in my last address.

The letter from Bro. Thomson on the subject of prayer, read from the *Millennial Harbinger* by Mr. Rice, was introduced for effect, and especially to hide his own retreat from the difficulty propounded to him on that very same subject. Why did he not read my answer to it? That would have set the matter in its proper attitude before you. My time will not allow me to read such disquisitions and comment on them. They are not called for. There are few who can comprehend the reasons of things. The best philosophy of prayer is, that God has granted the privilege, enjoined the duty, and given a promise. We, therefore, violate no decree, and sin against no revelation, in praying for all men. I believe, practice, and preach the necessity and propriety of praying for the salvation of our children, families, friends, etc., as much as I believe, preach, or practice any point of domestic and social duties and privileges. If I were to follow Mr. Rice into all these digressions into my writings, we should have scores of questions in discussion.

He says there is a certain power displayed in conversion, and so say I. And does it not come with as good a grace from me as from him? But he says he goes for a power beyond the naked Word, and that, too, an accompanying power. Well, the word "accompanying" explains not the nature of that power, and for that I have asked more than once, but I have asked in vain. He can neither expound what the "accompanying power" is, or can be, now how it operates, and therefore whether or not we agree, I could not say. I believe the Spirit accompanies the Word, is always present with the Word, and actually and personally works through it upon the moral nature of man, but not without it. I presume not to speculate upon the nature of this power, nor the mode of operation. I believe the Holy Spirit sheds abroad in our hearts the love of God, and dwells in all the faithful; that it sanctifies them through the truth; that "it works in them to will and do," and that it comforts them in all their afflictions.

But the Spirit of God does not thus enter into the wicked. When it fell from heaven on Pentecost, it fell only on the one hundred and twenty, and not upon the promiscuous assembly. For the multitude, after the Spirit's descent, did still upbraid the disciples with drunkenness. Those who first received it that day preached by it to the audience. The thousands who heard were pierced to the heart, and yet had not received the Spirit. They believed, and were in an agony of fear and terror, but had not yet received the Spirit. They asked what they should do, and yet had not received it. Peter commanded them to "Repent and be baptized, every one of you, for the remission of sins, and you shall receive the gift of the Holy Spirit." Of course, then, they had not yet received that gift. They, however, gladly received his Word, and were baptized. We have, then, the first three thousand converts regenerated by gladly receiving the Word and baptism. This is a strong fact for the first one in my fourteenth argument.

The second fact of conversion is found, Acts iv., and the question is, how were they regenerated? We shall read the passage: "Now that many of them which heard the Word believed, and the number of the men was about five thousand." We are now morally certain that these five thousand were converted by the Spirit only through the Word. We have already eight thousand examples of our allegation, and not one instance of one converted without the Word.

Our third exemplification is found, Acts v. 14: "And believers were the more added to the Lord, multitudes of both men and women." Women are here mentioned as well as men. We have, then, got multitudes of both sexes to add, in proof that the Spirit converted these, not without the Word, but by what they saw and heard.

We shall find a fourth example, Acts viii. 5, 6, 12. Philip went to Samaria and preached Christ to them. "And when they believed Philip preaching the things concerning the kingdom of God and the name of the Lord Jesus, they were baptized, both men and women." So the Samaritans were regenerated by the Holy Spirit through faith in the Word, which Philip preached.

A fifth example, is found in the eunuch: "If thou believest with all thy heart, thou mayest." He said: "I believe that Jesus Christ is the Son of God." Then he, too, was born of the water, and converted, not without the Word.

Paul furnishes a sixth case. When he had fallen to the ground, he heard "a voice saying to him, Saul, Saul, why persecuteth thou me? I am Jesus whom thou persecutest." His case is certainly one of indisputable certainty. He both saw, heard, and believed, and was baptized.

Eneas furnishes a seventh case: And Peter said to him, "Eneas, Jesus Christ maketh thee whole; arise and make thy bed."

The citizens of Lydda and Saron furnish the eighth case. Of them we read: "All that dwelt in Lydda and Saron saw Eneas" made whole by Peter, and they "turned to the Lord." The people of Lydda and Saron were converted by what they saw and heard. Conversion here, too, was not by the Spirit alone.

The inhabitants of Joppa furnish the ninth case. On Peter's visit, and the revival of Dorcas, through his preaching, many believed in the Lord. So that Peter tarried there many days.

Cornelius and his friends furnish the tenth case. That is so notorious, it needs only to be named. Peter told the words of salvation, and the Spirit miraculously sustained him. So that he, also, and his friends, were regenerated, through both the Word and the Spirit.

The Antiochans constitute the eleventh case. Common preachers, exiles from Jerusalem, came to Antioch Phenice and Cyprus. The hand of the Lord was with them. They spake unto the Grecians, preaching the Lord Jesus, and a great number believed and turned unto the Lord. (See also Acts xiii. 43-48.)

Sergius Paulus, deputy governor of Paphos, gives us the twelfth case. When he saw Paul strike Elymas, the sorcerer, blind, and heard Paul preach, he believed, being astonished at the doctrine of the Lord.

Lydia constitutes the thirteenth case. Lydia, a pious lady, a worshiper of God, whose heart the Lord had formerly touched, attended to Paul's preaching, believed, and was baptized.

The Philippian jailer heard Paul; he and all his house believed in God, and were filled with joy. This is the fourteenth special case.

Dionysius, the Areopagite of Athens, Lady Damaris and others with them, heard Paul, believed, and clave unto him and the Lord. These noble Athenians constitute the fifteenth case.

Crispus, the chief ruler of the Corinthian synagogue, and all his family, hearing Paul, believed on the Lord. This is the sixteenth case.

The Corinthians constitute the seventeenth example. Many of the Corinthians hearing, believed, and were baptized. The whole story is here beautifully told in the three words, "hearing, believing, and being baptized."

The Ephesians constitute the eighteenth case. Many of them hearing Paul, believed, came and confessed their deeds, burned fifty thousand pieces of silver worth of books, "so mightily grew the word of the Lord, and prevailed."

To these may I add the cripple at Lystra, as a nineteenth case; the people of Iconium as a twentieth—"To whom Paul so spake that a multitude believed"; and as the twenty-first example, the noble Bereans, "who searched the Scriptures daily, therefore many of them believed." Here are twenty-one clear and distinct cases recorded in one book, containing, in all, probably not less than from thirty to fifty thousand persons; in every one of which they heard, believed, and were baptized. So that, as far as sacred history goes, the Spirit of God never did operate in conversion without the Word.

Now I ask Mr. Rice to bring forward one single case of any one being converted to the Lord without the Word being first heard and believed! If the salvation of the world depended on it, he could not give it. It is, then, so far as the New Testament deposeth, idle, and worse than idle, to talk about sanctification or conversion, without the Word and Spirit of God. They are always united in the great work. No one is converted by the Word alone, nor by the Spirit alone.

Having then surveyed the premises, and heard the arguments and objections from the other side, I proceed, with great haste, to place in a miniature view the whole argument before you.

I. The first of this series of thirteen arguments was drawn from the constitution of the human mind, intellectual and moral. It was shown that the human mind, like the human body, has a specific constitution, which is never to be violated. In no instance does God, in the government of the universe, violate the laws and constitution which he has given, in effecting the ordinary objects of his providence, moral government, or in the scheme of redemption. He always addresses himself to man in harmony with his constitution: first addressing his understanding, then his conscience, then his affections. Miracles only excepted, he has never violated the powers given to man. He gives no new powers, annihilates no old powers, but takes the human constitution as he made it; and by enlightening the understanding, and renewing the heart by the gospel, effects, through his Holy Spirit, that grand moral change which constitutes a new moral creation.

II. Our second argument was deduced from the fact that from the earliest antiquity till now there never has been found a human being in any country or age possessed of one spiritual idea, impression, or feeling, where some portion of the Word or revelation of God had not been spoken to him, or read by him. So that it appears, in fact, indisputable that the Spirit of God rather follows, and in no case precedes, the progress or arrival of his Word. We have the history of man in the four quarters of the world, in attestation of this most significant and momentous fact.

III. By an induction of many cases of personal experience from observation, and, I may add, by a general concession, it appears, that amongst Christians the most gifted and enlightened, not one idea can be suggested from the most gifted, the most eminently illuminated with spiritual light and intelligence—not one idea can be expressed, not taken from the Holy Scriptures. Not one thought, idea, or impression, truly spiritual, can be heard from any man in Christendom, not borrowed from that Holy Book, directly or indirectly. These two matter-of-fact arguments, on almost any other subject, would be deemed all-sufficient.

IV. My fourth argument consisted in the avowal and development of that great law of mind, and of all organic existence, animal or vegetable, viz., that whatever is essential to the production of any specific result, is necessary in all cases. Whatever is essential to the production of any one effect, or offspring, vegetable or animal; any one result, intellectual or moral, is always and invariably necessary to the consummation of the same results. Therefore, whatever is essential to the conversion of one individual, is essential to the conversion of every other individual. It need not be urged that the same order and arrangement of things is necessary, because that is not implied as always essential; but so much of order, arrangement, and circumstances, as are essential to the production of one ear of corn, are uniformly and invariably necessary. Just so in the new birth. When called to assert and maintain any fact, we are not obliged to explain the whole nature, reasons, and contingencies thereof—I am only obliged to establish the fact itself. Natural birth is always the same thing. So is the spiritual. Baptism is always the same thing. Mr. Rice, without knowing it or designing it, was constrained to come to this result. While, in fact, seeking to oppose it, he came to the very same conclusion. He first argued for infant regeneration without faith; he then sought to have believers regenerated in some way different, but ultimately he asserted that regeneration was also before faith in adults, and thus, by the force of the universal law, he came to my grand conclusion, that whatever is necessary to the new birth, or regeneration, in one case, is necessary in all other cases. And so that point is decided.

V. My fifth argument, is deduced from the name "Advocate," given to the Holy Spirit by the Messiah, as his official designation, in conducting the work of conversion, convincing the world of sin, righteousness, and judgment. He was, then, to use words in pleading this cause; hence it is a moral argument, and a change effected by motives.

VI. My sixth argument is drawn from the commission given to this Advocate in pleading his cause. He was to convince the world of sin, righteousness, and judgment, by certain means. The Messiah prescribes the topics. He furnishes the arguments, and states them to the disciples in advance. The first topic is, "Because they believe not in me"; the second, "because I go to my Father, and you see me no more"; the third is, "because the Prince of the world is cast out." In this way, then, the work was to be conducted, and it has been conducted. And so proceeded the apostles through their whole ministry. All useful and successful pleaders, in all ages, have been obliged to adopt this course. And while the human constitution remains as it now is, the same course must be essentially and substantially pursued.

VII. My seventh argument is founded on that most significant and sublime fact, that the first gift the Spirit of God bestowed on the apostles was the gift of tongues. What could have been more apposite to teach, that the Spirit of God was to operate through the Word, than, as prefatory to the work, first of all giving to its pleaders the gift of tongues that by the machinery of words, he might accomplish his glorious work of regenerating the world. These seven arguments I distinctly stated in my first address on this subject. To some of these there was no reply whatever made. To none of them was a direct and formal refutation attempted. I regard them as I did at first, not only as unassailed, but unassailable.

VIII. My eighth argument was composed of the direct and explicit testimony of the apostles, affirming regeneration and conversion through the Word of God, as the seed or principle of the new life. The instrumentality of the Word was asserted by James as the will or ordinance of God. We had the united testimony of two apostles directly and positively affirming the very issue in our proposition. James affirming, that of his own will begat he us by, not without, the Word of Truth. And Peter saying, "We are born again," or according to McKnight, "We are regenerated, or having regenerated us, not by corruptible, but through," not without, "the incorruptible seed of the Word of God, which liveth and abideth forever." Here is as clear an indication of the instrumentality of the Word as can be expressed in human language. To explain these passages away is impossible, and you see how my opponent has evaded them. Paul, also, in various forms of speech, gives us similar views of the instrumentality of the Word. He told the Corinthians that he himself had "begotten them through the gospel." Thus making the gospel the indispensable instrument of regeneration. Peter, indeed, asserted before all the apostles in the convention at Jerusalem, that God purifies the heart by faith. But it was reserved to these later times to assume and teach, that God purifies the heart without faith, before faith, and independent of the Word of God.

IX. I elicited a ninth argument from the commission given to the Messiah, as reported in Isaiah, and from the commission given to Paul from the Messiah in person, with respect to the conversion of the Gentiles. This commission is reported by Paul himself in his speech before King Agrippa (Acts xxvi.). These commissions show the arrangement of means in reference to conversion, remission and sanctification, in the divine mind, purpose and plan. Illumination through the gospel is always first. The apostle was sent to "open the eyes" of the nations. He was "to turn them from darkness to light, and from the power of Satan unto God, in order to their forgiveness and participation of an inheritance amongst those sanctified through faith."

X. My tenth argument consisted of those Scriptures which show that whatever is ascribed to the Holy Spirit in the work of salvation is also ascribed to the Word; and that what is ascribed to the Word is also ascribed to the Spirit. The gentleman has not found a single exception to it. Are persons said to be enlightened, quickened, converted, sanctified, regenerated, comforted, etc., by the Word? they are also in some other Scriptures said to be so by the Spirit; and vice versa. This agent and instrument were so inseparably connected in the minds of the apostles and prophets that they could not conceive of the one without the other, in any operation or effect connected with the salvation of man.

XI. My eleventh argument was deduced from the fact that those who resisted the Word of God, or the persons that spoke it, are said to resist the Spirit of God. By not giving ear to the prophets that spoke by the Spirit, they resisted the Spirit. The Sanhedrim of the Jews, who resisted the words spoken by Stephen and by the twelve apostles, are represented by him as resisting the Holy Spirit. His words are: "As your fathers did, so do you always resist the Holy Spirit. Which of the prophets have not your fathers persecuted? and they have slain them that showed before the coming of the Just One, of whom you have now been the betrayers and murderers."

XII. A twelfth argument was deduced from another important fact: that the strivings of the prophets by their words, are represented as the strivings of the Holy Spirit. Thus spoke Nehemiah: "Thou sendest thy good Spirit to instruct them," through Moses, "and thou testifiedst against them by thy Spirit, in thy prophets, yet would they not give ear." Thus, in the Divine Word, the Spirit and the Word of God, and those who spoke it by the immediate authority of God, are so perfectly identified, that everything that is said to be done by, to, for, or against the one, is said to be done to, by, for, or against the other. So that we may still say that those who hear not Moses nor the prophets, would not be persuaded, though one rose from the dead! God still strives with men by his Spirit, and they still resist his Spirit, in and through the Word spoken by prophets and apostles. "Let every one hear what the Spirit saith to the churches."

XIII. My thirteenth argument consists in that most sublime and impressive fact, that God nowhere has operated without his Word, either in the old creation or in the new. In nature and in grace, God operates not without his Word. He never has wrought without means. He has, so far as earth's annals reach, and as the rolls of eternity have been opened to our view, never done anything without an instrumentality. The naked Spirit of God never has operated upon the naked spirit of man, so far as all science, all revelation teach. Abstract spiritual operations is a pure metaphysical dream. There is nothing to favor such a conceit in nature, providence, or grace. God broke the awful stillness of eternity with his own creative voice. He spoke, before anything was done. Speech, or language or a word, is the original and sublime instrumentality of all divine operations. God said, "Let there be light," and light was born. Does not the Bible say, "By faith we understand that the worlds were framed by the Word of God," so that the things that were made, were not made of things that did formerly exist? They were made out of the Word of God. All things having been created by the Word of God. Most evident it is, that his Word is the all-creative instrument. Without it was not anything made that now exists. Of course, then, if persons were to be created anew in Christ Jesus, without the Word of God, it would be a perfect anomaly, something wholly new in the history of the universe. If God operated upon absolute nonentity, and then upon inert matter, by his Word, and if his Spirit thus brooded on old chaos, what tongue of man can prove that in the new creation, he regenerates, renews, re-creates and sanctifies man without his Word! It never can be done, Mr. President. It is not only out of the power of Mr. Rice, but every other living man, to show that God moves at all in the affairs of redemption but through his Word. God's Spirit and Word operated conjointly on ancient chaos, and they still operate together on the chaos of the human heart in its sins. Read Psalm xxix. 3-9; Psalm xxxiii. 6-9. So my fourteenth argument details.

I am sorry that my time is always too short for the full development of the great elements of things, and mighty evidences of truth found in these propositions. I have arranged, however, such amount of facts and evidences as, I humbly think, never can be set aside by the ingenuity of mortal man. I am willing to commit these fourteen arguments to the world, fearless of the consequences. I think the case is a clear one, and one upon which we may say we have line upon line and precept upon precept. We have certainly the law and the prophets.

In conclusion, then, I must say that we have been much reproached and slandered on this theme. It is not from any aversion to preaching the Holy Spirit, (for we do efficaciously preach it,) that I have been constrained to take this ground, so offensive to some, and which has been made, in many instances, to retard the great and growing cause of reformation which we plead. I believe and teach the inspiration of the Spirit, the influences and effects of the Spirit of God in the hearts of all Christians, men and women. The man who represents me as opposed to a spiritual religion and to the operations, converting and sanctifying, of the Holy Spirit, does me the highest injustice, and blasphemes my good name in a way he must answer for to a higher tribunal. I have been long endeavoring to draw the proper lines between a wild enthusiasm and the true Spirit of our God—between what is spiritual and animal in some of the present forms of Christianity; and to save my contemporaries from a religion of blind impulses, animal excitements, and new revelations, by which I most sincerely believe vast multitudes are deluded to everlasting ruin. With Paul, and with me, there is but one body and but one Spirit, as there is but one hope of our calling—as there is but one God and Father of us all. (Time expired.)

MR. RICE'S CLOSING REPLY.

WEDNESDAY, NOV. 29, 1:30 o'clock P.M.

Mr. President.—I see not what advantage the gentleman expects to gain by attempting to blacken the character of Calvin—a man who was a blessing to the world, and who has long since gone to his rest. He says I have not a correct translation of Calvin's *Institutes*. I have one of the very best that has been made. But there are present in this large audience many scholars, who understand the Latin language. I was waiting to hear him read us the original. He certainly can not expect us to take his bare assertion in matters of this kind.

He emphasized the expression "horrible decree." Yet I presume he knows perfectly well that the Latin word *horribilis* is not precisely synonymous with the English word "horrible," derived from it. Calvin used it in the sense of awful. But, as I have already remarked, if Mr. C.'s interpretation of Calvin were correct, it would prove not that he held that some infants are lost, but that all nations, infants and adults, believers and unbelievers, perish without remedy; for he includes them all! Yet every one knows that he held no such doctrine. I will read from Calvin one passage which may throw some light on this subject. It is in the chapter on baptism.

"The mischievous consequences of that ill-stated notion, that baptism is necessary to salvation, are overlooked by persons in general, and therefore they are less cautious; for the reception of an opinion that all who happen to die without baptism are lost, makes our condition worse than that of the ancient people, as though the grace of God were more restricted now than it was under the law; it leads to the conclusion that Christ came not to fulfill the promises, but to abolish them; since the promise which, at that time, was of itself sufficiently efficacious to insure salvation before the eighth day, would have no validity now without the assistance of the sign."—Book IV., chap. xv., sec. 20.

Calvin here contends that it is unnecessary for laymen to baptize a child that is likely to die, because its salvation is secure without baptism. He never taught the doctrine the gentleman has charged upon him. The charge has been often made, but, I believe, never proved. If any passage can be found in his works that does teach the doctrine, I wish to see it produced.

Mr. C. still vainly strives to evade the force of the argument for a special divine influence, founded on the fact that God is said to grant or give repentance. He says God granted repentance, not to individuals, but to the whole Gentile world! The Bible does not say so. Peter had related to his brethren at Jerusalem the conversion of the family of Cornelius, a single Gentile family. When they heard the history of this interesting event, "they glorified God, saying, Then hath God also to the Gentiles granted repentance unto life" (Acts xi. 18). Did they say, God hath granted to the Gentiles the privilege of repenting? Had they not always this privilege? Was it ever refused to them? Was it not always their duty to repent? But the language of Paul to Timothy places the matter beyond cavil or objection: "In meekness instructing those that oppose themselves; if God peradventure will give them repentance to the acknowledging of the truth" (2 Tim. ii. 25). The gentleman says God had given repentance to the whole Gentile world; but Paul directs Timothy in meekness to instruct a certain class of wicked persons, if peradventure God will grant them repentance; so that they will acknowledge the truth. It is worse than vain to attempt to destroy the force of language so perfectly clear.

One of my most conclusive arguments against Mr. C.'s doctrine is, that it makes prayer for unconverted persons, as well as for the sanctification of believers, both unavailing and improper. To prove that this insurmountable difficulty had occurred to his own friends, as well as to me, I read a letter from a member of his church, published in the *Harbinger*. How does he answer it? Why, he says, I ought to have read his answer to the letter. It would have required rather more time than I have to spare; for of all men he excels in going round and round a difficulty which he feels himself incapable of meeting. Besides, it is my business to present arguments against his doctrine, and his to answer them. But he would have you believe that when I present an argument against his views, I am bound, if he have written anything on the subject, to read his answer! This is truly a singular demand.

I repeat the argument. If his doctrine be true, there is absolutely no propriety in praying. Why should we, and how can we, pray for blessings, which we verily believe God will never grant? He says he prays for the conversion of sinners.

When he enters the pulpit he stands before the congregation and prays that God will convert the unbelieving portion of it; and then he opens the Bible and tells them that God will not convert them; that the Spirit has dictated and confirmed the Word, and they must be converted and sanctified by it, or be lost! If his doctrine be true, what are his prayers worth? But he says he prays for the conversions of sinners. It is a happy thing when, as it sometimes happens, a man's heart keeps in the path of duty, when his head would lead him from it. The better feelings of the heart do not always yield to the frigid speculations of the head. I am happy to hear that he still prays that God would convert sinners, even though he tells them he will not do it!

I wish now to notice the list of some eight arguments, on which the gentleman has principally relied to prove the Spirit operates only through the truth.

1. The first was from the nature of the human mind—an argument purely metaphysical. But that God can, and does, exert a moral influence on the mind, distinct from words and arguments, was proved by the facts, that he created man upright, and that in protecting his church and people the Bible teaches us that he has exerted a controlling influence over the moral conduct of wicked men, not by words and arguments.

2. His second argument was that there are no spiritual ideas where the Word of God is not possessed. This assertion he can not prove. I have no objection, however, to admitting it; for the design of regeneration is not to make a new revelation, but to change the heart, and cause the sinner to understand and embrace the truths of the Bible. This argument, therefore, is worthless. It bears not upon the doctrine for which I contend.

3. Again, he argues that whatever is necessary to regeneration in one case is necessary in all cases, and consequently if the Word be necessary at all, regeneration can not occur without it, in any case. But the Bible says no such thing. God has never said that he will employ the same instrumentality in all cases. Sometimes, as I have proved, the living ministry is employed in converting men; and, at other times, it is not. This bold assertion, therefore, is without proof, and is contrary to fact.

4. His next argument is, that the Holy Spirit is called an Advocate. But does this name prove that the Spirit, in converting and sanctifying men, employs no other influence than that of words and arguments? Most certainly it does not.

5. On the day of Pentecost, he tells us, the first miraculous gift was that of tongues or languages; and the Spirit did employ words. Does the fact that God ordinarily employs the instrumentality of the truth in converting men, prove that he always employs it, or that he does not exert any other influence on their minds? Certainly it does not. These assertions, founded on such facts, are not worth a straw. The premises and the conclusion are the poles apart.

6. His next argument is, that believers are said to have been begotten by the Word. But God is said to beget them. So, then, God is the agent, and the Word the instrument. Does this prove that he exerts no other influence but that of the Word? The conclusion follows not from the premises. The expression, "purifying their hearts by faith," it would not be difficult to prove, militates against the doctrine of special divine influence.

7. Naked Spirit, he asserts, never operates on naked spirit. This is mere assertion. How can the gentleman prove it true? Does he know how one spirit influences another? Can he inform us how Satan can tempt men? Does he understand it? What are such unproved assertions worth?

But he says he does not pretend to know how the Spirit operates. He has tried to tell us both how he can, and how he can not operate. I will not misrepresent him. I will, therefore, keep his language before your minds. Let me once more read from his *Christianity Restored* (p. 350):

"But to return. As the spirit of man puts forth all its moral power in the words which it fills with its ideas, so the Spirit of God puts forth all its converting and sanctifying power in the words which it fills with its ideas. Miracles can not convert. They can only obtain a favorable hearing of the converting arguments. If they fail to obtain a favorable hearing, the arguments which they prove are impotent as an unknown tongue. If the Spirit of God has spoken all its arguments, or if the New and Old Testament contain all the arguments which can be offered to reconcile man to God, and to purify them who are reconciled, then all the power of the Holy Spirit which can operate upon the human mind is spent, and he that is not sanctified and saved by these, can not be saved by angels or spirits, human or divine."

The gentleman could not have employed language more clear and definite. He puts the Holy Spirit, in regard to conversion and sanctification, on a perfect equality with man, except so far as he may present more powerful motives than man. In the most definite terms, he denies any influence of the Spirit, other than that of his words and arguments. I hold that the Word is ordinarily used, but not always; and that when it is used there is also an influence of the Spirit distinct from it, renewing the heart, and inclining the sinner to receive the truth in the love of it.

In reply to my argument from the conversions on the day of Pentecost, Mr. C. says those persons were converted not without the Word. But did he prove that the three thousand were converted simply by the Word? He did not, and he can not. The apostles gave themselves not only to preaching, but to prayer (Acts vi. 4). Why did they pray? Because they knew that the Word alone could not convert men. They therefore prayed for the efficacious influences of the Holy Spirit. The very fact that they connected prayer with preaching proves conclusively that they believed the special and immediate agency of the Spirit necessary. The argument is conclusive.

But suppose I should admit that the Spirit operates on adults only through the truth, would it follow that the same is true of infants? I can easily prove that adults are saved by faith, never without it; but does it follow that infants must believe, or be damned? According to the gentleman's logic, it would; for he contends that whatever is essential in one case is essential in all cases. Neither reason nor Scripture will permit us to assume the principle that what is said of adults is applicable to infants. Mr. C. denies that infants are regenerated by the Spirit. So he leaves them to die in sin and be lost.

I will now resume the recapitulation of my argument. The necessity of the agency of the Spirit on the hearts of men, I have said, arises simply from their deep depravity. I have proved by a large number of passages of Scripture, that man by nature is destitute of holiness, and inclined only to sin; that he is born of the flesh and is carnal; that his thoughts are evil from his youth; that he is conceived in sin, and goes astray from his very birth; that his heart is deceitful above all things and desperately wicked, etc., etc. I have also stated and proved the fact that whatever is truly good in any man, is in the Scriptures ascribed to a radical change wrought in his heart by God. This most important fact, Mr. C. has not denied. Man being thus totally depraved, estranged from God, I have proved that he never will, and never can, love God, until he shall have experienced a radical moral renovation—a change which can not be effected simply by the Word of God.

I have offered several arguments against the doctrine taught by Mr. C. and in favor of the doctrine of a special divine influence in conversion and sanctification.

I. My first argument against his doctrine was, that it prescribes to the power of God over the human mind an unreasonable and unscriptural limitation. This I proved by two plain facts, viz.: 1st. God made man holy, upright, without words or arguments. In what manner he did it we know not, but most certainly the fact that such a power was exerted proves that God can sanctify the soul either through the truth, or without it. 2nd. I proved by several passages of Scripture, that he claims and has exercised a controlling influence over the moral conduct of men by an influence more powerful than mere motives. And if he can consistently control their moral feelings and conduct at all, without argument and motive, can he not exert such an influence as will lead them to Christ? To this argument Mr. C. has attempted no reply.

II. My second argument was, that the doctrine of Mr. C. necessarily involves the damnation of infants and idiots. He admits that they are depraved, that they "inherit a sinful nature," that they are "greatly fallen and depraved in their whole moral constitution." This being true, one of three consequences must follow, viz.: 1st. They go to hell; or, 2nd, they go to heaven in their depravity; or, 3rd, they are sanctified by the Spirit without the Word. He will not say they go to hell, nor will he pretend that they go to heaven in their depravity. The conclusion is, therefore, inevitable, that they are sanctified by the Spirit without the Word. This is our doctrine; and it is the doctrine of the Bible. Our Savior taught that all must be born again, because "that which is born of the flesh is flesh"—is carnal; and therefore it must be born of the Spirit. You have seen how the gentleman writhed under this argument, and to what absurdities and contradictions he has been driven to evade its force. I leave you, my friends, to determine whether it is more accordant with reason and Scripture, that infants should be sanctified by the Spirit without the truth, or that they should be forever lost.

III. My third argument was, that the doctrine of Mr. C. contradicts the teaching of the Scriptures concerning the depravity of man. They teach that men sin knowingly, willfully and deliberately; that their hearts are fully set in them to do evil. According to his doctrine, they sin only through mistake or error; and all that is necessary to convert them is to give them correct information. To this argument he has not even attempted to reply. He has not said one word concerning it—not a word.

IV. My fourth argument was, that a large number of passages of Scripture directly and most clearly teach that in conversion and sanctification, the Spirit of God exerts an influence powerful and efficacious, in addition to the Word, and distinct from it. "I will give them one heart and one way, that they may fear me forever, for the good of them and their children after them" (Jer. xxxii. 39). Does this language mean that God would reason with them? No. The time was coming when he would take the work into his own hands, and then his people would have one heart and one way. Again, "I will pour out water upon him that is thirsty, and floods upon the dry ground: I will pour my Spirit upon thy seed, and my blessing upon thine offspring; and they shall spring up as among the grass, as willows by the water-courses" (Isa. xliv. 3). Such are the blessed results, when the Spirit of God moves upon the hearts of men. Again, "A new heart also will I give you, and a new spirit will I put within you; and I will take away the stony heart out of your flesh, and I will give you an heart of flesh. And I will put my Spirit within you," etc. (Ezekiel xxxvi. 26). I need not repeat other passages, quoted from the Old Testament. To the most of them the gentleman has attempted no reply.

In the New Testament we find declarations equally strong in proof of our doctrine. Thus in Eph. ii. 10, Paul says: "We are his workmanship, created in Christ Jesus unto good works, which God hath before ordained, that we should walk in them." I endeavored to prevail on the gentleman to notice this text, but could not succeed. The word "create" is the strongest word in any language, and the apostle uses it without qualification, to express that change which is wrought in man by the Spirit, and which results in his doing good works.

Again, in the same chapter, the apostle represents man as dead in trespasses and in sins, and as being quickened by the power of God. Was a dead man ever made alive by words or arguments? Jesus stood at the grave of Lazarus and said: "Lazarus, come forth," but at that moment be exerted an almighty power to quicken him. So when God speaks to the sinner, who is spiritually dead, his Spirit breathes into his soul spiritual life—exerts an influence which causes him to embrace Christ as his Savior and rejoice in his service.

In the epistle to Titus, the apostle says, God saves us "by the washing of regeneration and renewing of the Holy Ghost, which he shed on us abundantly through Jesus Christ" (chap. iii. 5). And I have proved that in every instance where the expressions, "poured out," "shed upon," etc., occur, an immediate divine influence, distinct from the Word, is intended. When the Spirit fell upon Cornelius and his family, Mr. C. admits there was an immediate agency of the Spirit, entirely distinct from the Word; but when the same kind of expression is used concerning conversion and sanctification, he denies that any special and distinct agency is intended!

These and a number of other passages I have read, to most of which no answer has been attempted, prove conclusively that in conversion and sanctification there is an agency of the Spirit, distinct from the Word, renewing the heart and inclining it to the service of God. Most certainly such is the obvious meaning of these Scriptures; and they will bear no other interpretation.

V. My fifth argument was, that God is represented as giving repentance unto life—as granting repentance to the acknowledging of the truth. Faith, too, is declared to be the effect of regeneration. "Whosoever believeth that Jesus is the Christ, is born of God" (1 John v. 1). So in 1 Cor. iii. 5, Paul says, "Who, then, is Paul, and who is Apollos, but ministers by whom ye believe, even as God gave to every man." This passage I could not possibly induce Mr. Campbell to see! There are many others that teach most clearly that repentance, faith, and every grace, are the result of a change of heart, of which God is the author—all of which establish the doctrine for which I contend.

VI. My sixth argument was, that the doctrine of Mr. C. makes prayer for the unconverted, and even for the sanctification of believers, wholly useless and improper. Why should we ask God to convert men, and then preach to them, that he never purposed to convert any man, woman or child, by any other influence than that of arguments presented before their minds? Some of the followers of the gentleman are quite consistent. I have observed that in their public prayers they rarely ever ask God to convert sinners. If I believed as they do, I might reason with men; but I should never think of praying to God, to cause them to turn and live. And why pray at all? for Mr. C. teaches that both conversion and sanctification are to be obtained by reading or hearing the Word, and by this only. If Paul believed this doctrine, why did he pray for the Ephesian Christians, that they might be "strengthened with might in the inner man by his Spirit"? Paul believed in the special agency of the Spirit, and therefore prayed. This doctrine has been, and still is, the consolation of thousands of the followers of Christ, who regard it as one of their highest privileges, to pray for the conversion and salvation of dear friends, who are far away, or whose hearts are callous to the appeals of divine truth.

VII. My seventh argument was, that the conversions on the day of Pentecost and afterwards, prove a divine influence distinct from the Word. On that memorable day, three thousand souls were suddenly converted to God. With repentance for their sins and faith in Jesus Christ, they entered his church, and, to the day of their death, delighted in his service. Arguments and motives never produced in the minds of men such a revolution in an hour. "It was the Lord's work, and marvelous in our eyes." Thousands and tens of thousands have since experienced the same happy change. And even in these last days we are permitted to witness the fulfillment of God's promise to pour out his Spirit on all flesh. We often see a general religious interest gradually pervading a town or neighborhood, where no extraordinary efforts have been made to arrest the attention of the people. Christians become more prayerful. The unconverted pause and consider. They go to the house of God, which they had seldom entered, and hear with fixed attention the melting appeals of divine truth. The solemnity increases. The most careless become thoughtful. The proud are humbled. The most hopeless are reclaimed. They come "as clouds and as doves to their windows." Many are added to the church of God, and continue to adorn the doctrine of Christ by a godly life. Who can believe that results like these are the effect of mere argument and motive? No; it is the Lord's work. His Spirit is poured out as showers on the thirsty ground.

VIII. My last argument is, that the overwhelming majority of all the readers of the Bible, in all ages, have understood it to teach the doctrine for which I contend. From Methodists, Baptists, Episcopalians, and others, we differ in some things, but we meet at the cross of Christ. We hold the doctrine of human depravity and the absolute necessity of the special agency of the Holy Spirit in order to effect the conversion and sanctification of men. We can bow together around the mercy-seat, and unitedly pray to God that his Word may run and be glorified; that men may be convinced and converted, and that believers may be sanctified.

Indeed, so clearly is this doctrine taught in the Scriptures, that few have been found to deny it. Is the Bible a plain book? My friend admits that it is;

and if it is, he is certainly in error; for the overwhelming mass of the wise and the good are against him. If his doctrine be true, we must conclude that the Bible is one of the most obscure books ever written; for few indeed have been able to understand it on this vital point.

But I must bring my remarks to a close. I do rejoice and bless God that in the defense of this fundamental doctrine of Christianity I am sustained by so large a portion of those who profess to take the Bible as their only infallible guide. On this hallowed ground we meet, sensible of our need of divine aid in our preparation for heaven, and confident that in answer to our united prayers he who began the good work in us will perform it unto the day of Jesus Christ.

Here, too, we find our encouragement to go forth and preach the gospel which is "not after man." If I believed that no other influence but that of words and arguments would be exerted on the minds of men, I should have no heart to preach another sermon. I possess no eloquence that can melt the hardened hearts of men; no power to open their eyes and turn them from darkness to light, and from the power of Satan to God. My encouragement to preach the unsearchable riches of Christ is found in the promise that God will pour out his Spirit on all flesh, and will cause the wilderness and the solitary place to be glad, and the desert to bud and blossom as the rose.

Convince me that no such agency is promised, and I will weep for myself and for my race. There is no hope for man if this doctrine be not true. He is not, and never will be, pure enough to see God. Let me exhort those who have been induced to reject it, to a careful re-examination of the whole subject. If ninety-nine hundredths of the pious readers of the Bible were against me on a point so vital, I would examine again and again. I should greatly fear that I had fatally erred, and that, depending on my own efforts, with only motives before me, I should fail of preparation for heaven.

May God, in his infinite mercy, guide you and me into the knowledge of all truth; and may we be sanctified and fitted for the enjoyments of heaven by his Holy Spirit. (Time expired.)

END OF PROPOSITION.

www.ingramcontent.com/pod-product-compliance
Lightning Source LLC
Chambersburg PA
CBHW020420010526
44118CB00010B/344